Thirteen Festivals
A Ritual Year in Bengal

Thirteen Festivals
A Ritual Year in Bengal

Ralph W. Nicholas

Orient BlackSwan

RCS
Publishers

Published by
Orient BlackSwan Private Limited
1/24, Asaf Ali Road, New Delhi 110 002
E-mail: delhi@orientblackswan.com

And

RCS Publishers
40 Oxford Apartments, 11 I.P. Extension, Delhi 110 092
E-mail: rcspublishers@gmail.com

First published 2016

ISBN 978-81-923046-3-2

Typeset in
Goudy 11/13
by Manmohan Kumar, Delhi

Printed in India at
Rakmo Press, Greater Noida

Distributed by
Orient Blackswan Private Limited
Bangalore, Bhopal, Bhubaneshwar, Chennai, Ernakulam
Guwahati, Hyderabad, Jaipur, Kolkata, Lucknow
Mumbai, New Delhi, Noida, Patna

Contents

Preface

Anthropologists are often irritating. They show up from some alien world and move in on someone else's society for an uncertain length of time. They ask questions, write notes, and take photographs for reasons that do not make much sense. The people thus imposed upon are due an explanation for a lot of unintelligible behavior. For the anthropologist's part, explaining ethnographic research to people of limited education and little worldly experience is not a straightforward project. The term "social science" often does not communicate much to well-educated people, not to say village farmers, weavers, and housewives. "Participant observation" is not a part of their conceptual universe. Even success in making a case for the observation of everyday life and the annual cycle does not answer the question, "Why us? Why did you pick this village?" And, implicitly, "Why don't you go bother someone else?" I would like to offer this book to the many people in Kelomal who helped us when we lived there, and to the many others who tolerated us. I once overheard someone explaining to a visitor from another village that we went around asking questions, but seemed harmless and good-natured. In earlier books about Kelomal I have thanked the people who paved the way for our work; they are all now no longer here to receive my expressions of gratitude.

The present volume deals with the annual cycle of worship of Hindus in Kelomal, except for the two most consequential observances of the year. In *Rites of Spring* (2008) I analyzed the complex vernacular ritual of Gājan, which marks the end of one year and the beginning of the next around the time of the vernal equinox. In *Night of the Gods* (2013) I analyzed the complex Brahmanical ritual of Durgā Pūjā, and the subsequent worship of Lakṣmī, Kālī, and Jagaddhātrī that take place around the autumnal equinox. These are the nodal points of the ritual calendar throughout Hindu Bengal. In *Fruits of Worship* (2003) I went into more detail about the worship of the goddess Śītalā than I am able to do in this book; she is the mother of the village and has a place of great importance among the ordinary people of Kelomal.

My wife Marta and I lived in Kelomal, together with my late colleague and friend Tarasish Mukhopadhyay in 1968–69, then again during the autumn of 1970, during the season of Durgā Pūjā and the succeeding observances. In addition to a village census, collection of genealogies, and basic research on social structure, we attempted to witness every ritual we possibly could. Observing village-wide rituals, such as Śītalā Pūjā and Gājan was demanding but provided a single focus. However, we had to choose samples and collect oral information on the many occasions when there were multiple observances taking place at the same time. When rituals were taking place all three of us attended and kept notes, which we later compared and compiled. Those notes, and the photographs I took at the time, are the groundwork of this book, and of the earlier ones in this series. I bring up this rather obvious fact to point out that this is, at the bottom, an empirical, scientific study. The fact that it deals with religious practices might lead some readers to think it is speculative, metaphysical, or somehow not materialistic. I have taken an interest in the history of these observances and consulted scriptural authorities, but my aim is to explain what people understand by their rites. As I hope I have been able to show, there is an intellectual universe here, expressed in practical form.

Fortunately, Marta is still here, and I can thank her for her work and endurance in the field, and for editing all that I have written about this research. My friend and sometime collaborator Professor Aditi Nath Sarkar read the manuscript with careful attention to detail and recommended many improvements. I am grateful to Professor Kunal Chakrabarti for his constructive help with this book. I am also indebted to Aloke Roy Chowdhury and Joyati Sen, who have been the most cooperative publishers any scholar could ever hope for. A Fulbright-Hays Fellowship for Research in India supported the fieldwork in 1968–69. The Asian Studies Center at Michigan State University, where I was then a faculty member, supported the fieldwork in 1970. In 1971 I joined the faculty of the University of Chicago, where I had received my training in anthropology and South Asian studies when I was a graduate student in the 1950s. I have paid many intellectually rewarding visits to India since 1970, most in connection with my work on behalf of the American Institute of Indian Studies. I am indebted to these institutions and to the great South Asian Library of the University of Chicago. The extraordinary collection of publications from the Indian subcontinent, begun by Maureen Patterson, and developed with a clear-headed vision by James Nye, has been an asset of incomparable value as I have pursued my research.

A Note on Usage

There are many transliterated Bengali and Sanskrit words in this book. With a few small variations, I have followed modern spelling in transliterating from both languages and I have employed the most generally used diacritical marks. In written form, a great many individual words in Bengali and Sanskrit are *tatsamas*, indistinguishable from one another. Spoken Bengali, however, departs significantly from standard pronunciation of Sanskrit, and the rural dialect spoken in Kelomal departs from standard Bengali. In this book the most commonly used Bengali words are transliterated in a form that reflects standard spelling but with some recognition of Bengali pronunciation. For example, the retroflex voiced stop represented by *ḍ* is often a "flap" in Bengali, so it sounds like *r*; the word *bāṛī* "house" contains this sound. An *ṛ* followed by a vowel is the retroflex flap; an *ṛ* without a following vowel is the vocalic *r*.

The letter *c* represents a sound like English *ch* without the aspiration that usually accompanies *ch*. Thus *Caṇḍī* is pronounced more like *Chaṇḍī*. Even though the Sanskrit bilabial spirant *v* is assimilated to bilabial stop *b* in Bengali, I have used *v* where the word is recognizably Sanskrit (e.g., *navamī*), and where it is not pronounced, as in *tattva*. The common conjunct consonant *kṣm* is pronounced *kkh*; the name of the goddess Lakṣmī is pronounced approximately as Lokkhī. Initial *y* is pronounced *j*; I represent it with *y* except in the special instance of *yajamāna*, which appears here as *jajmān*, following the convention that has grown up in anthropological writing. In the dialect spoken in most of West Bengal, all three sibilants (*ś*, *ṣ*, *s*,) are pronounced *ś* and often written *sh* in English. The spelling I have used to refer to our generous host for most of these *pūjās*, the Ghosh Bari of Kelomal, is the spelling they themselves use in English, although in transliteration it would be *ghoṣ bāṛi*.

Bengali vowels are a source of good-humored joking in the rest of India. The implied vowel, represented by *a* in transliteration, is usually pronounced as an open *o*, though it is sometimes simply *o* depending on the following vowel. Whether the implicit vowel is pronounced at the end of a word usually—but not always—depends on whether the word ends in a conjunct consonant, in which case it is pronounced. Thus, Govinda, which is pronounced Govind in Hindi, sounds more or less like Gobindo in Bengali. I have not yet found a good rule for indicating the implicit vowel in word-final position where it is not pronounced; I have indicated it in all the cases where the word seems to belong more to the Sanskrit vocabulary than to spoken Bengali, but that is a very indistinct line.

1. Introduction

While there is no consensus among anthropologists about what "religion" is, there is a general agreement about the importance of a shared picture of ultimate reality in creating and maintaining a common culture. A widespread conviction that some truths cannot be challenged is at the root of a coherent society; it relieves the individual of the ceaseless burden of producing order out of what is in reality a random, uncontrollable, often chaotic world. This intellectual function contributes as much to the evolutionary adaptive value of a culture as do technology and social organization. However, it is often difficult to discern the central value of interpretability until it is challenged, until the worldview and settled truths of a cultural system are put to the test by conquest, asymmetrical cultural contact, or overwhelming, uninterpretable experience. In the modern world, the influence of industrialized societies on small, isolated ones has created numerous episodes of cultural disorganization and anomie, occurrences usually followed by the creation of new cultural syntheses and reintegration. Bengali cultural history began long before the relatively recent confrontations with Islam, colonialism, and industrialism. What is today called "Hindu" in Bengal is the precipitate of a very long succession of challenges to interpretability.

This is the fourth book I have written about Bengali religion as I studied it in some villages in East Medinipur District during fieldwork in the period 1968–70. The people in these villages were then and are today almost all Hindu, although there is a large, predominantly Muslim village nearby, and some households of Muslims were included in my area of study. When I wrote the proposal for this research in 1967, I used a common anthropological conception of religion based on sacred symbols deployed in rituals. In India, Hindus are generally distinguished from other denominations by their ritual practice rather than any belief or creed they are required to declare. "Hinduism"—whatever we mean by that term—has a plenitude of beliefs, but no dogma or orthodoxy. Islam has exercised a widespread influence on life and thought throughout Bengal, but it has not diminished the ritualism, polytheism, and idolatry of the Hindus.

In writing about the nodal rituals of the year for Hindus in Bengal—Gājan in the spring (Nicholas 2008b) and Durgā Pūjā in the autumn (Nicholas 2013)—focus on those particular, highly orchestrated acts that episodically organize the whole community allowed me to avoid engaging very deeply with the question of *if* or *how* they were "religious." Participants treated a god (Śiva) and goddess (Durgā, and her manifestations) with obligatory actions and physical offerings that were said to honor and satisfy them; there were accompanying myths that explained the powers and deeds that were attributed to them; and there were expectations of benefits that would be given to those who successfully honored and satisfied them. In each case the presence of deities, rituals, and myths seemed to make a prima facie case for referring to these observances as "religious."

In this book I deal with a more heterogeneous set of activities: the rituals that are undertaken during the rest of the year. As will become apparent, there are many other rituals that people in Kelomal think are very important; these rituals treat deities whose characters and powers are diverse, and whose modes of worship are quite different from one another. The Bengalis often say, in uncharacteristic understatement, *bāro māse tero pārbaṇ*, "In twelve months there are thirteen rituals." I have taken the title of this book from that expression. (*Pārbaṇ*, the Bengali form of the Sanskrit term *pārvaṇa*, refers to a day marked for a ritual; the expression *pūjā pārbaṇ*, "worship day," is often used. *Pārbaṇ* frequently takes the colloquial forms of *parba* and *parab*, terms that encompass both the worship and the specified day. I am using "ritual" to refer to acts of worship, and not to other common ritualized activities, such as bathing.)

The first objective of this book is ethnographic: describing the activity and explaining the meanings that attended the *pārbaṇs* as they cycled through the seasons. Beyond the ethnographic task, however, the diversity of the deities, the rituals, and the narratives that are celebrated around the year raise a further question: How did people in Kelomal see the universe, the world they inhabited? If the religion of a people provides them with a conception of ultimate reality, what was that conception for the people in Kelomal, people whose cultural inheritance was complex and apparently incoherent?

Religious History of Bengal

The religious landscape of Bengal has been complicated for millennia. Even when most inhabitants of the countryside remained close to their tribal origins, their rulers were promulgating ritual practices that originated among Indo-Aryan–speaking people. Some were Brahmanical practices, some were Buddhist, and some were Jaina. Both the Buddha and Mahavira came from nearby areas of what is today Bihar and propagated their teachings in the region. There were large Buddhist monasteries in Bengal from the sixth or seventh century. Jainism—although never as prominent as Buddhism—lingers faintly among the Saraks, an otherwise Hindu caste found in the border areas of West Bengal. Bengali Buddhists adopted tantric ritual practices, and gradually erased the distinction between Brahmanism and Buddhism, although the differences continued to be debated in learned circles. The Pāla kings (8th to 11th centuries) were Buddhists who patronized monasteries. They were succeeded by the Senas (11th and 12th centuries), who patronized Brahmans and instituted reforms in

Hindu institutions. The arrival of the Muslim Khiljis in western Bengal, early in the thirteenth century, added the pillars of Islam to the religious edifice. While ordinary people might not distinguish between Buddhism and Brahmanism, there was a clear-cut distinction between these practices and those of Islam. The Persian word "Hindu" began to appear in Bengali writing in the sixteenth century.

Richard Eaton (1993:132–34) assembled evidence from contemporary observers indicating that, although there were Muslim rulers over much of the region from the thirteenth century onward, it was not until the sixteenth century that there were large rural Muslim populations. Much of that information comes from Portuguese and other Europeans, who distinguished "Mohamedans" from "heathens" and "idolaters." Just how the heathens and idolaters identified themselves is unclear, and it is unlikely that we can ever find out. It is difficult to say how far down into the villages earlier Brahmanical and Buddhist practices might have extended. The rules and expectations of Islam did not penetrate deeply into Bengal until well into the nineteenth century, when pilgrims began to return from Mecca with the idea that Bengali Islam needed to be purged of non-Islamic practices.

Today, a great majority of Bengali-speaking people are Muslims. According to the 2011 Census of India, of the population of West Bengal (something over 91 million people), 72.5 % identify themselves as Hindu, 25.2 % as Muslim, and 2.3 % neither Hindu nor Muslim. The Bangladesh Bureau of Statistics puts the current population there at approximately 156 million, of whom 8.2% (about 12.8 million) are said to be Hindu. Thus, the combined Hindu population of the Bengali-speaking region is about 80 million people, or about 32% of the total.

What is it that the 80 million "Hindus" have in common? On what grounds can we say that all these people are "of the same religion," other than that they are not something else? Unlike the Muslim majority, they are not expected to subscribe to a creed or declaration of faith, or to join in any rituals that are common to all who call themselves Hindu. The highly visible worship of the goddess Durgā in the autumn is a pervasive feature of Bengali Hinduism; but, even though everyone visits the *pūjā pāṇḍāls* to view the images of the goddess, it is performed primarily by certain privileged sectors of society. The widespread practice of the Gājan of Śiva in the spring is a ritual of the ordinary people, especially in villages; it has no role for the high castes and wealthy families. As a rite of common villagers it is not publicized in the Bengali newspapers or attended by a frenzy of shopping for new clothes, but Gājan engages more of the Hindu population of Bengal than any other ritual. There are distinctions among Hindus well known in India: worshipers of goddesses are often called Śāktas, and worshipers of Śiva are called Śaivas, yet neither term is used very much by Bengalis. The Portuguese often called them all "Gentoo" or "Gentue," which seems to be a local adaptation of "gentile"; the British usually used "Hindoo."

Christian missionaries adopted the term *dharma* to speak about religion in Bengali. *Dharma* is an ancient concept in India; it refers to the intrinsic code for conduct of anything. Thus, the "idolaters" found the wide variety of their rituals and beliefs grouped together as *Hindu dharma*, a category that encompassed Śaivas, Śāktas, and Vaiṣṇavas, and lumped together the pious vegetarian followers of the Vṛndāvana Gosvāmīs with carnivorous Kālī *bhaktas*. This usage of *dharma* to translate "religion" or "denomination" has become widespread among educated Bengalis, who now also use it in connection with their rituals.

Other commonly used words refer to acts, not to beliefs; they are types of *karma*, "actions," often distinguished as *śubha karma*, "auspicious acts." *Anuṣṭhāna* ("performance" or "celebration") is used to refer to a social occasion or to the beginning of an event. *Dharmanuṣṭhāna*, a rather lofty term meaning "ritual" or "religious program," was not used in Kelomal or rural areas generally; however *ācāra-anuṣṭhāna*, meaning "customary performance or practice" was used by educated villagers to speak about rituals. A frequently used term, *ācāra-vyavahāra*, meaning "established custom or practice," extends beyond rituals to include conduct that is not concerned with deities or worship. While there is no Hindu orthodoxy, there is Hindu orthopraxy.

Rituals and Representations

As was the case in my previous books about the religious practices of people in Kelomal, my approach to religion is heavily influenced by Durkheim. However, while Durkheim sought a universal conception of religion, I have tried to approach Bengali rituals through Bengali categories. At the same time, I have followed generations of social and cultural anthropologists in a general acceptance of Durkheim's (1995:9) proposition that

> . . . religion is an eminently social thing. Religious representations are collective representations that express collective realities; rites are ways of acting that are born only in the midst of assembled groups and whose purpose is to evoke, maintain, or recreate certain mental states of those groups.

What Durkheim called "collective representations" are sacred symbols deployed in rituals by social groups, inspiring in individuals a sense that each person is part of something larger, a reality that transcends the individual. That reality is their society, society not as a collection of people but rather as something divine that has power over individuals, subordinating them to the whole. In this book I examine several levels of social organization to which rituals pertain: households, neighborhoods, villages, multi-village aggregations, and the "country" are the social universes of particular rituals.

Durkheim has been correctly understood by succeeding generations as a "functionalist." He sought to show how the creation of a sense of the sacred surrounding everything social—and the creation of a corresponding sense of the profane in everything arising from the individual—made societies cohere, subordinating the individual to the collectivity. However, he did not think there was a "group mind" of some kind; he recognized that the distinction between the sacred and the profane is created anew in each individual. Writing about how (as he thought) totems (or, as I would say, symbols) affect individuals, he said that although the totem appears to be a natural force it is in fact a moral, collective force; the totem provides the agency by which the moral force of society affects individual consciousness. The *conscience collective* was recreated in each person as a social rather than a biological inheritance. He thought that moral force was born in the individual during episodes of "collective effervescence," ritual-induced "hyperexcitement" during which a person is "in such a state of exaltation" that he ceases to "know himself"; without being aware of the origin, he experiences society as "collective consciousness," a force within himself (Durkheim 1995:218–22). Together with other contemporary scientific students of religion, I would go on to say that there is also an intellectual dimension to collective consciousness. As Catherine Bell (1997:12) put it, "religion is essentially a human project to formulate stable and meaningful dimensions behind the accidental, chaotic, and shifting realities of human existence." Not all rituals induce collective effervescence but they all create order.

"Stability" and "meaning" are keys to the way I have thought about religion in a universal context, and about the willingness—in fact, the need—of humans to act in relation to powers they cannot see and beings known only from myths. Stability is evident in the structure of the Bengali annual cycle of worship and in the close connection between the calendar and the rituals examined here. There is nothing unusual about a close relationship between the natural order of the annual cycle, the cosmology of a people, and their ritual cycle. The Hindu calendar is structured by a conception of a day and night of the gods; the fecundity of the earth, pregnancy, and birth, in the form of crops; and most notably in the opposition between the life-promoting increasing light ushered in at the vernal equinox and the dangerous increasing darkness beginning with the autumnal equinox. The physical world is quite undependable: the rain that is expected in Āṣāṛha (June/July) sometimes comes much later, and the much-anticipated change of seasons is often accompanied by unpredictable, destructive tropical storms. The spring season, which is regarded as an auspicious time of year, is also the time when infectious diseases spread most readily. The unreliability of crops is notorious. The progression of rituals does not make reality more predictable or controllable, but it is itself a reliable structure, an implicit statement of how things are supposed to be arranged.

After Durkheim, Radcliffe-Brown and the generation of social anthropologists who succeeded him were known as "structural–functionalists." Structure was understood to mean social structure, and social structure was supposed to exist as an empirically observable phenomenon. Lévi-Strauss recognized that, for all of the relationships among people we might observe, social structure is the conception of society they hold, acted out empirically to the best of their ability but inevitably always somewhat imperfectly. Structure is an intellectual construct, a model, encompassing social relationships but also extending beyond them to myth and ritual, and to the conception of the universe. Structuralism has been criticized for excessive formalism and abstraction from the chaotic world of everyday life. The same cannot be said of semiotic or interpretive anthropology, which focuses attention on meaning and recognizes, implicitly or explicitly, the central fact of humanity, which is our need to find a meaning for everything, a task that is most daunting when in fact there is no meaning in the random succession of events, of deaths and births, storm and tranquility, tragedy and joy. Interpretive anthropology has been criticized for failure to comprehend the ground reality of getting a living and political economy; but ignoring life as it is lived is certainly not a necessary part of interpretation. What I attempt to offer might be called functional structuralism and empirical interpretive anthropology, connecting people's conception of their universe to their workaday existence.

I use the term "symbol" quite often, although it does not correspond to anything in the vocabulary of people in Kelomal or their religious specialists. "Symbol"—a thing that stands for or represents something other than itself, and requires interpretation—is part of the meta-language of anthropology. A culture is a system of symbols that is shared by a human group; usually that group is "a society." People do not think that they are dealing in symbols, or symbolic actions; interpretation in the normal course of social life is automatic and unreflective. Although symbols (sometimes called signs) are given meanings by human beings, in India the usual view is that the meaning of anything is an intrinsic, natural part of that thing. In general, Bengali Hindu worship is grounded in the theory that ritual acts are efficacious, not merely representational. It is a theory not unlike that taught in Roman Catholic doctrine, in which the Christian sacraments—baptism, communion, marriage, etc.—are called "efficacious signs," symbols that accomplish what they represent. Whether or not people regard the meanings of their symbols as arbitrary, it is up to the anthropologist to open up the contents of symbolic transactions.

The applicability in Hindu India of Durkheim's distinction between sacred and profane realms has rightly been questioned. There are no analytical terms that correspond to such a distinction in Indian philosophy nor are there any in use among people in Kelomal, so why use it in discussing Hindu rituals? Whether we call them sacred or not, rituals are a class of activity sharply distinguished from everyday life—*śubha karma* vs. *kāj karma*. The use of "sacred" to identify the symbols employed in rituals directs attention to their distinctive characteristics. Sacred symbols are not necessarily different from the objects of everyday life, as is the ark of the covenant or the golden calf. As will be discussed later, there are many items used daily in Bengali households—such as pottery vessels, women's cosmetics, rice—that are transformed into sacred symbols by being employed in rituals. However, as sacred symbols they are given significance far beyond the ordinary; they convey more meaning than the things of everyday life.

Clifford Geertz (1973:89) wrote, "sacred symbols function to synthesize a people's ethos—the tone, character, and quality of their life, its moral and aesthetic style and mood—and their worldview—the picture they have of the way things in sheer actuality are, their most comprehensive ideas of order." Victor Turner (1967:27–28) identified three important features of symbols employed in rituals: (1) they are highly condensed, that is, they represent many things at the same time; (2) the meanings are disparate, that is, very different meanings are brought together in a single symbol; and (3) the meanings are polarized, with one end reaching the highest moral values while the other end is embedded in physiology—referring to birth, procreation, blood, or other emotionally charged meanings that are normally suppressed or repressed by the people who employ them. While these characteristics are important in the effectiveness of a sacred symbol, they are not sufficient in themselves to make anything sacred. Rather, it is their location in rituals that sacralizes them. Jonathan Z. Smith (1987:103–04) said, "Ritual is, first and foremost, a mode of paying attention." He goes on to illustrate with the example of a temple in which every feature is intentional and outside the ordinary. "A ritual object or action becomes sacred by having attention focused on it in a highly marked way. From such a point of view, there is nothing that is inherently sacred or profane. These are not substantive categories, but rather situational ones. Sacrality is, above all, a category of emplacement." And, we might add, the multivocality of sacred symbols is derived, in part, from their very appearance in rituals.

Sacred symbols often address fundamental issues in oblique ways. They speak about the nature of the universe and the meaning of our lives; and they arouse powerful emotions without exposing the unconscious roots of those emotions. In integral societies, religion constitutes the core of the culture; it informs other systems—kinship and other interpersonal relations, as well as education, politics, and economics—infuses them with values and valorizes the everyday code of conduct. Of course, there are not any truly integral societies left on the planet. Certainly, Bengal, with the division between Muslim and Hindu, has a visible break in its integrity. However, with respect to ordinary social relationships in Bengal villages, there is a supervening code for conduct that usually bridges the apparent cleavage. Small-scale societies tend toward integration and the creation of mutual intelligibility, features that are often more diffuse in large-scale urban settings. At the time of the fieldwork that underlies this book, Kelomal, though still a village, was more than slightly touched by modernity: it was an educational center for the surrounding area and there were many educated residents, although the small group of people with university degrees were employed outside the village and were usually present in the village only during the holiday seasons, especially Durgā Pūjā.

Interpretation

Durgā Pūjā and the other rituals that take place in the autumn represented the legitimate domination of the high-caste former landlords (a social order that was already largely in the past at the time of my fieldwork). Well-educated people in this group liked to discuss the meaning of their rituals. The image of a fierce, ten-armed goddess with numerous weapons trampling and spearing the Buffalo anti-god was said to enact the conquest of evil. At the same time, the idea that the goddess's autumnal visit represented the happy return of a married daughter to her natal family, bringing her children for a visit, was also an explicit theme of the observance. However, less often did anyone penetrate deeply into the meaning of the numerous animal sacrifices they carried out during each of the three principal days of Durgā Pūjā, as well as during the worship of Kālī and Jagaddhātrī—although these were moments of great emotional tension and ritual intensity. The contradictory image of a nurturing mother and a frightening female who was not satisfied without an offering of blood was apparently repressed by most people. The blood of the sacrifice that would have been polluting on another occasion was smeared on the sacrificers. They did not discuss these apparent contradictions, or why the goddess was satisfied only by offerings of uncastrated male animals. However, they did discuss the analogy between animal sacrifice and the goddess's slaying of the anti-gods. Also, senior men made much of the ritual's requiring the work of various servants of different castes in specialized roles, and of the redistribution of rice from their granaries, displaying a "proper" hierarchical social order of dominance and dependence.

While well-educated upper-caste people spoke about the meanings of their rituals, the common people—cultivators and artisans—who performed the Gājan did not often do so. Gājan revolves around the symbolism of fertilizing. The Śiva *linga* is the focus of worship, and the sexual union of Śiva with his consort Durgā, represented in the *Gaurī-paṭṭa* is the objective. Without ever being explicit, people from Kelomal and surrounding villages who had taken the status of ascetic renouncers for the duration of the Gājan spent hours on the penultimate night of the year chanting encouragement to the god and goddess, hidden inside the temple, to have intercourse. Their success was symbolized by the appearance of a certain fish that slipped out from the stone image of united genitals inside the temple, through a small sluice in the temple wall, into the eager hands of the ascetics, who cheered and raced to release the fish in a nearby pond. The ritual representation of the sexual act left little to be explained, even though it was not spoken about directly. There was little doubt that the ascetics, and everyone else attending that late-night vigil, understood what was supposed to happen. When we reviewed the ritual a few days later, the man who had been a principal ascetic was hesitant to discuss the meaning until my wife left the room.

There is a role for the anthropologist as an interpreter who goes beyond the exegesis of the practitioners. It is not necessary to be a psychoanalyst to see the physiological or the repressed elements in sacred symbols. The solidarity-creating functions of rituals are hardly taboo topics; they are not repressed, but they are also not discussed. Durgā Pūjā and the ensuing rituals in the autumn enacted and affirmed a hierarchical order that I call the sacrificial polity. Gājan represented community; the temporary ascetics, none of them of high caste, were empowered to bless the houses of everyone and to bring fertility to the fields and ponds of a large and undefined country. The hierarchical inversion represented by men of cultivator caste—temporarily transformed into *sannyāsīs*—blessing the houses of Brahmans and Kayasthas is obvious, and yet no one articulated it. Explaining the meanings of such ritual gestures and symbolic objects is the anthropologist's job.

Coping with Incoherence

Most people throughout history have never had to explain their worldview or how the universe runs; they do not have to discover for themselves the meaning of life or of the world. Whether seen or unseen, reality is self-evident to people who are busy getting a living, caring for families, and taking part in the social life of small communities. The meanings of the things they deal with are implicit; their shared cultural inheritance satisfies the usually limited intellectual requirements placed on it. However, there are abnormal moments when the capacity of a cultural system (ideology, belief system, cosmology) is seriously challenged by a calamity. Unprecedented epidemics have brought forth radical attempts at reinterpretation. Asymmetrical confrontations, as when Europe extended into the New World or to the islands of the Pacific, have generated famous "revitalization movements," new cultural syntheses that attempted to incorporate the challenge and restore coherence and meaning to the world. Such movements usually pass through phases during which they became more accurate in interpreting the new reality. Numerous examples of cultural resynthesis illustrate the basic human need for finding order in the universe and for making sense of unprecedented experience.

Indigenous peoples who were left alone were generally believed to have had fairly coherent worldviews and consistent cultural schemes that integrated everything from utilitarian activities (such as agriculture) to expressive ones (such as worshiping). Such people had no need of naming their religion, which was integral to their whole way of life and was all they ever knew; they did not have to distinguish a religion from something else. Coherent worldviews became known only after they had been disturbed, so we will never know much about the internal problems and inconsistencies of their primitive state; by the time Bengal entered history it was very far from a primitive state. Buddhism was a force, alongside the religious practices promoted by the Brahmans, long before the arrival of Islam. While it is difficult to tell how far a distinction between Buddhism and Brahmanism extended in village society, the difference was obviously consequential to the Brahmans who inveighed against Buddhism in doctrinal terms; there was dissensus in the religion of the Bengalis even without Islam. For many centuries there had been no undisturbed "traditional" society with a highly coherent cultural system to be torn asunder by Muslims or Europeans. It is well known that pre-Muslim Bengal had many temples, patronized by rulers, that housed very well-sculpted images of deities, Hindu and Buddhist. However, less is known about what went on in those temples, or about the rituals of ordinary people.

The vastly asymmetrical contact between industrialized and tribal societies produced a sharper discrepancy than did contact between the Afghans and Mughals, on one hand, and the farmers and fishers of rural Bengal, on the other. Even under Muslim overlordship, the extensive patronage by Hindu landlords of the authors of *maṅgal kāvya* narratives about Bengali gods was a critical element of the Bengali cultural response to Muslim rule. The devotional Vaiṣṇava movement initiated by Caitanya was even more influential. These two developments knit together the identity of the Bengali Hindus and established a core of practices that constituted a response to Islam, particularly in the Rarh tract of western Bengal. That response, which does not exclude elements drawn from Islam, defines what is "Hindu" in Bengal today.

As mentioned earlier, for Bengali Hindus the religious year is structured by the polarity between the rites of autumn and the rites of spring, Durgā Pūjā and the Gājan. The worship of the goddess Durgā in the autumn takes its authority from the Sanskrit *purāṇas*, though important Bengali elements are threaded through it. Today Durgā Pūjā is an expression of Bengali Hindu cultural identity, but it originated in privileged sectors of society. The Gājan of Śiva in the spring has no puranic authority; it belongs to the vernacular tradition, and it engages ordinary people, especially villagers. Most Hindu rituals are carried out on specific *tithis*, lunar days in particular lunar months. Important rituals that have dates fixed not on the lunar calendar but by seasonal concerns take their authority from the Bengali *maṅgal kāvyas*: the worship of Śītalā, goddess of poxes, is held in the dry weather when smallpox was most contagious; Manasā, goddess of snakes, is worshiped particularly at the beginning of the rainy season when snakes are most often encountered.

While the great importance of both *paurāṇika* and *laukika* ("popular") deities is quite evident, the everyday religious life of most Hindus in rural Bengal comes from what may be generally identified as "Bengal Vaiṣṇavism." The influence of the Vaiṣṇava exemplar Caitanya colors the lives of most Bengali Hindus of all castes and orientations. The devotional religious movement known as Gauṛīya Vaiṣṇavism (Gauṛa being an ancient name of Bengal) claims Caitanya as its founder, Lord Kṛṣṇa as its preeminent deity, and the love of Rādhā for Kṛṣṇa as the model for human devotees. However, though the two are related, Gauṛīya Vaiṣṇavism, with its elaborate prescriptions for the conduct of devotees, is not the same thing as Bengal Vaiṣṇavism—the practices of the people in the countryside.

Vaiṣṇavism in Rural Bengal

The legacy of Caitanya's Kṛṣṇa *bhakti* has attracted a great deal of attention from students of Bengal: it has produced beautiful lyrical poetry and music, and it has given a sweet flavor to much of Bengali Hindu culture. However, Bengal Vaiṣṇavism stretches far beyond Radhā and Kṛṣṇa. Many people who are called "Vaiṣṇava" (a word

Figure 1. This singer is a *kanthi-dhārī*; he wears a necklace of *tulasī* beads indicating his status as an initiated Vaiṣṇava. The man playing the *khol* drum on the right is also wearing the *tulasī mālā*.

rendered as *baiṣṇab* or *baiṣṭom* by village people) have been initiated by a guru and can be identified by a string of *tulasī* beads wrapped tight around their necks (for which they are called *kanthi-dhārī*, "necklace-wearers"); such people are often observant of dietary and ritual restrictions. There is a second group of Vaiṣṇavas in the villages, people who are called *jātīya baiṣṭom*, "born Vaiṣṇavas," or "Vaiṣṇavas by caste." Such people are usually the direct or indirect products of illegitimate births. A widow who is found to be pregnant may be compelled by the community to undertake a conversion from her caste to *baiṣṭom*. Once she becomes a Vaiṣṇavi, her child is then Vaiṣṇava by caste. People of this background are often observant of the restrictions that govern initiated Vaiṣṇavas, converting their flawed genealogies into emblems of piety. But most villagers are Vaiṣṇavas neither by initiation nor by caste. They are "Vaiṣṇava-oriented," attentive to their *tulasī* shrines and participating in *kīrtan* parties on full-moon nights; Kṛṣṇa is the foremost deity of their everyday life.

Though the influence of Caitanya runs very deep in rural West Bengal, it does not prevent most people from participating fully in the worship of many other deities. Other deities of the Vaiṣṇava pantheon are worshiped just as attentively as Rādhā and Kṛṣṇa throughout rural Bengal. Foremost among them is Lakṣmī, who most often appears in Sanskrit texts as the consort of Nārāyaṇa, a name of Viṣṇu. However, in Bengal this fickle goddess of wealth and prosperity is treated as an independent female power; she is worshiped around the year in rituals that span the register from Sanskritic Hinduism to unwritten practices that accompany the harvest. The numerous stories of simple people to whom Lakṣmī brings prosperity and the powerful ones whom she reduces to beggary are told often in conjunction with her worship. There are two sides to this goddess: an ancient one who is revered simply as a divinity, and a far more familiar one who resides in the houses, rice fields, and granaries of Bengal.

Satya Nārāyaṇa, a marked form of Viṣṇu, is worshiped very frequently throughout the year. In Kelomal, different families had very different schedules and occasions for the worship of Satya Nārāyaṇa, but he was worshiped by all. A deity with the same name is also revered in other parts of India, but only in Bengal is he identified with—even identical to—a Sufi saint known as Satya Pīr. A mandatory element of the worship of Satya Nārāyaṇa in Bengal, though not elsewhere in India, is the offering of *śirni* or *śinni*, a Persian term used in Bengal for a preparation of banana, sweet items, and milk that is offered at the graves of Muslim saints and at the shrines of Muslim "deities," such as Olābibi, the cholera goddess. Offerings of *śinni* are normally made by Muslims, but in the worship of Satya Nārāyaṇa they are made by Hindus, including Brahmans. The Bengali Satya Nārāyaṇa is a Hindu–Muslim hybrid peculiar to Bengal.

Caitanya

Bengal has contributed a significant element to the practices of a great many Hindus throughout India (and far beyond) in the form of devotional worship of Kṛṣṇa. Not until Rabindranath Tagore (1861–1941) did Bengal give birth to a figure of such wide-ranging influence on Indian civilization as Caitanya. Often called Caitanya Deva and Mahāprabhu (Great Lord), he was a Brahman born Viśvambhara Miśra in 1486 CE in Navadvīpa, a well-known center of traditional scholarship, about 75 km north of present-day Kolkata. (The last Hindu king of Bengal, Lakshmana Sena, fled Navadvīpa just before the arrival of the first Muslim ruler, Muhammad Bakhtiyar Khilji, at the beginning of the thirteenth century.) Viśvambhara had a Brahmanical education and began teaching after the death of his father. At the age of 22 he went on a pilgrimage to Gaya, in Bihar, to perform the *śrāddha* obsequies for his father. Something happened to him in Gaya that caused him, after an early life of restraint and quiet scholarship, to become emotional and expressive. His biographers attribute the transformation to his meeting there with an ascetic named Īśvara Puri who had earlier attempted to attract Viśvambhara to the life of a renouncer. After Īśvara Puri initiated Viśvambhara with a Kṛṣṇa *mantra*, he was transformed into the ecstatic Caitanya (De 1961:71–81).

When Caitanya returned to Navadvīpa the staid Brahman community feared for his sanity. He began the practice of group-singing of *kīrtans* (songs about the earthly career of Lord Kṛṣṇa and the fervid love of Rādhā for Kṛṣṇa), accompanied by loud drumming and dancing. Outgrowing the courtyard where they began, his *kīrtan* parties took to parading through the streets of the town in what became known as *nagar* ("town") *kīrtan*. *Nagar kīrtan* is a persisting feature of the movement Caitanya originated. His passionate expressions of love for Kṛṣṇa attracted many followers, and created a pattern for subsequent generations of devotees. Some time during his early years in Navadvīpa, Caitanya met Nityānanda, an *avadhūta* ascetic, who came to form one pole of Bengali Vaiṣṇavism characterized by a tendency to ignore education, caste, and strict observances in favor of simple, direct expression. It seems likely, as well, that the followers of Nityānanda included Sahajiyās among whom a yogic sexual *sādhana* was practiced (Dimock 1966:11–25). The lineage of Nityānanda is widespread today in rural Bengal, where the simplicity of practice, without elaborate, expensive rituals, gives ordinary people unmediated access to god. The other pole of the movement was created by the Gosvāmīs, Brahmans who established their center in Vṛndāvana, and who lived by a detailed and strict code of conduct based on the Sanskrit *Hari Bhakti Vilāsa* (De 1961:448–529). The more elaborate ritual life of the Gosvāmīs is confined to those initiated Vaiṣṇavas who adhere closely to the teachings of learned gurus.

Caitanya renounced worldly life and became a *sannyāsī*, an itinerant renouncer. Vṛndāvana, the scene of Kṛṣṇa's life among humans and of the love of Rādhā, was naturally attractive to Caitanya. In his love for his Lord, he identified strongly with Rādhā, and was thought by his followers to embody both Kṛṣṇa and Rādhā. However, Vṛndāvana is approximately 1200 kilometers from Navadvīpa, while Puri, in Odisha—an important Vaiṣṇava center and one in the dominion of a Hindu king—was only half as far, about 600 kilometers away. His journey to Puri, through western Bengal and northern Odisha, is remembered as the beginning of his distinct variety of *bhakti* religiosity in the countryside. Caitanya's initial stay in Puri, in about 1510, was rather brief. He undertook an ill-documented journey of about two-years' duration through southern and western India before returning to Puri. There, the annual outing of the god Jagannath on his gigantic *rath* at the beginning of the rainy season is a time of great intensity in the Vaiṣṇava calendar; these became occasions for visits of Caitanya's followers to Puri (De 1961:83–102).

Almost all of the accounts of Caitanya's life are hagiographical and describe miraculous powers. Even discounting some of the more improbable attributions, it is clear that he was charismatic in the original sense of the term—his spontaneous ecstasies and expressions of *bhakti* attracted people to him. About two years after his return to Puri, Caitanya decided to make his long-desired pilgrimage to Vṛndāvana. He traveled from Odisha through Bengal where, it is said, a large group of disciples attached themselves to him with the intention of joining in the journey. He was persuaded that such an entourage was not appropriate to a pilgrimage, so he returned to Puri. After a short stay he started out again more quietly, accompanied only by a Brahman and the Brahman's servant. According to the accounts of the disciples in Vṛndāvana, Caitanya was in an uncontrollable ecstasy throughout his stay; they soon took him on the road back to Puri in order to prevent him from hurting himself. Caitanya is said to have converted people into Kṛṣṇa devotees everywhere as he traveled, both inside Bengal and out.

The movement that he began is significant throughout India, but it is most influential among the ordinary people of rural Bengal—the agriculturalists, artisans, and fishers who constitute the vast majority of Hindus, both middle and lower castes. There are very few Hindu houses in rural Bengal that do not have a sacred basil (*tulasī*) plant, usually growing in a small pillar (*tulasī mañca*) near the doorway, marking the presence of Viṣṇu devotees in the house. Tending the *tulasī* is a very inexpensive expression of *bhakti*; moreover, it is said—with exaggeration characteristic of Vaiṣṇava teachings—to be equivalent to a Vedic sacrifice. In house after house, sons are named for Caitanya and his disciples. Small shrines with various representations of Caitanya and his closest followers are found throughout the villages.

Vaiṣṇavism was integral to the religious life of rural Bengal before the fifteenth century. Cults and modes of worship that preceded the appearance of Caitanya continue in the twenty-first century, though often colored by the pervasive effects of the movement he initiated. (1) Most old *zamindār* families have *kuladevatās*, clan deities. While the representations of these deities that are found in family temples are usually *śālagrāms*—fossil ammonites from the Gandaki River—they are given identities mostly drawn from the Vaiṣṇava repertoire. Their worship is often related to the career of Lord Kṛṣṇa as told in the *Bhāgavata Purāṇa* and to the prescriptions laid out in the *Hari Bhakti Vilāsa*. (2) As noted earlier, the worship of Satya Nārāyaṇa is one of the most common religious practices of people at all levels of society and on a wide variety of occasions. Nārāyaṇa is generally regarded as a form of Viṣṇu; they are often depicted as identical. Satya Nārāyaṇa is a particul ar name and form of this god, distinguished by his identification with a Sufi saint known as Satya Pīr, and by Bengali narratives unknown in other parts of India. (3) Nārāyaṇa or Viṣṇu has as his consort the goddess Lakṣmī, whose worship goes on year-round in rural Bengal. As the goddess responsible for the prosperity of a house and family, abiding in the crops, she is often represented—in various forms—in households at all levels of society. (4) The cult of Kṛṣṇa and of Rādhā–Kṛṣṇa is spread throughout Bengali Hindu society. Many middle- and lower-caste villagers are vigorous participants in the Kṛṣṇa *kīrtan* parties that move through the villages on full-moon nights. There were three main constituents of Vaiṣṇava practice in Kelomal: processional *kīrtans* and celebrations of Kṛṣṇa *bhakti*; commemoration of noteworthy events from the *Bhāgavata Purāṇa*; and, for the initiated Vaiṣṇavas, observance of the demanding "opinion of the Gosvāmīs" of Vṛndāvana (*gosvāmī mat*), practices that are often different from general Bengali usage.

Maṅgal

The significance of Śītalā and Manasā among rural people in West Bengal leads one to think of a long line of functionalist explanations of religion as the struggle of helpless humanity against existential insecurity. Infectious diseases and snakebites are difficult to prevent through practical action, so magical or ritual defenses are attempted. However, although there have been cyclones that were remembered by people in Kelomal as having done more harm than disease and snakes combined, there is no god of cyclonic storms. The gods may be human creations, but they are not reflexive reactions to problems large or small. Every cultural system provides a scheme from which deities are created, and each perpetuates the products of past efforts. (The term "understood" can be substituted for "created"; the issue is what people think gods are and what gods do, not their "existence," whatever is meant by that word.) The Abrahamic religions, which assert that god is singular, provide work-arounds: trinitarianism, Mariolatry, saints, *pīrs*, *jinn*, or at least the promise of a *mehdi* or a messiah in the future. The Indian religions that are usually gathered under the heading of Hinduism, provide a less-tortured path to deity creation, declaring that there are 33 crores (330 million) of gods, most of them still undiscovered.

In Bengal, the process of discovery is guided by a cultural scheme under which the gods manifest themselves, then show humans why they need to be worshiped; in their narratives, they create their own places in the pantheon. Existential threats cause some deities to reveal themselves; there is not a theogony of existential threats, but rather the self-revelation of gods is built around the concept of *maṅgal*. In its most general sense, *maṅgal* means "well-being"; and it is well-being that is the fruit most generally sought by Bengalis in worship—from the simple offering of water to the *tulasī* and sounding of the conch-shell at twilight to the most elaborate ritual observances, such as Durgā Pūjā. The forces of nature, such as rain and storms, can give or take away *maṅgal*, just as can disease and poisonous serpents, and they can be approached through gods of deliverance, such as Kṛṣṇa or Śiva, who also belong to the all-India pantheon. But the deities especially known to the Bengalis—those celebrated in the *maṅgal* poems—have distinctive narrative ties to Bengal, even when, like Śiva and Caṇḍī, they are deities also known to the rest of India.

The life-long quest for *maṅgal* brings people into daily contact with the gods mentally, collectively, and ritually. However, no one ignores the obvious fact that the well-being of a family or household, or a clan, a caste, or a village, is also brought about by practical activity that is not ritual. Cultivating crops; weaving cloth; making baskets, plows, and pots; excavating ponds and canals—all conduce to the well-being of people and communities. But these are activities that are considered to be work (*kāj*, *kām*, *karma*) or labor (*pariśram*). They belong to the realm of *saṃsāra*, which in a philosophical sense means "worldly attachments," in a more ordinary sense "worldly life," and in its most common usage "family" or "family life." These are the difficult activities that are obligatory to sustain a family, and they are also the activities that tie people to this world, as opposed to helping them toward "release" or "liberation" (*mukti*). While *mukti* or *mokṣa* is understood by some people simply as release from rebirth, Vaiṣṇava-oriented people have an image of a heaven (*svarga*), a place of infinite delight (*ānandaloka*) where Kṛṣṇa engages in eternal play. Ritual—like work and other action—is also considered to be *karma*; but rituals are usually qualified as *śubha karma*, "auspicious action." Both work and ritual have results: *phal*, "fruit." The fruits that are sought through ritual—whether they are limited ones like preventing infection or increasing growing crops, or the ultimate fruit, release from *saṃsara*—are *māṅgalik*, "auspicious," "propitious."

Some *śubha karmas* are what anthropologists recognize as life-cycle rites. Ronald Inden and I analyzed the Bengali Hindu life-cycle rites (*saṃskāra*), including the rites for the dead (Inden and Nicholas 1977:35–66). The life-cycle rites are classified as *naimittika karma*, acts that are "special," done on contingent "occasions," and not regularly repeated. They contrast with *nitya karma*, auspicious acts that are done regularly and repeatedly. The language of *śubha karma* and *nitya karma* is used mainly in priestcraft, and in the manuals used by priests. In ordinary language, *nitya karmas* are usually called *pūjās*, meaning "worship," or *utsava*, "festival," "celebration," or "ceremony." Durgā Pūjā, which is widely regarded as the hallmark of Bengali Hindu culture, is traditionally based in individual houses (*bāṛi*), which means a particular clan or descent group, normally of a high, dominant caste in a village (Nicholas 2013). Gājan, which is performed by ordinary people—cultivators and artisans—is based in the *deś*, the land, or country, extending indefinitely beyond the boundaries of the village in which it takes place (Nicholas 2008b). Śītalā Pūjā, which addresses the mother of a village, is based in individual villages; it distinguishes between villages, and treats each one as a total social unit, inclusive of all castes (Nicholas 2003:62–211).

These three *pūjās* were of great importance to the people in Kelomal, but they were not by any means the totality of *māṅgalik* religious life in the village. As noted earlier, the rites and symbols of Vaiṣṇavism were displayed in many aspects of daily life and were the most common expression of religious thought and action (Nicholas 2003:28–61). Then there were the *pūjās* that were done by individual households throughout the village and throughout the year. Most families that performed household *pūjās* strove to do so on a regular (*nitya*) schedule, though contingencies arose that interfered with the best of intentions. And there were *pūjās* that were done out of individual desire (*kāmya*) or a personal commitment (*mānasik, mānat*). I shall say something about all of these types of worship. The fact that so much of the religious life of Kelomal remains to be described and interpreted is testimony to what I call the center of gravity of Bengali Hindu culture. Neither ceaseless labor in pursuit of a better standard of living, nor the emotional engagement of Bengali politics—both of which are of visible importance in the lives of ordinary people—outweighs the value of the expressivity, performance, and delight they manifest in rituals. Most people find *ānanda*, "joy," in beautiful rituals.

History and the Present

The fieldwork described in this book was done in 1968, 1969, and 1970; so what is being described is now history. I cannot chronicle the changes that have taken place since that time, so there is a sense in which this is an account of a moment in history, a moment that had a deep history of its own. Ordinary people in Kelomal had a sense about history, which they brought with them when they offered explanations of their customs and practices. Most often their historical sense was based on their respect for what they thought had been the practices of their ancestors. A frequent answer to the question "Why perform such and such a ritual?" was " Our ancestors have done this for fourteen generations, so we do it." Underlying such answers was a theory of inheritance that makes the perpetuation of custom seem close to a biological necessity.

Though sometimes tinged with a bit of golden-ageism, among educated villagers in the 1960s there was a clear idea about the differences between past and present; many people remembered the fierce cyclone that struck the district in October 1942, killing thousands of people and destroying the principal rice crop along with many buildings, followed by the 1942/43 famine; then Independence in 1947 bringing electoral politics, land reform, and other radical changes to local society. Most people understood what had changed in their world, but they strove to maintain what they regarded as their ancient customs and their duty to their forebears. I have looked back into history, before the 1960s and before the 1940s, to try to understand how the religious and social systems that I saw were put together. The apparently heterogeneous assembly of gods, myths, and rituals that pervaded the lives of people at every level of this small society seemed to them to be quite coherent, to constitute a well-organized system of beliefs and practices. Trying to understand how that system came together has been a fascinating pursuit in its own right, though to some extent it has led away from ethnography.

Bengali Hindu Society

Bengali Hindu society is still today predominantly rural. Among the 91 million people who live in West Bengal, even though the percentage of urban dwellers is the highest in history, 62 million (68 %) live in rural areas. In 1951, at the first Census of India after Independence, West Bengal was approximately 75% rural. As in other parts of India, villages in Bengal include a range of occupationally specialized castes, although agriculture is the principal source of the livelihood of most people. The anthropological study of peasant societies was begun by Robert Redfield, whose influence was greatest in the post-war 1940s and '50s. He visualized villages as situated on a cultural continuum between more or less culturally autonomous tribes (whose members were generally non-literate) and more cosmopolitan urban societies, which were differentiated by class and occupation, and were dependent on literacy to conduct their affairs. Contemporary West Bengal, has moved some way along what Redfield called the "folk–urban continuum." Many, if not most, adult villagers have visited Kolkata and 73% of them are literate; these are no longer isolated and illiterate peasants.

Weber (1946:283), who probably had a very slender knowledge of any actual peasants, characterized peasant religion as "inclined toward magic" and "bound to nature." However, he noted one phenomenon of importance for understanding India:

> Only tremendous transformations of life-orientation have succeeded in tearing them away from this universal and primeval form of religiosity. Such transformations have been derived either from other strata or from mighty prophets, who, through the power of miracles, legitimize themselves as sorcerers.

He noted (1968:447–48) the recurrence in India of such "prophets," whom he called "mystagogues." (Students of contemporary India will recognize the attraction many people—not all of them unsophisticated villagers—find in the legerdemain practiced by some popular religious figures.) However, in contrast to the mystagogue there is the "exemplary prophet . . . who by his personal example, demonstrates to others the way of religious salvation," a figure "particularly characteristic of India." Buddha was Weber's prototypical exemplary prophet. His life of renunciation and contemplation was at the heart of his teaching, and his example laid the foundation for a world religion (though it largely disappeared from India). The religion of monastic Buddhists today is predominantly other-worldly; that is, oriented toward release from this world and from the endless chain of mortality. Caitanya was also such a prophet; during his own lifetime the influence of his example was extensive, and it continued after his death. Although, unlike the serene Buddha, Caitanya was an expressive ecstatic, like the Buddha his aim was other-worldly. Still today, for some who follow Caitanya, the objective is Vaiṣṇava heaven, the dwelling place of Kṛṣṇa and the *gopīs*. However, despite the pervasiveness of Caitanya's influence, and his other-worldly message, the great weight of Bengali Hindu practice is this-worldly; the objectives are mostly near-term and related to this life and its hardships. People seek the birth of sons, or good crops, or relief from suffering; ritual is supposed to bear fruit (*phal*). For most people the language of deliverance, of "reaching the other shore," that figures so strongly in Vaiṣṇava hymns, pertains to life in the present. People know about *mukti* or *mokṣa*, about release from the pain of rebirth, but that is not what they say they are seeking when they worship.

Kelomal

There are hundreds of villages in East Medinipur District—exactly how many there are depends on who is counting. There are villages (*grām*) that are socially recognized as communities by their inhabitants but not entered as such in the revenue rolls, which list *mauzās*, the Mughal Persian term still used to designate revenue-villages. There are *mauzās* that encompass more than one socially recognized village. Recently the West Bengal Ministry of Drinking Water and Sanitation has added a second set of names after "Village Names," which it calls "Habitation Names" to recognize socially significant residential units. Kelomal is truly an odd combination: there are five *mauzās* and eight *grāms*, all of which together are seen by their inhabitants as constituting a single community. When a resident of any of these villages is asked by an outsider for his or her village, the usual response is "Kelomal"; internally, however, the name of one of the socially recognized villages is offered. The post office and schools all bear the name of Kelomal. I have elsewhere discussed the social history of Kelomal, its settlement, social composition, and speculation about the origin of its name (Nicholas 2008a). Google Maps affords a view of the locality with the names of six of the villages; Bhubankalua (spelled "Bhubunkalua"), Murarikalua, Satkalua, Narsinghkalua, Balikalua, and Ramkalua. Banamalikalua and Dubkalua are omitted. The name Kelomal appears on the post office and on the Sarojbasini Girls' High School. Radhamani Hat, a major bi-weekly market that falls within Murarikalua, is identified on the map as a bus stop.

In 1970 there were representatives of 21 castes resident in the eight Kelomal villages: 20 of them were Hindu; there was one settlement of Muslim Weavers (Jola Tanti) that lived on the edge of one village. The Māhīṣya caste, whose preferred occupation was farming, was the largest single group in Kelomal, with 2143 persons, 57.6% of the total population. Closely connected to the Māhīṣyas was a population of 79 caste Vaiṣṇavas, comprising 2.1% of the population.

The dominant caste in Kelomal was Dakṣin Rāṛhi Kāyasthas; there were 277 persons of this caste, 7.4% of the population. Before independence Kayasthas, whose hereditary occupation is usually given as "scribe" or "writer," were often employed in the courts of petty rulers and the administration of local estates. The Kayasthas in Kelomal obtained their dominant position through such roles of two of their ancestors, one in the court of Tamluk and one in Mahishadal. These houses had once organized many lower caste people in an arrangement of hierarchical dependence that I call the sacrificial polity, which was made explicit in the ritual of Durgā Pūjā and in the subsequent autumn rituals. Another caste, Karaṇ, has the same traditional scribal occupation as the Kayasthas. Karan appears as a synonym for Kayastha in pre-modern Bengali writings, but the Karans in Kelomal (323, 8.7% of the population) said they originated in Odisha (Uṛiyā Sṛṣti Karaṇ).

There were four different Brahman castes in Kelomal. Brahmans of the "Middle Order" (Madhya Śreṇī Brāhmaṇ) filled the priestly office for Kayasthas and for the nine high Sudra castes (*navaśākha*); for their caste, they constituted an atypically large group (105 persons, 2.8 % of the population), were mostly well educated, and many men had occupations besides priesthood. There were seven households, with 40 persons (1.1%), of Vyāsokta Brāhmaṇs, who were priests for the Mahisyas. There were also fifteen Brahmans whose ancestors came from Odisha (Utkal Śreṇī Brāhmaṇ); they performed rituals for the Karans and also served as cooks on ceremonial occasions. There were thirteen Rāṛhi Śreṇī Brāhmaṇs, refugees from erstwhile East Pakistan who had settled in Kelomal after Partition. Although four Brahman castes seems ample, there were other endogamous Brahman castes resident in other nearby villages who provided priestly services for castes outside of the "nine-branches" (*navaśākha*), the higher-ranking Śūdras. Agradānī or Agraśrāddhī Brāhmaṇs who dined and accepted gifts at services for the dead (*śrāddha*), and Ācārya Brāhmaṇs who were astrologers and who performed rituals for some low castes also visited Kelomal to provide their specialized ritual services.

There were members of five of the nine *navaśākha* Sudra castes, from whom Brahmans were permitted to accept water: Tili (Merchants), Mālākar (Garland-makers), Nāpit (Barbers), Svarnakār (Goldsmiths), and Kāmār (Blacksmiths), numbered 232 persons or 6.2% of the population. In addition to the Māhīṣyas, who predominated among the Sudras, and whose priests were Vyāsokta Brāhmaṇs, there were several other Sudra castes, each of which had its own priests (sometimes called *patit* "fallen" Brahmans): Śuklī Tānti (Weavers), Rājbaṅgśī (Fishers), Dhopā (Launderers, who in Kelomal had become weavers and makers of the images of deities), and Karaṅgā (Cattle-traders and Veterinarians). There were 310 persons among these castes, constituting 8.3% of the population. The lowest Hindu castes were Ḍoms (Basket Makers and Musicians) with 28 persons, and Mucis (Leather-workers) with 8 persons, together constituting 1% of the population. There were 74 Muslim Weavers (Jolā or Julāhā Tāntis), who were 2% of the population, though socially they belonged to the village of Kumorganj, which lay directly across the road from Kelomal. Muslims predominated in Kumorganj, where there was a mosque.

In writing about the Māhīṣyas, together with the Karans and *navasakha* Sudras, I often refer to "ordinary" or "common people." These terms translate the Bengali expression *sādhāraṇ lok*, which is somewhat more respectful than *choṭo lok*, "little people," the term higher-caste people usually used to refer to them. Those "ordinary people," in turn, spoke of the high-caste dominant families as *baṛo lok*, "big people."

Most villages in East Medinipur are demographically similar to four of the Kelomal villages, the ones that lie farthest from the neighborhoods where Kayasthas and Brahmans dwell. Balikalua was 72.8% Mahisya, Satkalua was 79.7% Mahisya, Ramkalua was 94.4% Mahisya, and Narsinghkalua was 100% Mahisya. The

Mahisyas are the descendants of the frontier settlers who cleared the jungle, embanked the fields, cultivated rice, and caught fish. Their descendants predominate throughout the region. When the Census of British India was done in 1881 the name Mahisya did not appear: in its place was a populous caste of farmers and fishers called Kaivartta. The Census Report, and the ethnological compendium prepared by H. H. Risley (1892) discussed the social status and rank of the Kaivarttas, noting that while there were five ancient kingdoms in Medinipur that had Kaivartta rulers, high-ranking Brahmans and *navaśākha* Sudras would not accept water offered by persons of this caste. By the end of the nineteenth century there were many educated Kaivarttas who were offended or embarrassed by this official characterization of their low status. They created a caste organization along the lines of a modern voluntary association dedicated to obtaining an improved standing for their group. During the first decades of the twentieth century the cultivating section of the caste—called Hālī ("plowing") or Cāsī ("cultivating") Kaivarttas—separated itself from the group that relied primarily on fishing for its livelihood; they chose Māhīṣya, a name from the *purāṇas*, to distinguish themselves from the Jālī ("netting") Kaivarttas, the name that remained to designate the fishing section. The Fishers soon took their turn at name-changing, adopting Rājbaṅgśī as a caste name, though they were still often called by less elevated names such as Tiyar or Dhibar. The changes of names undergone by the former Kaivartta caste, however, did not win them the service of high-ranking Brahmans.

The attention given to caste names and other indicators of dignity are signals of the continuing importance of caste differences in rural Bengal. The distinction between the "big people" and the "little people" was to a significant degree a register of caste difference, which corresponded to the differences in occupation, income, education, and life style that are markers of social class in other social contexts. The very large proportion of Māhīṣyas in the population of Kelomal and all the surrounding areas mitigated the low rank they occupied as outside the *navaśākha*, "high Sudra" caste group. The Mahisyas represented the villages as communities; the headman of each village was a Mahisya. While they symbolically acknowledged their status as *prajās*, dependents of the Kayasthas, during Durgā Pūjā, they also were the sole masters of the Gājan and the worship of the village tutelary goddesses. The abolition of *zamindāri* land tenure strengthened the position of the Māhīṣyas in relation to the Kayasthas (although it did little to improve the position of castes below them). Voting in democratic elections established an advantage in numbers unknown in the old order, but factional cleavages divided the Māhīṣyas and other villagers, creating contests rather than the "vote blocs" seen elsewhere in India, where local caste groups vote as units. The enduring if imperfect power of rituals to represent and restore a coherent society in the face of powerful social changes will be told in the following chapters.

In my earlier research in East Medinipur I had worked in villages that had the more typical caste demography. In 1968 I selected Kelomal because it offered a more complete society as completeness is conceived of in Bengali culture. Among the Māhīṣyas the ritual calendar is naturally weighted toward the agricultural cycle, with great importance placed on the spring Gājan and its symbols of fertilizing. Among Kayasthas and Brahmans, Durgā Pūjā and the subsequent rites of the autumn are considered most important. I wanted to see all of the elements in the annual cycle, which turned out to be very numerous.

The Kelomal Economy

Most Kayastha and Brahman houses were relatively well-off and educated. Apart from a few Brahmans who lived primarily from priestly work, there were teachers and employees who worked in salaried positions in the town of Tamluk, then the Subdivdisional Headquarters, and now the Headquarters of the District of Purba Medinipur. Most Kayastha households also had members who worked far from Kelomal, in Kolkata, Medinipur town, and Jamshedpur. People who lived far away visited the village only occasionally, especially in the autumn at "*pūjā* time," although they regarded Kelomal as "home," that is, the address they gave when asked for "permanent residence" or *nivāsa*, which might be understood as "ancestral abode." Kelomal had good privately operated schools, one for boys and one with residential facilities for girls. Teachers in the schools were mostly Brahman and Kayastha men from Kelomal. These families also owned more than the average amount of agricultural land and fish ponds. Before independence much of the cultivation was done by share-croppers. When West Bengal's land reform program began to grant land to the tiller, some of the share-cropped land was shifted to "self cultivation," that is, farmed by day laborers rather than share-croppers. Some land was held as tax-exempt *devottar* property, that is, the deed was in the name of a family deity. A family member was declared to be the "servant" (*sevāit*) of the deity, responsible for worship, care of the temple, and management of the land and its produce, putatively to support the deity and temple.

The rural economy of Kelomal in the late 1960s depended primarily on agriculture, handloom weaving, and betel leaf (*pān*) cultivation. Mechanization had not yet reached the area in 1968. Rice agriculture was the primary activity of farmers, and most of it was rain irrigated. Fields were cultivated with bullocks, planted and weeded by hand. High-yielding rice varieties were extensively farmed, and wherever water was available, a second crop was cultivated after the main harvest in Agrahāyaṇa and Pauṣa (November/January). Though most men, from the highest castes to the lowest, caught fish for home consumption, fishing provided a principal source of income for the Fishers. When they were offered the opportunity, they caught fish in the ponds belonging to other villagers in return for a share of the catch. Some of them occasionally went on fishing voyages into the Bay of Bengal with relatives who lived in villages nearer to the sea and who operated large boats.

The population density in the Kelomal area was very high; agricultural land was insufficient to support all of the families that might have preferred to farm, and many households supplemented their income with one or two handlooms that they operated for many hours of the day (and night). Weaving was sometimes called *ṭak-ṭaki kāj*: the sound of the shuttle striking one side of the frame then the other in a steady rhythm, with a sound like "*ṭak*." That sound could be heard coming from many houses far into the night, especially on the night before *hātbār*, one of the two days a week when the market at Radhamani Hat convened. Radhamani was the main market for the Kelomal locality. There were many shops belonging to Kelomal Tili families that were open daily. Marwari cloth merchants came from Howrah twice weekly. Most weavers worked on the putting-out system: they received thread from the merchants and returned woven cloth on market day in return for a "making charge" (*bāni*). A majority of weavers took advances on the making charge from the merchants and were perpetually in debt, a condition that the merchants fostered because it guaranteed them a steady supply of cloth. The most common product of the Kelomal weavers was cotton bed-sheets made of locally dyed yarn. These sheets were mostly a uniform color except for the borders, which were a simple pattern of stripes in contrasting colors. A few people with less sophisticated looms made loosely woven *gāmchās*, usually in large, brightly colored checks. *Gāmchās* ("body wipers," i.e., towels) are ubiquitous; they are used for towels, head-wraps, garments when bathing, and sometimes by men to cover their torsos. Cloth was delivered to the middlemen in the market on Sunday or Wednesday, the days the market met, stacked together in bales, taken to the railway station by bus, and delivered to Howrah where there was a larger wholesale cloth market. In the years since we did fieldwork, the scale of the cloth market has increased greatly; Radhamani Hat is now the second largest cloth market in West Bengal, and it now has a bank branch.

Pān, "betel leaf," is the major ingredient in the masticatory often called "betel." The "betel nut," the fruit of the areca palm (*supāri*), which contains an alkaloid compound, is widely used throughout tropical Asia and is one of the ingredients of a prepared *pān* in India. When it is ripe and dried, the areca or betel nut is hard and has to be cut into bits with a special cutter. A small amount of cut-up *supāri*, some spices, and sometimes a bit of tobacco, are wrapped in a betel leaf that has been smeared with lime and a red dye. Calcium oxide in the lime releases the alkaloid from the areca nut. The main flavor of the preparation is provided by the betel leaf. It is the quality and characteristics of the leaf that determine the quality of the *pān*. Kelomal and its vicinity were blessed with appropriate conditions for cultivating betel leaves, and it was a cash crop that enabled a number of families to prosper despite having limited agricultural land. *Pān* cultivation is labor intensive but can be done profitably on a plot of land as small as 5–6 meters by 10–15 meters.

The plant from which betel leaf is harvested is a variety of pepper; the vine grows in fertile, moist soil shaded from direct sunlight. The plentiful fine alluvium of the Kelomal area is well suited to *pān* cultivation. In this area, *pān* gardens (*baroj*) are made with the dried stalks of a tall marsh grass called *khaṛi*. Slender stiff stalks of *khaṛi* about 180 centimeters tall are placed close to one another around the outside and across the top of the *baroj*, so as to admit only a small amount of sunlight. Inside, deeply cultivated rows of soil are mixed with oilseed cake and manure. Vine cuttings are planted about 30 centimeters apart, each with its own *khaṛi* stake extending to the top of the *baroj*; rows are separated just enough for a person to pass between them. As gardens mature, more soil and manure are added, so that older gardens may be elevated as much as a meter or a meter and a half above ground level; thus elevated, a garden is not likely to be flooded during heavy monsoon rains. The monsoon is generally advantageous, since the *baroj* does not have to be watered when it rains. However, the price of *pān* goes up in the dry season, so watering a garden to keep it producing is very rewarding. When we were doing fieldwork there were no pumps and no good method of watering *pān* gardens except laboriously by hand. Potters in a nearby village made special pots, called *baroj kalasi*, that could hold about five liters of water. During dry weather the *pān* cultivator and/or his wife and children filled these pots in a pond near the *baroj*, climbed up from the pond with the pot on one hip, an arm hooked around its neck, to the *baroj*, where they poured the water carefully between the rows of vines. It was exhausting work, but the income made successful *pān* cultivators prosperous.

Pān leaves were plucked by hand on the day before market day. The *pān* market at Ramtarak Hat was a bit further away than Radhamani Hat. Often working late into the night, the cultivator arranged the leaves, one at a time, in spiral layers in a circular basket, then sprinkled them with water to keep them fresh. Early on market day he put the basket on his head and walked to Ramtarak Hat. There he sold them to a middleman who resold them in Howrah to dealers who in turn, transported them by train across northern India. A cultivator who grew valuable *miṭhā* or *sānci pān* might come home from a market day with Rs.50, a large sum in those days, when a day laborer was paid only Rs.1.25 (along with a mid-morning snack and a meal) for seven or so hours of work. The *pān* cultivators were the people who first built domestic Hari Mandirs, Vaiṣṇava shrines representing Caitanya and his principal disciples. However, *pān* cultivation is also subject to catastrophic uncertainty: a virus could wipe out an entire *baroj*; and, once it appeared, it was almost impossible to eradicate. Although they were generally devout Vaiṣṇavas, around the time of Kali Puja in the autumn *pān* cultivators held a special *pūjā* for Baroj Kālī to protect their gardens from blight.

In long-settled parts of Bengal, *pān* cultivation is done primarily by a specialist caste, Bārui or Bārujībī, "those who live by the *baroj*." However, there were no Baruis (nor Tāmbūlīs, betel-leaf sellers) in Kelomal or surrounding villages; *pān* was grown almost entirely by Māhīṣyas. Most handloom weavers in Kelomal were also Mahisyas. There were also local caste groups that claimed weaving as their caste occupation, both Sukli Tantis and the Weavers whose ancestors were Launderers. The Muslim settlement on the edge of Kelomal also included many weavers.

There was some electrification in Kelomal in 1968. Power had been brought in to run irrigation pumps, but some of the more prosperous householders had managed to get connections. The supply was fitful, usually a few hours a day. No one had a television receiver at that time. Since then, the increased availability of electricity and the popularity of television have influenced the knowledge and worldview of villagers to a far greater extent than radio and newspapers, the media to which they had access in 1968.

2. Hindu Rituals in Bengal

Ritual Universes

Most of the rituals seen in Kelomal had this-worldly objectives. All rituals were supposed to bear fruit—usually for some social group, although occasionally for a single person. For people in Kelomal, the most inclusive of the social universes was the *deś*, the "country." The Gājan, the most important ritual of the spring season, had the goal of fertilizing the world, which in Kelomal was thought of as extending approximately as far as one could see. The boundaries were indefinite; success in worship would be enjoyed by an extensive region. Even though the ritual was performed in one village and at one Śiva temple, participants could come from anywhere, which, in practice, meant any of the surrounding villages.

By contrast, worship of the village mother—as in Śītalā Pūjā—had a village (*grām*) with definite boundaries as its object. Most villages are made up of a few *pāṛās* (neighborhoods), cohesive residential units with a high degree of solidarity even in the absence of ties of kin or caste. In the case of the minority castes in Kelomal, the *pāṛā* was coextensive with the local caste group. Thus, groups such as the Fishers, Launderers/Weavers, or Doms, a neighborhood-based *pūjā* had the local caste group as its social universe, though they always referred to the occasion as "our *pāṛā pūjā*" rather than "our *jāti pūjā*."

A great many acts of worship take place in "houses" (*bāṛi*), a term that may be used inclusively to refer to an entire clan or descent group (*vaṃśa*, pronounced *boṅgśo*) or shrunken to refer to a single domestic group (*paribār*). For example, the Durgā Pūjā of the Ghosh Bari included all of the male descendants of the founding ancestor, a figure from the nineteenth century, as the worshiping universe. Many of the rituals that are conducted within individual houses are *bratas*, which usually impose austerities on women. The expectation that a bride would be brought into the house to live in a joint family with the husband's parents and siblings remained very strong; a part of becoming a member of the marital household includes learning the domestic rituals practiced there. After the death of the parents, married brothers normally divide their property and create separate economic units. In Kelomal, many houses had partitioned their property several times over across three or four generations, but were still living close together, if not in the same house. Many such groups continued to share their domestic rituals although the families were economically independent of one another. Localized descent groups (*kula*) held domestic rituals in common unless conflict over the division of their joint property had created an irreconcilable cleavage.

Finally, on some occasions, a single family or even a single person undertook a ritual independent of any other houses or any wider social group. Many such *pūjās* were held to honor a *mānsik* or *mānat*, a personal commitment to worship a particular deity if some desire—such as birth of a son or cure of an affliction—were fulfilled.

The Structure of the Year

People in rural Bengal are attentive to the calendar because of the dictates of agriculture in the monsoon climate and also because of the cycle of rituals. The four cardinal points on the calendar, the equinoxes and the solstices, are ritually marked transitions. Each solar month begins when the sun moves from one sign of the zodiac (*rāśi*) to the next; these transitions are called *saṃkrāntis*. The four transitions that mark the key moments of the ritual year are not perfectly aligned with the equinoxes and the solstices, though it is difficult to notice the discrepancy in tropical latitudes. Two of the nodal observances, Durgā Pūjā and the Śayana ("lying down") of Viṣṇu, are set on the lunar calendar so they rarely occur on the *saṃkrānti*, although the date is always close. Makar Saṃkrānti (the winter solstice) and *paylā* Baiśākh (the first day of the new year) are set on the solar calendar and occur on the *saṃkrānti* days, which do not vary much from one year to the next, although they are also not exactly on the solstice and the equinox.

For the people in Kelomal, and for rural people throughout West Bengal, the four nodal points in the calendar, and the observances that take place on those occasions, provide a structure for the year. The principal polarity is between the rites of autumn and the rites of spring, which I have written about in detail (Nicholas 2008b, 2013); they are opposite one another on many dimensions. Spring (*basanta*) is the time of the Gājan and the beginning of the new year on the Bengali calendar. Some villagers from agricultural and artisan castes take very stringent vows and become ascetic renouncers (*sannyāsī*) for the duration of the ritual. During the principal days of the Gājan—in most villages a week-long period—the temporary ascetics perform arduous ordeals and chant for long periods in an effort to arouse Śiva from his yogic slumber. Gājan enacts the marriage of Śiva and Durgā; it culminates in their union, late at night on the penultimate day of the old year. The high castes of the village have very limited roles in Gājan, though they are counted among the beneficiaries of its fertilizing power; social distinctions are subordinated in this ritual. There is no Sanskrit text for the Gājan; written sources alluding to the ritual are middle-period Bengali works pertaining to the god Dharma. The ritual practices are passed down orally and are leading examples of *lokācār* (popular customs).

The rites of autumn (*śarat*), by contrast, are detailed in ancient Sanskrit texts and heavily reliant on learned Brahmans. They are the observances of the high castes whose members, until comparatively recent times, held the dominant economic and political power in rural Bengal. These rituals are leading examples of what I will call "the rulers' schedule of worship." The agricultural and artisan castes, whose members have the most important roles in the Gājan, are engaged as servants and dependents during the worship of Durgā and the other goddesses whose *pūjās* follow. Durgā Pūjā is symbolically centered on the sacrifice and the relationship between the rulers, who satisfy the goddess with blood offerings, and their subordinates, who receive a share of these sacrifices but cannot offer them. The popular customary rites of the Gājan address the village as a unity: families and clans are all in it together regardless of caste or wealth. By contrast, the Durgā Pūjā of the rulers, and the subsequent *pūjās* of the autumn enact the hierarchies of caste and wealth, arranging the local community in a ranked social order that I call "the sacrificial polity."

The solstitial rites are secondary to the equinoctial ones, but they are nevertheless very important in providing the structure of the year. The vernal equinox is marked by observances on the lunar calendar, so it is rarely on the day of the equinox. On the second day of the bright fortnight of Āṣāṛha (June-July), which may occur before or after the *saṃkrānti*, the god Jagannāth in Puri is taken out from his temple on a journey in his chariot (*rath-yātrā*). This is an occasion of central importance for Vaiṣṇavas; there are *rath-yātrā* observances all over West Bengal, including one at Dimari Hat, near Kelomal. The chariot returns to the temple on the tenth day of the bright fortnight, and the eleventh day is known as Śayanaikadaśī, "Lying-down eleventh," the day Viṣṇu is said to lie down for his sleep, beginning the night of the gods. The night of the gods ends on the eleventh day of the bright fortnight of Kārtik (October/November), the day after the end of the cycle of goddess worship begun with Durgā Pūjā. Jagannāth appears to have originated among common people in Odisha, but, in keeping with the Vaiṣṇava custom of painting everything with a Vedic brush, his rituals have been heavily Sanskritized. The Puri temple has become one of the most important Vaiṣṇava *dhām* in India.

The end of the night of the gods corresponds to the beginning of the main rice harvest in eastern Medinipur District. Harvesting and threshing rice is, of course, very hard work but it is also the happiest time in agricultural families (providing that the harvest is at least normal). Lakṣmī is visible in heaps of golden grain on the threshing floor. The harvest culminates in the winter solstice, known as Makar Saṃkrānti, when the sun passes into the *rāśi* of the Makar, an imaginary creature with an elephant's trunk and the body of a dolphin, the conveyance of the goddess Gaṅgā. Being connected with agriculture, Makar Saṃkrānti is an event on the solar calendar. In an observance called *nabanna* ("new rice"), newly harvested rice is first eaten on this day, in the special form of *piṭhā*, sweet cakes of rice flour. There are numerous ritual observances that span the range from the most local and vernacular (*laukika*) to the most Sanskritic.

Between the Brahmanical rituals of the formerly ruling dominant castes and the *lokācār*, or *laukika*, rituals encoded in popular custom are two intermediate levels. *Sadācār* ("good practice") and *śiṣṭācār* ("polite practice") are terms used to describe rituals that are observed by refined households, usually equated with the high castes but also including some cultivator and merchant caste households who qualify as *bhadralok* (roughly "genteel people"). These are households that are reasonably prosperous, so they can afford to perform rituals properly; also, they are attentive to their conduct. They often regard their rituals as *kulācār*, "clan customs." I refer to this schedule of worship as "cosmopolitan"; it is not confined to a village or a locality but is known and followed by Hindu *bhadralok* throughout Hindu Bengal. *Deśācār* ("custom of the country"), by contrast, is restricted to a particular locality. In Kelomal that locality is the kingdom of Tamluk. ("Kingdom" in rural Bengal should usually be understood as a *parganā*, a unit of revenue administration under the Mughals that became a "*zamindāri* estate" under the British. Such kingdoms are nothing like the princely states that were found elsewhere in colonial India.) However, the customs of other nearby kingdoms—Kashijora, Mandalghat, and Moyna—were followed by people who originated there. As will become clear in chapter 4, the distinctions among these levels of ritual practice are most clearly drawn between the various occasions of the worship of Lakṣmī.

In previous books I pointed out that, although they may be intensively engaged in the worship of Śiva or Durgā, the people of Kelomal cannot be characterized as Śaivas or Śāktas. Along with some other important deities, the present work adds a Vaiṣṇava leg to the tripod. In addition to what I have said earlier (Nicholas

2003:28–61), here I expand the picture to indicate more about the pervasiveness of Vaiṣṇavism in Bengali Hindu society. While the religious year is structured by the observances of the solstices and the equinoxes, the very numerous Vaiṣṇava rites that go on around the year create a continuous ground, to use a musical analogy. In addition to the calendar of Kṛṣṇa worship that is related to events described in the *Bhāgavata Purāṇa*, there is also a cycle of Lakṣmī worship that is tied to agriculture. The worship of Satya Nārāyaṇa, which is also important throughout the year, follows many calendars—some set by individual households and lineages, and some set by no calendar at all but rather by transitory piety.

In a literate civilization with a specialized hieratic class there is an inescapable connection between historic and textual religious practice; however, ethnography also brings to light many elements that have emerged from local usage. This book begins with ethnography and the life and activity of the people in Kelomal. They thought of themselves as participating in the civilized practice of Brahmanical Hinduism, even when they were engaged in rites that are wholly or largely indigenous and unscriptural. The mythic or folkloric narratives that correspond to the *pūjās* described here generally offer a this-worldly return for worship, and, correspondingly, this-worldly suffering attributed to failure to worship. However, as I said earlier, *bhakti*—devotion—is a different matter. Love for Kṛṣṇa offers some serenity in this life, but the goal is an end to the cycle of rebirth.

According to learned Advaita teaching, the self (*ātmā*) of a person who has achieved a complete cessation of desire will not be reborn, but will merge with the uncreated ground of being (*brahman*) and become extinguished (*nirvāṇa*, *mukti*), losing its individual distinction. Rather than offering the bliss of extinction, the Vaiṣṇava gurus who taught villagers in Kelomal emphasized an all-consuming love for Kṛṣṇa, with *mukti* interpreted as union with Kṛṣṇa and eternity in a heavenly Vṛndāvana. However it is conceived of, the goal of *mukti* is quite different from the worldly rewards people sought in the worship of Lakṣmī and Satya Nārāyaṇa, as well as Śiva and Durgā. The complex and elaborate character of "Hinduism" as a religion is clearly expressed in the large number of deities and open-ended character of the pantheon, and in the richly detailed modes of worship they are supposed to receive. However, within this vast aggregation of beliefs and practices there is a clear distinction between devotional practices and those rituals that aim to satisfy deities and thus obtain their favor—by and large a distinction between other-worldly and this-worldly objectives. The *Bhagavad Gītā* recommends "desireless action" in support of dharma, but there were few people in Kelomal (or anywhere else in the world) able to afford such a luxury; the fruits they sought from worship were as varied as their gods.

The Composition of Rituals

The number of ritual observances found in a Bengali almanac is astounding. The almanac is called a *pañjikā*, a term that refers to its five essential components: solar days (*divasa*), lunar days (*tithi*), stars (*nakṣatra*), asterisms (*yoga*), and divisions of the day (*karaṇa*). Modern Bengali almanacs contain a great deal more information than the five essentials, including both tables for use by astrologers and brief guides to ritual procedures for the use of priests. Many people consult the almanac to determine propitious and unpropitious times for various mundane activities, and to find out when to conduct rituals.

The calendar lays out a succession of rituals, which are called simply *karma* (actions) in the almanac and in other priestly guidebooks. As noted in Chapter 1, there are two types of *karmas*, in the restricted sense of the term meaning "rituals": *nitya karma*, actions that are repeated regularly, and *naimittika karmas* or *saṃskāras*, actions that are "special" and that are performed only once in a person's lifetime. The *saṃskāras* are very ancient Hindu rituals, conducted with Sanskrit *mantras*, although in Bengal they also include many Bengali customary practices that are not found in other regions of India. This book treats *nitya karmas*, rituals that are repeated—often at regular intervals—and that are dedicated to worshiping the gods. Unlike the *saṃskāras*, the *nitya karmas* belong to an open-ended set with an indeterminate number of observances in honor of an extensive and expandable pantheon of deities. Some *nitya karmas* are said to be obligatory (*kartavya karma*), while others are undertaken because of a personal desire (*kāmya karma*) and do not recur on a regular schedule. This chapter deals with the construction of *nitya karmas*.

There are many layers of textual tradition underlying most Hindu rituals; Bengal has both absorbed ancient ones and produced some of its own. The *sūtra* literature, which belongs to the "end of the Vedas" (*vedānta*) period, roughly 500 to 200 BCE, contains extensive instructions on the proper performance of rituals. Fire offerings (*homa*) are a feature of these ancient rituals; *homa* offerings occur frequently in contemporary Bengali rituals that are otherwise a thousand years more recent. The great Sanskrit *purāṇas* (*mahāpurāṇa*), which were composed between about 300 and 1000 CE, contain directions for the worship of many deities, both those recognized in the Vedas and those introduced later—including many goddesses. Lesser Sanskrit *purāṇas* (*upapurāṇa*) composed in Bengal after about 1000 CE contain myths and rituals that are regarded as particularly important in Bengal and eastern India but are often unknown outside this region (Hazra 1963).

It is well known that Hindus frequently worship deities that they regard as embodied in statues (*mūrti*, *pratimā*, *vigraha*, "image") or in less iconic representations, such as a Śiva *liṅga* or a pair of feet representing Viṣṇu (*Viṣṇupada*). The *purāṇas* say that in the earlier ages, when dharma was upheld, humans could see the gods directly. In the *kṛta* age, when complete order prevailed, there was no need for images. In the successive *tretā* and *dvāpara* ages, although the gods were still visible to humans, they prepared images of them for worship. However, in the present, degraded, *kali* age, humans are no longer able to see the gods; they need to make images on which to focus their worship. Vedic ritual centered on sacrifices (*yajña*); the rituals for images in the *kali* age center on worship (*pūjā*) that is supposed to satisfy deities with honor and glorification.

There are textual descriptions of the gods that enable humans to make images that are worthy of receiving *pūjā*. The most comprehensive descriptions are in the *purāṇas* and *tantras*, usually in the form of *dhyāna mantras*. *Dhyāna* means "contemplation"; an adept should be able to bring a deity into his presence by a mental recitation of the *dhyāna*. *Dhyāna mantras* also serve as guides to the preparation of images. Numerous finely wrought images of deities in stone and bronze from the Pāla and Sena periods of Bengal testify to the attention given to accurate representation of forms described in *dhyāna mantras*. In more recent times, smaller images made of stone, of bronze, of an alloy of eight metals (*aṣṭadhātu*), or even of gold, have been created for the clan temples of wealthy households. Deities are often represented in sculptures made of unfired clay built up on frameworks of bamboo and straw, painted and decorated to create images faithful to their *dhyāna mantras*, images that are subsequently allowed to return to the earth either through immersion or abandonment to the elements. Most common of all are simple "pot" (*ghaṭ*) representations: a deity is invoked into a pot, while it is being immersed in a pond or stream, by means of a *mantra*. The pot is usually given a green coconut "head" and clothed in a simple cotton cloth (*gāmchā*).

Underlying *dhyāna mantras* and images created after them is the non-dualistic premise that the gods have bodies. They may live in heaven and be immortal, but they are beings with bodies just like humans. The distinction between spiritual and material worlds is largely absent in Hindu cultures. Rituals, when they are properly carried out, are regarded as physically effective, which is important in understanding what might otherwise be regarded as "merely symbolic" actions. The assumption of non-dualism underlies the ritual procedures for creating a body for a deity and for inducing the deity to inhabit it, procedures that are laid out in the *tantras*.

Unless one is discussing weaving (the word originally meant "loom"), *tantra* is a difficult subject. It usually refers to texts relating to the worship of Śakti, that is, one or another of the manifestations of a totalizing goddess. Buddhism acquired an elaborate tantric repertoire that was widespread in India, particularly in Bengal, and persists most notably in Tibet. There are comparable practices contained in the Śaiva *Āgamas* and the Vaiṣṇava *Pañcarātra* texts. The number of tantric texts is not known, and relatively few have been subjected to scholarly study. There is something of a cult interest in the subject because of the sexual *sādhanā* and "left-handed practice" (*vāmācāra*) in some of the texts, although these practices are in fact quite rare and are irrelevant to the widespread use of *tantras* in worship, except perhaps amongst Westerners. Like the *purāṇas*, the *tantras* are constructed as dialogues, and they often deal with many of the same subjects. However, the *tantras* prescribe many ritual practices that cannot be traced to other textual sources, and they rely heavily on the magical power of words for their effectiveness. They evidently emerged out of unwritten popular customs and, over some centuries, were integrated into the worship of the gods prescribed in the earlier texts. In addition to instructions about worship, some *tantras* also contain spells (*baśīkaraṇ*) that are supposed to bring others under one's control. Thus there is an odor of black magic attached to the term *tantra*. Most of what appears as tantric practice in contemporary Hindu rituals is reliant on yogic physiology and anatomy, which treats the body of the worshiper as a microcosm, and makes use of verbal formulas and gestures that mobilize the *śakti* in the body.

Dhyāna mantras are descriptions, intelligible at the level of ordinary language; they make it possible to visualize a deity. However, *tantras* also contain several types of semantically

Figure 2. A Brahman forms the *kūrma* (tortoise) *mudrā* while invoking the goddess Manasā before worship.

uninterpretable *mantras* that are employed in *pūjās*. Intrinsically powerful *bījā* ("seed") *mantras* are said to represent or contain particular deities or powers, even though they are single syllables such as *auṃ*, *hriṃ*, *kliṃ*, with no apparent meaning; in fact "this unmeaningness is their real meaning" as Shashibhusan Dasgupta (1962:21) perceptively wrote. The late Agehananda Bharati (1965:101–63) dealt comprehensively with *mantras*, both tantric and Vedic, as well as Indian theories that explain the origin and powers of *mantras*. Occult *mantras* are used extensively in even the most ordinary occasions of worship performed by Brahmans in Kelomal.

Most *pūjās* make some use of *yantras* as well as *mantras*. A *yantra* (pronounced in Bengali something like *jontro*) is a diagram thought to embody the deity to be worshiped, although the diagram does not have any obvious connection with the deity in question. Even in the absence of complex diagrammatic *yantras*, Brahmans routinely draw vermilion stick-figures called *puttalikā* on objects of worship, including everything from the pots embodying deities to trees, doorposts, and walls of places of worship. (*Yantra* is also used colloquially to refer to many kinds of device or machinery, such as a rice mill or a loom, or to a musical instrument.) Generally, knowledge of *mantras* and *yantras* is the province of Brahmans; ordinary villagers understand and respect their specialized knowledge and think employing Brahmans to perform worship on their behalf is beneficial. Many houses are adorned with *puttalikās*—on doorways, walls, and pots—drawn by Brahmans during bygone *pūjās*. There are also gestures called *mudrā*, mostly done with the hands, that are prescribed by *tantras* for the invocation of deities. Thus, a Brahman is the custodian of a monopoly in practices—*mantra*, *yantra*, and *mudrā*—essential to worship, comparable to that of a Roman Catholic priest whose ordination qualifies him to transform the communion wine and host into the blood and body of Christ.

Brahmans

The Brahman monopoly on rituals has sometimes been given credit for their caste superiority, even when economic and political power is held by another caste. The role of the Brahman as mediator between man and god is generally accepted throughout India, and, as elsewhere in India, it was usual for Brahmans to perform worship on behalf of householders and villages in Kelomal. But there are Brahmans and there are Brahmans. There are different orders (*śreṇī*) of Brahmans for different categories of castes. Raṛhī Śreṇī Brahmans (Brahmans whose ancestral homes are in the Rāṛh region of West Bengal) are the most highly ranked among Bengali Brahmans. There were a few families of Raṛhī Śreṇī Brahmans in Kelomal, but they were refugees from erstwhile East Pakistan who did not practice priesthood. Medinipur District belongs to the Madhyadeśa (the "middle land" of Bengal, the region between Bengal and Odisha, not the Madhyadeśa of Āryavarta); its high-ranking Brahmans are Madhya Śreṇī Brahmans. They performed the worship for the higher castes in Kelomal: for Kayasthas and sometimes for Karans, for their own Brahman *śreṇī*, and for the castes (*jāti*) of the *navaśākha* (the nine high Sudra castes). The ancestors of the Brahmans known as Utkal Śreṇī Brahmans came from Odisha, which is adjacent to Medinipur District; their only "natural" *jajmans* in Kelomal were the Karans, who also originated in Odisha, and they sometimes performed rituals for them. In addition to secular occupations, Utkal Brahmans often worked as cooks at feasts; food cooked by Brahmans is acceptable to people of all castes.

Bengali Hindus recognize Brahmans who perform priestly services that are not acceptable to the *navaśākha* as *varṇabrāhmaṇs*, and sometimes as *patit* ("fallen") Brahmans. These Brahmans sometimes have stories that explain how they came to occupy a low status, but they do not acknowledge the non-Brahman origins sometimes attributed to them in local lore. The Brahmans who perform the rituals of the Mahisyas are called Vyāsokta Śreṇī Brahmans. Vyāsokta means "declared by the sage Vyāsa," implying that they are Brahmans "created by decree." However, the Vyāsokta Brahmans describe themselves as Gauṛādya Vaidika Brahmans, "Original Vedic Brahmans of Gaura." In Kelomal, they performed rituals on behalf of Mahisyas, Jatiya Vaiṣṇavas (whose ancestors were generally Mahisyas), and for villages as communities. The fact that they presided in such important rituals as the village Śītalā

Pūjās and Gājan is an indication of the extent to which the villages as communities belonged to the more-or-less indigenous Mahisyas.

The Fishers received the service of other low-ranking Brahmans, apparently a section of the Vyāsokta Brahmans severed from those who are priests of the Mahisyas. There are still other priestly Brahman groups that perform the rituals of the lowest castes (Karangas, Dhopas, Doms, and Mucis). Ācārya Brahmans are astrologers but they sometimes also preside at rituals for low-caste groups. Agradānī or Agraśrāddhī Brahmans are guests at feasts for the dead where their function is to accept food and gifts that take death impurity away from the relatives of the deceased.

In short, the people of Kelomal were full-fledged participants in the system of Brahmanical ritual intermediation. Yet, at the same time, there were many domestic rituals that were conducted by householders—and especially by women—that did not involve Brahmans at all. And, in the Gājan, one of the most important, most visible rituals of the annual cycle, the weight of performance rested with non-Brahman villagers, mostly Mahisyas, although the Vyāsokta Brahmans had a role.

Customs

The mixture of Brahmanical and non-Brahmanical corresponds to some extent to the mixture of Sanskritic and non-Sanskritic. However, there are many purely Bengali elements in rituals of all kinds. Durgā Pūjā, which is the most Sanskritic of Bengali rituals, is nevertheless laden with popular customs that are honored as strictly as are those in the scripture. Some popular practices are presided over by Brahmans while others are done without any intermediation. A typical example of an elaborate but unscriptural customary practice is provided by a nineteenth-century account, which begins preparation for Durgā Pūjā around the summer solstice, on the day of *rath-yātrā*, three months before the beginning of the *pūjā*. The prescription calls for the preparation of a split bamboo that will be used in the framework of the clay image of the goddess. It is to be smoothed by a Potter (i.e., the maker of the image) and taken by the domestic priest to the household temple or gods' room (*ṭhākur ghar*) where, after worshiping Hari, he is to anoint the bamboo with sandalwood paste and to invoke Durgā into it. The bamboo remains in the temple for about six weeks, until Janamāṣṭamī, the birthday of Kṛṣṇa—another Vaiṣṇava observance—when it is handed over to the person who will prepare the framework (*kāṭhāmo*) for the image of the goddess (Ghosh 1871:1). Details of that sort do not appear in the *purāṇas*, which mention simply that a temporary clay image of the goddess should be prepared if there is no permanent image.

The Sanskrit *Upapurāṇas* composed in Bengal often prescribe practices of purely local origin. For example, Bengalis say that during the autumn season, when Durgā Pūjā takes place, the gods are sleeping and it is necessary to awaken her "untimely" or "out of season" (*akāl bodhan*) for worship. There are several Sanskrit *upapurāṇas* composed in Bengal that are cited as authoritative for the worship of Durgā. The earliest of these, the *Devī Purāṇa* (c. 6th century CE) says nothing about awakening the goddess. The later *upapurāṇas* relate the awakening to a story in the *Rāmāyaṇa*: Rāma is said to have awakened the goddess for worship to gain her favor before his invasion of Lanka. That story does not appear in the Vālmīki *Rāmāyaṇa*, but it is included in the fifteenth-century Bengali *Rāmāyaṇa* of Kṛttivāsa. In the sixteenth century this tradition was given the authority of Raghunandana, a renowned Bengali *smārta*, in his widely consulted *Durgā Pūjā Tattva*. This is an illustration of the way in which an observance that began as the custom of the country was transformed into an authoritative Sanskritic practice commonly regarded as very ancient (Sarkar 2012, Nicholas 2013:52–59).

There are two or three priestly offices in Durgā Pūjā: the *pūjaka*, the "worshiper," is the Brahman who performs the main rituals, the *tantra-dhāraka*, the "holder of the book," is the Brahman who has the manual for the ritual, from which he provides directions and *mantras* to the *pūjaka*. In some cases there is a dedicated reader (*pāṭhaka*) who reads or recites aloud the *Devī Māhātmya* section of the *Mārkaṇḍeya Purāṇa*, which is generally called simply *Caṇḍī* in Bengal; it is the verbal narrative on which the ritual is based. In the Durgā Pūjā I have described, the *pūjaka* was also the *pāṭhaka*, who read the *Caṇḍī* aloud each day, from the awakening of the goddess until her departure, a total of sixteen complete readings. The ritual manual that guides the work of the *pūjaka* is a composite of procedures derived in part from very ancient texts, classed as *śruti* ("heard," or revealed, putatively Vedic sources), but largely from more recent ones, called *smṛti* ("remembered" or learned sources, including *purāṇas* and *tantras*).

The later *upapurāṇas* composed in Bengal incorporate tantric procedures: purifications of the parts of the body and seat of the priest (*śuddhi*), identification (*nyāsa*) of parts of his body with those of the deity, creating auspicious gestures (*mudrā*), drawing diagrams (*yantra*) that constitute deities in themselves, and the recitation of *bīja* ("seed") *mantras* that contain the deities in the form of sound. Once the priest is prepared he is able to accept the commitment of the worshiper's *saṃkalpa*, his resolution to worship the deity, which identifies the worshiper as the beneficiary of the ritual. (The worshiper is known as the *yajamāna*, "sacrificer," a term that has become *jajmān* in anthropological writing.)

The priest's power to invoke the deity into the inert clay image with *mantras* and *mudrās*, giving it vision (*cakṣura dāna*) and establishing its breath (*prāṇa pratiṣṭhā*)—elements of ritual drawn from the ancient *śruti* and *smṛti*, later *purāṇas*, and still later *tantras*—is not viewed as a composite but rather as a unified procedure, a seamless set of acts dedicated to the single purpose of showing honor and reverence to a powerful deity; if she is satisfied she protects her worshipers. The aggregation of components into a coherent Sanskrit ritual is the work of learned Brahmans, scholarly *smārtas* such as Raghunandana, who distilled received learning into guidebooks. Although the village Brahmans in Kelomal were not capable of such scholarly work, those who practiced priesthood had some understanding of the meaning of their ritual acts. The Brahmans who came from outside the village to perform Durgā Pūjā were more learned and able to discuss the meaning of their words and gestures.

Some practices that are customs of the country originated with the little kings who held positions of power under the Mughals, and sometimes under the British as well, if they were able to survive in the status of *zamindārs*. The Banāi Pūjā illustrates the influence of local rule on ritual practice. Although Kelomal was a part of the kingdom (*parganā*) of Tamluk, it was settled by people from several adjacent *parganās*. All of them practiced a very popular, non-Sanskritic ritual called Banāi Pūjā to mark the principal rice harvest at the winter solstice, Makar Saṃkrānti. As noted earlier, this is a significant observance throughout Bengal: many people make a pilgrimage to Sāgar Island, where the Hugli River (which has sacred standing as a distributary of the Ganges) meets the Bay of Bengal, and where the pilgrims bathe in the sea. In Tamluk, it is the day of a major festival at the temple of Barga Bhīmā, the ancient and powerful goddess of the kingdom. Because many people throughout Tamluk *parganā* were accustomed to going to town for the festival and fair, Banāi Pūjā was done on the day preceding Makar Saṃkrānti. In the adjacent kingdoms of Moyna and Kashijora there was no such fair, so families that originated in those *parganās* held Banāi Pūjā on the *saṃkrānti* day. There were also families that originated in Mandalghat *parganā*, which held a bathing festival on Makar Saṃkrānti; those Mandalghat people held Banāi Pūjā on the first day of the following month, Māgha (January/February). Differences such as these are likely to erode as marriages mix families from different *parganās* and the old boundaries lose relevance. In 1960 I was told that the king of Tamluk had the right to collect a special cess (*abwāb*) if one of his subjects married a girl from another kingdom. That custom—already rarely honored in 1960—was no longer observed a decade later.

The Hindu ritual calendar emphasizes lunar cycles, which trace a distinctive path through the year, since lunar months of approximately 28 days are shorter than solar months. Raghunandana's treatise on rituals is called *Tithi Tattva*, "Doctrine of Lunar Days." However, as noted earlier, agriculture—and much of rural life—runs on the solar calendar, which tracks the seasons that govern planting and harvest. *Saṃkrāntis*, such as Makar Saṃkrānti, belong to the solar calendar; these are days on which the sun moves from one sign to another, marking the change of solar months. In Kelomal there is one principal rice harvest each year. However, across Bengal there are three different seasons in which rice is grown; there is a ritual for the harvest of each of these crops. Farmers who have only one rice crop each year do not practice the rituals for the other harvests. However, more cosmopolitan people—in Kelomal generally high-caste, educated people—follow the all-Bengal schedule of three harvest festivals. They save rice from the winter harvest for use in the spring and rainy-season *śiṣṭācār* harvest rituals, which are recognized in the almanac and in Bengali language sources, but not in the Sanskrit *pūjā* manuals. Worship of the dangerous goddesses Śītalā and Manasā also follow the solar calendar, though not for reasons connected with agriculture: smallpox epidemics occurred during the hot, dry months preceding the rainy season, and snakes became a threat when the rains came, flooding them out of their dry-season hiding places.

Bengali Narratives

Although Brahmans who perform rituals use Sanskrit *mantras* and consult Sanskrit sources, such as the *Purohita Darpaṇa* (Mirror for Domestic Priests) and manuals (*paddhati*, "pathway") for particular *pūjās*, they also use Bengali language texts. Among the most usual activities of priests is performing the simple offerings that are part of *brata* observances. *Brata* (Skt. *vrata*)—an ancient word for many kinds of religious action—has taken on a specific meaning in Bengali: A *brata* is a self-denying observance—most often undertaken by women and most often requiring a fast of a day's duration—that is an act of worship of a particular deity. There are numerous *bratas* through the year; only a few of these are observed in any household, and many are confined to particular regions within Bengal. Although the worship is simple, each *brata* is accompanied by a *brata kathā*, a Bengali language narrative explaining the significance of the act and often extolling exemplary women who adhered to their commitments despite adverse conditions. In earlier times, when there were few literate women, a Brahman often read the story to the women observing the *brata*. As female literacy became widespread in the twentieth century it became increasingly common for a woman to read the *brata kathā* aloud to other women of the household. In families where women worshiped daily in the domestic shrine, performing the simple worship accompanying a *brata* also became more common, though engaging a Brahman to carry out the ritual remained an indicator of *bhadratā*, refinement and social standing.

There are other Bengali language narratives called *maṅgal kāvya* (meaning something like "poems of auspiciousness"), unknown in Sanskrit, that play important roles in the construction of Bengali rituals. Chapter 6 takes up the influential Bengali story of Śiva as a cultivator. It begins with a figure of Śiva well known throughout India, addicted to narcotics, getting a living as a beggar. His wife, Durgā, and his sons Gaṇeśa and Kārtik, do not fare well under this domestic economy, and Durgā urges him to get an occupation. In an outcome peculiar to Bengal, he settles on farming; and the narrative mixes images from the *Purāṇas* with abundant details about the practice of rice agriculture in deltaic Bengal. These stories appear not only in Bengali Śaiva mythology, but also in the myths of the god Dharma, a Bengali deity known only from Bengali language sources that lack any Sanskrit counterparts. Neither the *brata kathā* nor the *maṅgal kāvya* are freestanding narratives; they get their power as constituents of rituals, they are ritual performances and not simply stories.

Vaiṣṇavism lies like a thick syrup over much of Hindu Bengal. The influence of devotion to Kṛṣṇa exemplified by Caitanya pervades rural West Bengal, even invading the worship of other deities. The narratives that frame Kṛṣṇa *bhakti* are the stories of the life of this god among the cattle-keepers of Vṛndāvana as told in the *Bhāgavata Purāṇa*. The followers of Caitanya went in two different directions: the Brahmanical keepers of a canonical faith, known as the Gosvāmīs of Vṛndāvana, adopted the complicated, Sanskrit, non-Bengali *Hari Bhakti Vilāsa* as a ritual guidebook. The people in the Bengal countryside, for the most part, adopted the enthusiastic devotional practice of *kīrtan* singing, using Bengali and Brajabuli verses about the love of Rādhā and Kṛṣṇa. In house after house of cultivators and fishers there are sons named Gaur (Caitanya), Nitai (Nityānanda), Advaita, and Śrīvāsa, or

Bistupada (Viṣṇu-pada), Keṣṭopada (Kṛṣṇa-pada). What I have described as the "predominant religious orientation" of ordinary Hindus in rural West Bengal is Vaiṣṇava. Ordinary people in Kelomal identified their strand of Vaiṣṇavism as having descended from Nityānanda, rather than from the Vṛndāvana Gosvāmīs. They extended *bhakti* devotionalism, derived from Caitanya's teaching and example, to deities such as Śītalā and Manasā, even though they were worshiped with animal sacrifices, which are anathema to most Vaiṣṇavas. Some older or particularly observant Vaiṣṇavas abstained from meat, or even fish, but most people were untroubled by any contradiction between strictures laid down in Brahmanical Vaiṣṇava texts and their customary practices. In general, the tension between equality and hierarchy expressed in the opposition between the organization of the Gājan and the organization of Durgā Pūjā is also expressed in Vaiṣṇavism as the opposition between the commoner followers of Nityananda and the elite followers of the Vṛndāvana Gosvāmīs.

The difference between the everyday practice of Vaiṣṇavism and the dense scriptural practices of the followers of the Vṛndāvana Gosvāmīs was recognized by some people, but I never found anyone who regarded it as a problem. People in Kelomal rarely mentioned sectarian differences. The potentially much greater gulf between the worship of goddesses, with blood sacrifices, and the Vaiṣṇava abhorrence of blood-letting, was managed by a kind of shift of ritual attention, often within the same household, not to say within the village. Although the rituals of the high castes were often costly, while the devotional practices of Vaiṣṇavism are mostly inexpensive, the economic issue was not often mentioned. Rather, the distinction between the practices of the lower and upper castes were described as differences of mental inclination (*mat*). Everyone loved the rituals, the display, the emotional power, and the opportunity to perform. The economic rationalist might have said that there was a good deal of waste in the display of some rituals, and that the money might be better spent on food, education, or medical care. In Kelomal most people would have responded that the deities must be worshiped. But it was very clear that worship was as much for the worshiper as for the gods.

The Pantheon

Caitanya preached that *bhakti* is the true means of worship and implicitly turned his back on the complex and sometimes expensive rituals prescribed in the *purāṇas*. However, although the influence of Caitanya spread widely in western Bengal, Bengalis still practice elaborate rituals alongside the expressive devotionalism of Caitanya's Vaiṣṇavism. The attitude people adopt when worshiping Śiva, or Śītalā, or Manasā, or Lakṣmī is confusing to the observer, since each deity is treated as preeminent among the gods when he or she is being worshiped. Examination of the total system of gods and goddesses reveals, however, that most deities have specific domains or responsibilities. In Kelomal, for example, Viśvakarma *pūjā* was considered obligatory for families that had "machines" (*yantra*), such as rice mills or looms. People who cultivated betel leaves held Baroj Kālī *pūjā* in their *pān* gardens (*baroj*), but no one else did so. Manasā, goddess of snakes, was worshiped in most households during the rainy season. Śītalā was most often worshiped by villages as communities, rather than by individual families, in recognition of the communal spread of epidemic infectious diseases. Durgā was not worshiped in most households, only in those whose agricultural land was formerly extensive enough to create a group of subordinate cultivators and dependents. (As such inequality shrank, collective forms of Durgā worship grew, and are now very widespread.)

Lakṣmī is the domestic goddess, personified in the married women of a family, present in the rice stored in the granary, and abiding (or not) as the prosperity of the household. Sarasvatī, the beautiful goddess who is worshiped by students for success in their studies, and who is the deity of artists, especially musicians, is a sister to Lakṣmī. Her annual *pūjā*, which occurs in the winter month of Māgha (January/February), is a very popular event, and one that elicits a lot of social activity, especially among students and in schools. Gaṇeśa, the elephant-headed son of Śiva and Durgā, is also quite popular. He is worshiped frequently, and often at the beginning of the worship of other deities, in his role as "overcomer of obstacles." Shopkeepers worship him at the beginning of a new year, the first of Baiśākh, as they open new account books. And he appears with Lakṣmī, Sarasvatī, and Kārtik as the children of the goddess in the great Durgā Pūjā ceremony. However, Gaṇeśa is not a dominating figure in the Bengali pantheon. Kārtik, often called Kumār, is depicted as the god of warriors, with a bow and arrows (though improbably mounted on a peacock). Kārtik rarely receives any attention outside of his appearance as the son of Durgā and Śiva. The last day of the month that bears his name is designated for his *pūjā*, but it is observed in only a few locations in West Bengal.

Kṛṣṇa is different; his domain is not specialized: he is the deliverer, the god who transcends limitations and offers salvation to humans whose existential condition—worldly life (*saṃsāra*)—is sometimes called "the pain of the womb" (*jaṭhar yantraṇā*), that is, the inevitable consequence of birth. The devotional worship of Kṛṣṇa relies heavily on *kīrtans*, poems that relate episodes from the *Bhāgavata Purāṇa* in lyrical Bengali. Although Kṛṣṇa receives food offerings like the other deities, they are usually simple ones and the role of the Brahmans is not elaborate. Non-Brahman *kīrtan* parties moving around the village singing devotional lyrics, accompanied by double-headed *khol* drums and small brass cymbals, are the foremost vehicles of Kṛṣṇa worship. By contrast, Kṛṣṇa rituals expounded in the Bengal *upapurāṇas*, heavily reliant on the *tantras*, are somewhat mysterious and inaccessible to ordinary people.

Although I have dealt with this elsewhere, it should be noted here that in the Gājan, the springtime worship of Śiva, the methods of worship are not textual; they belong to the oral tradition, to Bengali conceptions of Śiva and Durgā, and to the vernacular language. The Bengali Śiva is a puranic god, eccentric and addicted to narcotics, crossed with a Bengali farmer who plows, plants rice, and supports his family by labor. This Śiva is not the god who dances at the dissolution of the world, but a source of fertility. In his relationship with fertility he is also closely connected to Sūrya the Sun god and the god Dharma, a Bengali deity who has been gradually merged into Śiva over the last few centuries. These three male gods are present together in the Gājan.

Throughout Hindu Bengal there is usually a goddess who stands as mother of the village. In Kelomal and much of East Medinipur and Haora districts, Śītalā is the village mother. And in this region, when Śītalā is worshiped, so is the Muslim hybrid deity Olābibi. To the east, across the river in South 24 Parganas district, there are several other Muslim hybrid deities who are worshiped by Hindus. In West Medinipur and areas outside the delta region,

Figure 3. Grām Caṇḍī in Narsinghkalua is simply several lumps of laterite at the base of a neem tree. A brick platform for the goddess was a later addition.

the village mother may be Manasā, goddess of snakes. Throughout Kelomal and rural West Bengal there are numerous shrines to Grām Caṇḍī, often little more than piles of laterite chunks at the base of a tree (*gāch talā ṭhākur*). These goddesses are sometimes called "mother of such-and-such village." When such inchoate forms are recognized by an unusual level of attention from the public, when they are thought to possess particular powers, they often begin to acquire bodily attributes: eyes made of cowrie shells, silver noses, limbs, and clothing are added to shapeless rocks, so that a vaguely anthropomorphic figure begins to emerge, together with a growing reputation and a distinctive personality. If such a *gāch talā ṭhākur* seems to be very lively (*jāgratā*), a temple may be constructed for her, though the temple may stand somewhat incongruously at the foot of the tree where she emerged. I have written about the village mother elsewhere (2003:62–77). Manasā *pūjā* is quite important in Kelomal, though it is not as elaborate as the Manasā *jhā̃pāns* that are performed in West Medinipur and Bankura. Manasā is worshiped at various times during the rainy season, when snakes are flooded out of their holes and when snakebite is most frequent. A special occasion of Manasā Puja is *arandhan*, "no cooking," a day when the hearth is not lit.

The earth is herself a goddess. The divinity of the earth is recognized when clay images of deities are made; the man who takes the clay for making the figure bows reverently and touches his forehead to the ground before digging. Farmers observe the menses of the earth, Ambubācī, by refraining from plowing or digging during this three-day period at the beginning of the rainy season just as they refrain from sexual intercourse during the menses of their wives. Nal Saṃkrānti, a ritual that is observed by farmers in Kelomal on the last day of solar Āśvina (September-October) is intended to increase the crops in the fields; it corresponds to the life-cycle ritual of *sādh*, indulging the desires of a pregnant woman for the benefit of the child, and is directed to the earth as the mother of the crops.

Motherhood is a constant concern of families; the goddess Ṣaṣṭhī is responsible for maternity and the welfare of children. Ṣaṣṭhī means "the sixth," and refers to the sixth day of a lunar fortnight. Though no one performs all of them, there are eight Ṣaṣṭhī *bratas* observed on bright fortnight (*śukla*) *ṣaṣṭhīs* around the year in Kelomal. There is a very important ninth Ṣaṣṭhī *pūjā* that does not take place on a lunar *sasthi*; this is the Nīla Ṣaṣṭhī, a very widely observed *brata* that occurs on the penultimate day of the year, which corresponds to the sixth day of the Gājan in Kelomal, the day on which the union of Śiva and Durgā is consummated. There are other *bratas* as well; most of them require women to undertake self-denying observances for the benefit of others.

There are also deities worshiped by special occupational groups, as was mentioned earlier, such as Baroj Kālī Pūjā by betel leaf cultivators. People who work with machines—handloom weavers or operators of rice-husking mills—hold an annual *pūjā* to Viśvakarma, builder of the universe and patron of tools. Shopkeepers worship the goddess Gandheśvarī, goddess of spices and by extension, the goods one finds in a shop.

Yet another category of worship is formed by some of the *pūjās* of lower caste groups. In Kelomal there was a densely settled neighborhood of 74 people who said they belonged to a weaver caste. But they were not the Weavers (Tantubāy) of the Bengali *navaśākha*, who would not make marriages with them. Kayasthas said that this group was Launderers (Dhopā), whose ancestors were settled in Kelomal on *cākrān* land—that is, land provided in return for their caste-specialized service. As Launderers, they were considered low caste by most other people in the village. They conducted an annual worship of Satya Nārāyaṇa, which they describe as being "for our neighborhood (*pāṛā*)." Their neighborhood consisted entirely of people of the same caste. Likewise, there was a large group of Fishers (Rājbaṅgśī, or Tiyar, 131 people) all of whom lived in a single *pāṛā*. They held festive annual Sarasvatī and Satya Nārāyaṇa *pūjās* for their neighborhood. Both Satya Nārāyaṇa and Sarasvatī are deities worshiped by most other people in Kelomal, but by staging especially elaborate versions of these *pūjās* for the benefit of their castes and neighborhoods, they were able to hold a more grand celebration of the type enjoyed as collective clan or village rites by the higher castes.

Figure 4. Viśvakarma, Builder of the Universe, worshiped in a rice mill on Dharma Saṃkrānti. The god is seated on his *vāhana*, an elephant, and holds a ruler in his right hand and a hammer in his left. The cloth decoration is made of handloom bed sheets woven in Kelomal.

Although most deities that were worshiped in Kelomal during the period of our fieldwork were well-known to earlier generations, there were also newer members of the pantheon. Śani, the personification of the planet Saturn, has been recognized as a potentially malign force throughout Hindu India for centuries. However, the appearance of numerous small Śani shrines in Kolkata in the 1960s, where people made donations to ward off evil, brought him to the attention of people in rural areas who had not previously paid much heed to his propitiation. While there were not many people in Kelomal who paid attention to Śani, the practice of

Figure 5. Sarasvati *Pūjā* in the Fishers' neighborhood. Participants are shown as they wished to be seen, posing piously before the goddess. In fact, however, they spent most of the night dancing and drinking. This *pūjā* takes place in the winter month of Māgha (January/February); the men are wrapped against the cold.

making a small offering to him on Śanibār (Saturday), his day, was gaining ground. A Vyāsokta Brahman performed Śani *pūjā* on Saturdays in a Kālī temple. A more surprising addition to the Kelomal repertoire was seen not in the 1968–70 period, but in 1981, when I visited Kelomal during Gājan. Santoshi Ma ("Satisfaction Mother"), whose cult had been invented out of elements of other deities in Hindi-speaking North India in the 1960s, was the subject of a popular Hindi movie, *Jai Santoshi Mata*, made in 1975. A year or two after the release of the film she was accorded a place among the deities saluted in the Gājan in Kelomal. Practice of the Gājan was also influenced by another film: *Bābā Tāraknāth*, released in Bengali in 1977, was treated by many common people as factual testimony to the power of the Śiva of Tārakeśvar. It brought about a considerable increase in the number of people making the pilgrimage to the Tārakeśvar temple from all parts of Bengal, including Bangladesh, and also from neighboring states, thanks to a Hindi-dubbed version of the film.

It is difficult to think of this collection of religious observances as a "system"; it looks more like a historical accumulation. It is difficult to create a theology that would unite these pieces or demonstrate their coherence. Certainly, most people in Kelomal in the later 1960s were not highly educated, but they spoke intelligently about their views on religious matters and occasionally even about what they presumed my views to be. One intelligent Kayastha woman prefaced each statement she made about her own practices by telling me, "You don't believe this." The pervasive influence of devotional Vaiṣṇavism often led people to talk about *bhakti* as an appropriate religious attitude regardless of the deity being worshiped. Thus, the reality of their practices often seemed to be in contradiction to their stated beliefs. Men whose Vaiṣṇava piety was evident in everyday life also took part in blood sacrifices to Śītalā. It would be difficult to assemble a theology out of the apparent beliefs of most of these people. However, if the inquiry begins with consideration of rituals rather than beliefs, the problem of internal coherence appears to be contingent. One of the first facts that emerged from observing rituals in Kelomal is that the particular deity being worshiped was, at that moment, the preeminent deity in the pantheon; the other deities were consigned to the residual category of "all the gods and goddesses" (*sarva deva-devī*). All of the other gods and goddesses are not ignored when one god is being worshiped, but they are demoted for that moment to secondary status. Many people in Kelomal were unsophisticated, but they were not indifferent to contradictions or incoherence in their worldviews; however, they compartmentalized both what they regarded as the spheres of authority of particular gods and the social universe to which that authority pertained.

Trying to understand the calendar of heterogeneous observances that make up the ritual year in Kelomal, and most other Hindu villages in Bengal, requires a focus on the rituals first, and then on the beliefs and narratives that are adduced to explain them. The annual cycle of worship is coherent even though it is constructed out of rituals drawn from diverse sources and different historical eras. In considering such an array of religious occasions it is helpful to keep in mind the great emotional and aesthetic pleasure people took in performing these rituals. People in Kelomal—and Bengalis in general—enjoy and get satisfaction from conducting rituals. There is usually a fine aesthetic sense to the arrangements for worship, whether it is expressed in *ālpanā* drawings by women or decorations carved from pith by the Garland Makers. There is a choreography to the gestures of Brahmans who conduct rituals, from *mudrā* hand gestures, to the postures used in making offerings to, the graceful movement of oil lamps before the image of a deity. Whenever possible Bengalis like to have music; drums are obligatory for major ceremonies, and brass bands are hired when resources permit. Best of all are the theatrical performances of the companies that sing the *maṅgal* poems of Śītalā. Bengalis worship their gods out of respect for their power, and sometimes fear of that power, but they do so with immense pleasure.

3. Vaiṣṇavism

Throughout West Bengal, on the night of the full moon (*pūrṇimā*) each month, small bands (*dal*) of five or six men gather to sing *kīrtan* songs narrating the deeds of Lord Kṛṣṇa and the love of Rādhā for her dark lord. There is always at least one *khol* (the double-headed drum used especially for religious songs) and one pair of *karatāls* (small cymbals that have a high-pitched ring). These *kīrtan* parties include no trained singers—indeed, hardly any of them are good singers—but they are people whose passion and devotion are evident in their performance. There were four such groups in Kelomal; in what they call "strolling" (*beṛā*) *kīrtan*, each group made its way around a section of the village, visiting certain houses, all of the Hari Mandirs both public and domestic, and other Vaiṣṇava sites.

At each location they sang and danced, and a crowd would gather—usually about 30–40 local men, women, and children. In each place, the performance began with a slow rhythm and somewhat intelligible recitation of verses, then rose in intensity, with faster rhythms, louder singing, and less narrative. Members of the company danced with increased fervor, adopting the posture with upraised hands that is thought to be that of the ecstatic Caitanya and his disciples during their processional *nagar kīrtans* around Navadvīpa. All began to sing "*Hari bol! Hari bol! Bolo bolo Hari bol!*" ("Say the name of the lord"). When the enthusiasm had reached its most fevered pitch, the householder or temple *sevait* brought out a large basket filled with *bātāsās*, small, round sugar wafers that he flung into the crowd in a gesture called Hari *luṭ* ("Lord's plunder" or the "Loot of Hari"; the word "loot" is from India). Youngsters scrambled to get as many of the sweets as possible, and everyone attempted to pick up at least one *bātāsā* and to consume it with reverence as the *prasād* ("grace") of Lord Kṛṣṇa.

The *khol*, the drum used in *kīrtan* singing, is the foremost sacred symbol of these occasions. When a *khol* is brought out it is an announcement that a religious narrative or song of praise is about to be sung. The drum is worshiped before performances and, referred to as *śrī khol*, treated almost as a personified being.

These joyous occasions were intended to capture the spirit of *bhakti* religiosity that characterized Caitanya's own ecstatic frenzies. The terms *kīrtan* and *saṃkīrtan*, meaning "singing the praise of the lord," are used to describe these enthusiastic hymns. Simply reciting the names of a god, *nām saṃkīrtan*, is considered to be a path to salvation; and narratives are punctuated with shouts of "*Hari, Hari bolo, Hari bol.*" The verses of the *kīrtans* describe the deeds of Kṛṣṇa among the cowherds, his dalliance with the *gopis*, and—most favorite—the love of Rādhā for Kṛṣṇa, her longing to hear the sound of his flute. Rādhā's love is offered as a model for the human devotees. Their attachment is often described as something different from erotic love, though the images in the *kīrtans* are earthy. In Bengal Rādhā is considered to be a married woman who is drawn to Kṛṣṇa. Traditional accounts of Caitanya's experience when he chanted the name of Kṛṣṇa appear to describe a man possessed, often described as "madness"; his love for Kṛṣṇa is said to be identical to that of Rādhā. His followers attribute divinity to Caitanya, whom they call Śrī Kṛṣṇa Caitanya, and whom they say embodied both Kṛṣṇa and Rādhā. Singing and chanting the name of the Lord to the increasing rhythm of the sacred *khol* drum and *karatāl*—sometimes augmented by cannabis, hot humid weather, and hunger—may induce a mild possession in members of the *kīrtan* party; possessed or not, the participants take great pleasure from their performance.

Beyond sincere expressions of devotion in their songs, these village Vaiṣṇavas are not expected to perform any rituals or observe any discipline. The elaborate code for conduct laid out by the Vṛndāvana Gosvāmīs was largely unknown to them, and would have constituted an insuperable barrier to the religious practices of people who had to do a lot of demanding manual work. Even their choice of occasions for worship failed the test. The full moon—illuminating paths through the darkened villages—as the occasion for *kīrtan* parties is not mentioned in the texts, which emphasize *ekādaśīs* rather than *pūrṇimās*. *Ekādaśī*, the eleventh day of each lunar fortnight, is a fast day for those who follow the Gosvāmīs.

Besides fasting, observant Vaiṣṇavas are strict vegetarians. Some Bengali Vaiṣṇavas consider themselves vegetarian because they do not eat meat, although they do not hesitate to consume fish and sometimes other creatures of the water, including tortoises. In fact, most Bengali Hindus are meat-eaters, although meat is expensive and thus an infrequent treat for most. Some members of the Karaṅgā caste, who dealt in cattle and served as veterinarians, were also butchers who served Hindus. They butchered only goats, not cattle, and they did not slaughter on Thursdays (Lakṣmī's day), *ekādaśīs* and *pūrṇimās*, or *amāvasyās* (new-moon nights, which are unpropitious and connected to death). Strict dietary discipline is difficult for people who must work in the field or at other arduous tasks. The ascetics who participate in the Gājan in the very hot spring season follow a difficult fasting regime, eating and drinking only before dawn and after dark, with a very restricted diet; and they do so for a week or ten days. However, they are excused from labor during that period of temporary renunciation.

Vaiṣṇava Shrines

Bhakti, personal devotion, replaces a great deal of expensive Hindu ceremony. In Bengal no one in living memory has performed the Vedic *aśvamedha* horse sacrifice; the claim that chanting the name of Kṛṣṇa is equal to a horse sacrifice in its capacity to deliver the worshiper to liberation is a kind of antique fantasy. However, invoking ancient Vedic images to support contemporary practices is an important feature of those who hold the *Bhāgavata Purāṇa* above other scriptures. Van Buitenen (1966) argued that this text, which was completed by about 1000 CE, is written in artificially archaic language in order to give it Vedic authority. Certainly, contemporary adherents of Gauṛīya Vaiṣṇavism do not tire of speaking of their texts and practices as "Vedic," although they have nothing to do with the Vedic hymns or sacrifices. *Bhakti* relieves common people of a religious obligation to make expensive offerings or to engage in elaborate rituals. And a great deal of the beauty of devotional practice in Bengal centers on the *tulasī*, the sacred basil.

As noted earlier, almost no Hindu house in Kelomal lacked a *tulasī mañca*. The *tulasī* plant is the most visible sacred symbol of Vaiṣṇavism in Kelomal. Caring for the *tulasī* is a simple act of devotion that is possible even for the poorest people. *Mañca* refers to a platform or pedestal, a structure in which a small *tulasī* plant grows. The simplest ones, usually at the houses of the poor, were mounds of compacted earth piled above ground level near the entrance to the house, with a *tulasī* plant growing in the top. Some were built of bricks and stood 25 to 50 centimeters above the ground, always just outside the house entrance. Some Potters who did specialized work made beautifully ornamented *tulasī mañcas* in terra cotta. Those were sometimes round in cross-section, tapering up to a small opening in the top for the earth in which the *tulasī* was planted. The most favored shape was square in cross-section, decorated with bas relief figures of Caitanya and Nityānanda dancing. If there were human figures on the other sides, they were Caitanya's other principal disciples, also usually shown dancing.

Simple or elaborate, the *tulasī mañca* received daily attention—most often provided by a woman, though some pious Vaiṣṇava men considered service of the *tulasī* to be one of their duties. The plant is to be watered daily, by someone who has just bathed and, thus, is in a pure state. And an honorific light is to be displayed before the *tulasī mañca* at twilight, the dangerous liminal transition from day to night (*sandhyā belā*). At that time, in most dwellings, women blew conch shell trumpets—three sustained notes—to clear any malevolent presence from the house. The sound of the conch

Figure 6. A *tulasī mañca*. This one is more elaborate than most, but the concept is always the same: the *tulasī* or sacred basil plant is grown in a pedestal at which it receives daily worship

shell issuing from every direction as the village grew dark evokes life in rural Bengal with a serenity that obscures, momentarily, the hardship of life for many people. The housewife, her head modestly covered, carrying a lamp at twilight to display before the *tulasī*, bowing to touch her head at the base of the pedestal as at the feet of a goddess, is a scene of simple grace. These are acts of worship that are everyday Bengali religion. They are overlooked by most of the accounts of Bengal Vaiṣṇavism, though they are the most common expressions of *bhakti*.

Tulasī, the name of the sacred basil plant, is the name of a woman renowned in the *Brahmavaivarta Purāṇa* (II, Ch.15–22) as a model wife deceived by a devious Lord Viṣṇu. In a previous life she had been a *gopī* in Vṛindāvana, banished by Rādhā for making love with Kṛṣṇa. Reborn, Tulasī became the wife of the powerful anti-god (*asura*) Śaṅkhacūṛa. Although Śaṅkhacūṛa was powerful and virtuous, being on the opposite side of the eternal conflict with the gods, Viṣṇu was at war with him. Viṣṇu could not kill Śaṅkhacūṛa unless his wife was unfaithful to him. Viṣṇu, using his power of *maya*, disguised himself as Śaṅkhacūṛa and had sex with Tulasī. She realized too late that she had been deceived; and her husband was killed. She told Viṣṇu that she was obligated to curse him for his deceit. He persuaded her to spare him the very dangerous curse of a faithful wife (*sati*) by promising her that she would be reborn as the beloved *tulasī* plant (Sen 1922:I,129–51). The plant is often said to be the darling of Hari, a name that ambiguously refers both to Viṣṇu and Kṛṣṇa.

The Hari Temple

Beginning in the 1920s, corresponding to the time when the modern identity of the Mahisyas was being established, a new style of temple began to be constructed in eastern Medinipur District, where Mahisyas are numerically preponderant. Although the tradition of family-owned temples is ancient, they were for centuries constructed and maintained exclusively either by high-caste families or by the families of local rulers. The kings of Tamluk and Moyna were Kaibarttas (as the forebears of the Mahisyas were known) who maintained elaborate temples as parts of their estates. The Rādhākṛṣṇa Temple of the Tamluk Raj is the foremost temple of the Rāj Bāṛi (although the more ancient temple of the Goddess Barga Bhīmā is the most important temple in Tamluk town). Moyna, with a much smaller capital, has a Rādhākṛṣṇa Temple as its principal shrine, and a Śaivaśakti temple as second in renown. The Moyna fort also contains a shrine (*thān*) for Dharma Ṭhākur, a Vaiṣṇava *samādhi* (a shrine to the former head priest of a Vaiṣṇava temple), and the grave of a *pīr* (a saintly Muslim teacher). Less prominent families did not have so many shrines, but it was usual for Brahman and Kayastha clans to maintain temples—whether a room in the house or a separate structure—for their clan deities (*kuladevatā*), which, as discussed in chapter 1, was almost always a *śālagrām* stone embodying a form of Viṣṇu.

Viṣṇu, as the supreme ruler, was generally regarded as appropriate for families in dominant positions at every level from the kingdom to the small *zamindāri* estate. However, ordinary

Figure 7. The Hari Mandir in Dubkalua. Some pillars are wrapped in colorful paper and a colored streamer is strung inside the roof during worship. "Moon garlands" (*cā̃d mālā*) made of pith decorate the five *tulasī mañcas* and the priest has painted a fresh *puttalikā* on the central *mañca*. The image of Garuḍa is not visible in the photograph.

Mahisya cultivators had no such claims. Their Vaiṣṇavism emanated from Caitanya and the *bhakti* movement. The *tulasī mañca* found in every Mahisya household became the basis for the new style of Hari Mandir.

Hari Mandir is a generic term for any kind of Viṣṇu Temple, but the style that became most popular in the last century in eastern Medinipur has a characteristic form. A platform made of brick and cement, about 3 meters square, is raised about a meter above ground level. Four *tulasī* pedestals are constructed on one section of the platform in a square arrangement, the sides of the pedestals paralleling the sides of the platform, with a fifth, larger pedestal at the center of the group. A four-sloped roof covers the platform, supported by pillars along the sides of the platform. The sides are left open; the steps mark the front of the temple. After construction the temple must be ritually "established" (*pratiṣṭha*), making it the residence of a living deity. At the time of its establishment, an image of the great bird Garuḍa, conveyance of Lord Viṣṇu, is installed, facing toward the *tulasī* pedestals, emulating the way Śiva's bull, Nandi, is placed at Śiva temples. This is the only example I know of in which the term *mandir* is applied to a structure that is not fully enclosed. Other open-air shrines are called *thān*, which is probably derived from *sthāna*, meaning simply "place." When conducting worship, a Brahman sits facing the array of *tulasī* pedestals. Daily service is provided by the person or family designated as *sevāit* (servant) of the temple. After bathing, the *sevāit* is to water the *tulasī* plants and sweep the platform.

The Hari Mandir of Satkalua village was built in the Bengali year 1335 (1928/29 CE), and the one in Murarikalua was built in 1338 (1931/32). Construction dates were not shown on those in other villages. The Hari Mandir of Narsinghkalua, the only village in which the entire population was Mahisya, was the only temple common to that village; their village Śītalā was kept in the temple of the Brahman who performed her worship. In the 1950s and 60s some Mahisya households that had become relatively well off, thanks to income from betel leaf cultivation, began building Hari Mandirs as domestic temples, analogous to the temples of the *kuladevatās* of the higher castes, but expressing the *bhakti* piety of the followers of Śrī Caitanya.

In some Hari Mandirs, particularly the newer ones, the sides of the *tulasī* pedestals were decorated with images of Caitanya and his principal disciples molded in bas relief cement sculptures, and painted appropriately. They depicted Caitanya, Nityānanda, Advaitya, Śrīvās, and Gadādhar dancing ecstatically, arms upraised. The favorite figures are Caitanya, known as Gaurāṅga (Golden Bodied), or simply Gaur, and Nityānanda, commonly called Nitāi. Gaur-Nitāi is nearly a unity in the common usage, and Gaur and Nitāi were favorite names for first and second sons in many Mahisya families when I was doing fieldwork. The choice of Nityānanda over the other disciples was an indication of the divide between the stiff discipline of the Vṛndāvana Gosvāmīs and the ecstatic Nityānanda *vaṃśa*. Elsewhere I have discussed the various interpretations people placed on these temples (Nicholas 2003:57–59). Commonly, people said the five *tulasī* pedestals represented Caitanya, at the center, and the four disciples around him.

Hari Mandirs were the places for *Hari bāsar*, "gatherings of the Lord," on the special days of Kṛṣṇa. The most popular of these occasions were the congregations on full-moon nights, when *kīrtan* parties sang about the deeds of Kṛṣṇa and Hari *luṭ* is flung into the crowd. However, there were also gatherings on *ekādaśīs*, when *maṇḍalīs* met. A *maṇḍalī* is a congregation—more exclusive than those of the everyday Vaiṣṇavas of the village—of men who had taken initiation (*dīkṣā*) from the same guru. As the day of choice of the Vṛndāvana Gosvāmīs, *ekādaśīs* were preferred by the extra-pious and those who sought the respectable status of *kanthi-dhārī*, described in chapter 1. However, the celebrations on *pūrṇimā* nights were more festive and accessible to everyone. These were supported by the village, with each house, ideally, taking a turn (*pālā* or *bār*) paying the cost of the offerings.

Samādhi

Much less common than Hari Mandirs, *samādhis* are Vaiṣṇava shrines that express an important set of cultural constructs. A *samādhi* (commonly pronounced *samāj*, which usually means "society") may be the grave of a Vaiṣṇava guru (*gosāiṅ*). It is well known that Hindus are cremated at death; burial is quite uncommon. Cremation (*sava dāha*) releases the *ātmā* ("self," often misleadingly rendered in English as "soul") from the body, allowing it to move to the ancestors, to be venerated, fed by descendants, and to take birth again. A few extraordinary people are thought to attain liberation from rebirth while still in their bodies (*jīvana mukta*) and, thus, not to require cremation. Among Vaiṣṇavas in Kelomal, it was sometimes the practice to bury *jīvana muktas* (in a seated posture) and to erect platforms over their burial places, the resulting structures resembling nothing so much as the graves of Muslim *pīrs* (*dargāh*). Some pious people accorded the distinction of *jīvana mukta* to deceased parents, and established small *samādhis* near their own houses, usually marked by a mound of earth, or sometimes by three mounds. These domestic *samādhis* were cleaned daily, and the conch shell was sounded nearby in the evening. It was usual to mark the death anniversary of a *jīvana mukta* by feeding a small group of observant Vaiṣṇavas. The *samādhi* of a venerated *gosāiṅ* was usually a more elaborate shrine and the gathering place of a much larger group, the *maṇḍalī* of that *gosāiṅ*, in an event reminiscent of the *'urs* of a *pīr*. The patterns of social organization and worship developed by the ordinary Muslim and Hindu cultivators and artisans of rural Bengal have a lot in common (Nicholas 2003:28–46).

The Puri Program

The time that Caitanya spent in Puri, in Odisha, at the famous temple of Jagannāth, influenced the ritual program of his followers in Bengal. Medinipur is the district in West Bengal physically and culturally closest to Odisha; Caitanya traveled through Medinipur when he moved between Navadvīpa and Puri. The distinctive calendar of rituals of Jagannāth is well known in West Bengal; dates and activities are noted in the Bengali almanac. The most important occasions are the *rath-yātrās*, the chariot trips, in which the image of Lord Jagannāth, his brother Bālābhadra and his sister Subhadrā, together with the Sudarśana Cakra (discus) that identifies Jagannāth as a form of Viṣṇu, are taken out of the great temple on huge, elaborately decorated chariots—really, rolling temples—drawn by hundreds of devotees pulling on heavy ropes. (The story that devotees who fell while performing this sacred act and were crushed beneath the huge wheels of the *rath* led to the English "juggernaut," referring to an overwhelming, unstoppable vehicle of, usually, destructive force.) Neither the images of the deities, which are rather crude wooden figures, nor the ritual observances that take place in Puri are at all typical of Hindu practice. The indigenous origins of these gods and their rituals are apparent, yet they are recognized as among the most sacred images and observances of Hindus. Both the example of Caitanya and the practices of the kings of Odisha with respect to Jagannāth have elevated this temple to the highest level of Hindu holy places (*dhām*).

There are three major festivals at the Puri Jagannāth temple, all at the beginning of the rainy season. The first is the *snāna-yātrā* or "bathing journey," in which the images are taken from the

Figure 8. *Rath melā* in Dimari Hat. The chariot is in the distance, with five spires like a Hari Mandir. The large wheels are invisible because of the crowd. Artisan castes bring their products for sale at the fair; a Potter is in the foreground.

temple to a designated bathing place. This festival takes place on the full-moon day of Jyaiṣṭha (May/June), which corresponds to the beginning of the Bengali observance of *ambubācī*, in which the earth is said to menstruate. Jagannāth is drenched in 108 pitchers of water drawn from a particular well. The pitchers are gold, a measure of the patronage of the temple by the royalty of Odisha and its standing as a pilgrimage place for all of India.

The *rath-yātrā* or "chariot journey" is the largest event of the year. Thousands of pilgrims gather in Puri for the festival beginning on the second day of the bright lunar fortnight of Āṣāṛha (June/July), normally 16 days after the *snāna-yātrā*; the deities are brought out of the temple, each on its own grand chariot, and drawn along a three kilometer route to a secondary temple, where they remain for eight days. On the tenth day of the bright lunar fortnight the third festival, the "return journey" (*punar-yātrā* or *ulṭarath*) takes place.

There are smaller versions of the grand carriages of Puri serving village temples in West Bengal. There was not one in Kelomal but there was one in nearby Dimari Hat, where there was a *melā* (fair) on the day of the *rath-yātrā*. Hundreds of people from throughout the vicinity came; in addition to ordinary purchases, there were unusual items for sale, including images of deities made by Paṭuās and seedling coconut trees, sprouted and ready to plant at the beginning of the rainy season. The chariot was constructed in the nineteenth century, with heavy iron wheels, and an elaborate temple-like structure on top. Brass images of Rādhā and Kṛṣṇa from the Dimari temple sat on the highest seat; Garuḍa sat on a lower level; and the Brahman who performed the worship sat on the level below as the carriage was drawn along an established route about three-quarters of a kilometer in length to a point near the main road between Tamluk and Mechada, where it remained for eight days before being returned to Dimari Hat. The images normally resided in a temple and the chariot sat, devoid of ornamentation, until the following year.

KṚṢṆA *BHAKTI*

Ordinary village people in East Medinipur manifest their attachment to the deeds of Lord Kṛṣṇa in many ways. For example, displayed on the walls of modest mud-built houses of cultivators are lithographed pictures showing scenes from the *Bhāgavata Purāṇa*—Kṛṣṇa dancing in a circle with the *gopīs* on Rās Pūrṇimā, the full-moon night of Kārtik (October/November), or sitting with Rādhā as the *gopīs* push them on a swing on Dol Pūrṇimā, the full-moon night of Phālgun (February/March). Among the most popular expressions of *bhakti* are the *Bhāgavata* stories known as *Kṛṣṇa Līlā*. *Līlā* means "play," and it also refers to the actions of deities in relations to humans. *Yātrā* (pronounced *jātrā*) is a medium of cultural performance developed in Bengal over some centuries; how long is not very clear. It is costumed drama staged by actors who are villagers themselves and who have other occupations, often agriculture, when they are not performing. During agricultural down-time, troupes of *yātrā* performers, carrying trunks with their costumes and stage gear, travel through the countryside seeking villages that can pay for their performances. In the 1968–70 period, a troupe of 8–10 performers agreed to stage a performance for three nights for Rs.150, plus food and lodging. Food meant the ordinary diet of rural people in Bengal: rice, dal, vegetables, and fish. Lodging was a place on a verandah where bedding could be rolled out.

There are some recently composed dramas that deal with modern themes. Beginning in the 1930s, leftist dramatists, recognizing an authentic medium of the common people, organized "people's theatre" *yātrā* companies in Kolkata. Rural *yātrā dals* were not yet much affected by such developments in 1970. I cannot say what has happened after the arrival of television in the countryside. In the late 1960s *Kṛṣṇa Līlā* was still the most popular *yātrā* drama, with scenes from the *Bhāgavata* stories and the relationship of Rādhā—another man's wife—with Kṛṣṇa. People in Kelomal particularly liked *yātrā dals* from the southern part of the district, Kanthi (Contai) subdivision, where the dialect is closer to Oriya. "Oriya *yātrā*" was said to be a particularly suitable vehicle for telling the stories of Kṛṣṇa's deeds and of the devotion of humans to their god, perhaps because of the importance of Puri as a pilgrimage place and as the scene of Caitanya's ecstasies.

Performance by Paṭuās was another enduring medium of popular expression in East Medinipur. The Paṭuā caste is small and not widely distributed; it is distinctive in the ambiguity of its religious identity. Many people have both Hindu and Muslim names, and recite Muslim prayers although they deal in Hindu images. Paṭuā performers formerly traveled through the villages carrying cloth bags of hand-painted scrolls, each consisting of a series of colorful pictures illustrating episodes in a story that is sung in rhymed couplets by the Paṭuā as he unrolls the scroll. In recent years the stories have been expanded to include contemporary events. Health care workers have enlisted Paṭuās to tell stories about the transmissions of AIDS. Some of them composed the story of the attack on the World Trade Center, with illustrations gathered from images seen on television. Painting scrolls for sale has become more lucrative than performing in villages, but still there is a song for every scroll, whether or not it is intended for sale. *Kṛṣṇa Līlā* remains a staple. In 1961, when I first encountered a couple of itinerant Paṭuās, I copied down the words to their version, which are given here in translation. A separate picture illustrated each exchange between Kṛṣṇa and Rādhā.

Narrator: Beneath the *kadamb* tree, who is it Rādhā? Is Kānāi playing? His back against the tree playing the flute?

Leaning against the *kadamb*, calling with his flute, is Śyām. Hearing it, the many *gopīs* of the Vraja pastures cannot resist.

Rādhā, veiled as a modest wife, goes gently to the water, thinking of Kṛṣṇa with each rhythmic step.

Rādhā: "Are you not my husband's sister's son? Am I not your mother's brother's wife? Don't make sexual jokes with me! Be quiet Kānāi.

"Soon I will see Āyan Ghoṣ [my husband]. He will put an end to your error. He will make you sell the cow from your cowshed [impoverish you]. He will destroy your pride."

Kṛṣṇa: "What pride is there in a herd of cows? I can get cows. Where can I get a woman like you, fair princess?"

Rādhā: "First, lover, look. Why are you working up such a desire? Go home and tell your parents to arrange for your marriage."

Kṛṣṇa: "I tried to get to get married, Rādhā, but fortune intervened. Now I am seeing and hearing that I will marry one whose name is sweetest Rādhā."

Rādhā: "First, love, look. Why are you working up such lust? Tie a pitcher to your neck and drown yourself."

Kṛṣṇa: "To buy a pitcher, Rādhā, where will I get cowries? To tie it to my neck, Rādhā, where will I get rope?

"Your breast, that is my pitcher. The braid of your hair is my rope.

"The stream of your love, that is my sacred Yamunā. To drown myself in that body, that is my desire."

"Don't call me 'black, black' daughter of Vṛṣa Bhānu. The water of the Yamunā is also black, but everyone drinks it.

"The water of black clouds relieves the whole world.

"The water of the Yamunā is surely black; why do you put it in your pitcher?

"Why do you put black shadow in your beautiful eyes, sweetheart?

"Don't call me 'black, black,' daughter of Vṛṣa Bhānu. Fortune has made me black. What shall I do?"

Narrator: Having heard so much, Kṛṣṇa felt despondent. He spoke to the bamboo flute in his hand: "Become a black snake!" A black snake appeared, crawling on the path. It wrapped itself around Rādhā's right leg and bit her on the left.

Rādhā: "What you asked for Kānāi, that I will give. The black snake has bitten me. Make it well."

Narrator: Hearing this, Kṛṣṇa uttered an incantation from a distance.

Kṛṣṇa: "Now tell me truly, sweet Rādhā, how far has the poison gone?"

Narrator: Seeing the poison gone, Rādhā's senses returned.

Rādhā and Kṛṣṇa embracing, man and woman, became as one.

This vernacular version of *Kṛṣṇa Līlā* sits athwart the conventions of more elevated Vaiṣṇava theology. Kṛṣṇa is a seducer of married women; he is not above using magic to get his way. Like many villagers, he is self-conscious about his dark complexion. Metaphorical interpretations of the love of Rādhā and Kṛṣṇa are replaced by more familiar, earthy ones that are well understood by peasant farmers and artisans.

A few devout Vaiṣṇavas expressed their *bhakti* through renunciation. The anthropology of India was preoccupied for a time with the issue of Hindu renunciation, since it was thought to be the one institutional method of expressing individuality in a society that incorporated each person into a collectivity. Kelomal afforded me rich experience of individuality among ordinary people who were living under the worldly obligations of *saṃsāra*, imbedded though they were in collectivities. However, there were also renouncers, people—usually men—who had given up worldly obligations.

Saiva renouncers who belonged to the Daśnāmi order, called *sannyāsīs*, were known to villagers, but never visited during my time in Kelomal. However, Vaiṣṇava renouncers, called *bairāgis*, often made the rounds, going from house to house begging for food, occasionally singing Kṛṣṇa *kīrtans* with enthusiasm and cracked voices. Giving rice and lentils to a *bairāgi* was considered a virtuous act. Such people often lived at temples, sometimes in the company of women who were usually widows who had been badly treated in their marital households and became *sevā dāsīs*, "serving women," in Vaiṣṇava temples.

Clan Deities

The clan deities (*kuladevatā*) of the high-caste houses are on a different plane from the devotional religion of the peasantry. Clan deities are usually *śālagrāma* stones, described in chapter 1, identified by their markings as one or another of the forms of Viṣṇu. Dāmodar, Raghunāth, and Nārāyaṇa are the names of several of the *kuladevatās* in Brahman and Kayastha family temples in Kelomal. Possessing a clan deity is a mark of distinction; it means "our house is old and aristocratic" (*banedi/baniyādī*). At the same time it is also a continuing obligation: a *kuladevatā* has the legal status of a minor person. He must be served, attended to, provided with proper priestly attention daily, and brought out for major *pūjās*. Old landed families often wait for the third generation before dividing their property; acrimony and lawsuits frequently accompany such delayed partitioning. The *kuladevatā*, however, is indivisible and must continue to receive service and financial support from all segments of the clan even if they are in serious conflict with one another. Responsibilities and expenses are painstakingly divided into "turns" (*pālā*), shares of responsibility proportional to the number of coparceners. Land for which the deed (*patta*) is in the name of the deity (called *devottar* property) cannot be partitioned, so the produce must be divided among the descendants, all of whom remain servants (*sevāit*) of the deity. There may be considerable ill-will between the sides, but most people think that abandoning a *kuladevata* will lead to terrible consequences for the clan.

Attending to a clan deity sometimes resembles child-care. It must be wakened, bathed, clothed, and fed in the morning, then worshiped; and again in the evening, it requires feeding, worship, and being put to bed. The *śālagrām* stone is seated in a miniature throne (*siṃhāsana*) during the day and lies in a very small bed at night. It has its own utensils for bathing and dining. A typical morning offering consisted of *ātap* rice (rice that is husked without parboiling and is thus quite pure because it is uncooked), together with sweets and fruits. The evening meal, called *śītal khāoyā* (cool food), might include only sweets and milk. *Śālagrām* are not even faintly anthropomorphic; it is difficult to see the connection with the divine figures who are accorded such ceaseless care.

There are numerous special occasions throughout the year, some of them enacting the deeds of Kṛṣṇa as described in the *Bhāgavata Purāṇa*, and some that are peculiar to Bengal and unknown in Sanskrit literature, that bring special attention to the *kuladevatās*. There are eight such observances among high-caste families in Kelomal.

1. *Chānā-pānā*. Through the month of Baiśākh (April/May), the first month of the year, when the weather is hot and dry, the *kuladevatā* was given a daily refreshing drink made with milk curd (*chānā*), which is the basis for most Bengali sweets. The *kuladevatā* was not the only deity who was given this hot-weather refreshment, though it was the only one that received a daily offering. One Kayastha house sent *chānā-pānā* to the village Śītalā and Pañcānan on one day during the month. In another household, *chana-pana* was also offered to the Śivas in four domestic temples.

2. *Gajā-mug*. *Mug* is a variety of lentil or pulse that is a common item in the Bengali diet. If it is soaked in water and allowed to sprout (*gajā*), *mug* is a common item of *jal khāoyā* ("water food," a snack accompanying a glass of water), food that is uncooked and pure, suitable for offering to a deity. In the rainy season month of Āṣāṛha (June/July), on the second day of the bright lunar fortnight, the day when the chariot of Jagannāth was taken out, sprouted mug was offered to the *kuladevatā*.
3. *Jhulan-yātrā*. The "swinging festival" takes place in the rainy season month of Śrāvaṇa (July/August). The rainy season is regarded as the most romantic time of the year, and the image of lovers sitting together on a swing under a large tree is particularly evocative. Kṛṣṇa and Rādhā are depicted sitting close to one another on a swing that is pushed by the *gopīs*. *Jhulan yātrā* takes place inside the temple over five days, from the eleventh day of the bright lunar fortnight until the full-moon night. Temples that had images of Rādhā and Kṛṣṇa placed them on swings. The domestic temples that housed *kuladevatās* had only their *śālagrām* stones, which they placed on miniature swings, then swung for the entertainment of the deity. Offerings to the deity on each day of this festival were much larger than normal and the Brahman who performed the worship received a larger honorarium than usual (Rs.1 in 1968). The additional offerings became *prasād* that was distributed to the houses of neighbors and dependents, as well as being eaten solemnly by family members.
4. *Janmāṣṭamī*. The birthday of Kṛṣṇa is observed on the eighth day of the dark lunar fortnight in Bhādra (August/September). This is an auspicious day on calendars throughout India, and it is marked in various ways by Vaiṣṇavas everywhere. In Kelomal, the *kuladevatās* received extra offerings, though not on the same scale as the swinging festival.
5. *Rās yātrā*. The autumnal month of Kārtik (October/November) is full of important religious observances. The new-moon night of Kārtik is the occasion of Kālī Pūjā, a dark and dangerous event that takes place on the same night as the more famous festival of illuminations—Dīwālī—that is widely

observed throughout India. During the bright lunar fortnight following Kālī Pūjā, the worship of the goddess Jagaddhātrī is held. The image of Jagaddhātrī is immersed on the tenth day of the bright fortnight and, on the following day, the night of the gods is said to end. On each night throughout Kārtik a lamp, called *ākāś pradīp* or *svarga pradīp*, "the heaven lamp," is lit for the ancestors.

The full-moon night of Kārtik is a major event in the Vaiṣṇava calendar. It is called *Rās Purṇimā*, the night on which, according to the *Bhāgavata Purāṇa*, Kṛṣṇa danced with the *gopīs*. He appeared to each individual *gopī* to be dancing with her, even while he danced with all of the others at the same time. The scene, which is often depicted, is sometimes used to demonstrate that Kṛṣṇa is the giver of individual salvation. The occasion was a special one in all of the domestic temples in Kelomal. One Kayastha family, markedly richer than the others, had constructed a fine *rās mañca*, a nicely painted brick and cement tower in an open area at the top of which was a sheltered platform where the clan deity was taken out to enjoy the occasion. Bringing a deity out of its regular abode is a ceremonial event. There is a procession with drummers; the deity should be carried in its throne by a Brahman beneath an honorific umbrella. The daily offerings were augmented for *rās yātrā* as they were for the other special observances.

6. *Makar saṃkrānti*. The month of Pauṣa (December/January) is the time of the principal rice harvest. Pauṣa ends when the sun passes into the house of the Makar, an imaginary sea creature, part dolphin, part fish, and part elephant. The last day of Pauṣa is the conjunction (*saṃkrānti*) with the Makar. The rice harvest is the province of the goddess Lakṣmī, and I shall say more about the events on *makar saṃkrānti* in discussing her worship. However, although this is not predominantly a Vaiṣṇava observance, the *kuladevatā* is not ignored. A special food called *makar*, made of cut-up raw fruits and vegetables mixed with milk and molasses, is prepared for the clan deity, thus including it in the family circle on a predominantly social occasion.

7. *Dol yātrā.* The full-moon day of Phālguna (February/March) is another observance taken from the *Bhāgavata Purāṇa. Dol* also refers to a swing, but in this case it is the swing of the baby Kṛṣṇa. However, *dol* is far better known throughout India as Holi, the festival of colors, on which Kṛṣṇa and the *gopīs* sprayed one another with colored fluids. Today it is considered by many in India to be the ritual that marks the beginning of spring. In most places it is generally just a big, boisterous, playful holiday. Bengalis use a lot of colored powder called *ābir*, although some colored liquids— including some indelible ones—are also sprayed around. McKim Marriott's justly famous essay, "The Feast of Love" (1966), records his experience of Holi in a North Indian village in 1952; there, a lot of hierarchical inversions took place. It is certainly true that my wife and I became very colorful in Kelomal in 1969, but many of the people who might have been even more attractive targets simply stayed out of sight, content to exchange a little color within their own houses.

All of the *kuladevatās* got special attention on *dol purṇimā*. However, on the night preceding the full moon, two households, the Ghosh Bari and the Karkun Bari, also performed a special ceremony, called *c̃ācar*. The *c̃ācar* is a combination of outdoor worship and a bonfire. Each of these families constructed, in an open field, a kind of hut or shelter. A frame of freshly cut bamboo was prepared. Inside was a banana tree with its blossom. The structure was covered with straw. After dark, a Brahman brought the *kuladevatā* out of the family temple. The procession was accompanied by drums and by servants, one of whom carried an umbrella over the deity; others carried articles needed for the *pūjā*. The *kuladevatā*, seated on its miniature throne, was placed inside this hut for worship. After the completion of worship, which included a *homa* fire offering, the Brahman brought the deity and the articles used in the *pūjā* out of the *c̃ācar*, and it was set on fire. There was some merry making by youngsters around the fire. The Brahman held the deity, in its throne, so that it could witness the burning. The Brahman said that the fire represented the destruction of the

Figure 9. *Cā̃car* fire on *Dol Yātrā*. After the Ghosh Bari *kuladevatā* was worshiped in the shelter in the agricultural field, the shelter was set ablaze and the deity was returned to its temple in a procession. The priest carried the deity, under the honorific umbrella. People from the Ghosh Bari carried the offerings and lamps; a Barber carried an honorific fly-whisk and a water pot to cleanse the path before the deity passed. Two Dom youngsters provided rhythm on a *ḍhāk* and gong.

anti-god Holikā or Holākā, and the deity needed to witness this. There were several other bonfires in the empty fields, but these two were the only ones where there were *pūjās*.

8. *Basudhārā.* Meaning "stream of plenty," *basudhārā* is a parochial ritual with a fancy name. On the last day of Caitra (March/April), which is the last and hottest month of the year (and also the occasion for the Gājan), an apparatus was created that allowed a slow stream of cooling water to drip on the *kuladevatā*. A small hole was pierced in the bottom of an earthenware pot, and the cover of another earthenware pot was similarly pierced. The *śālagrām* stone was seated in the concave pot lid and the pot with the hole suspended above and filled with water so as to create a steady stream of water over the *śālagrām*. Having bathed the deity, the water then flowed into the intact pot beneath. A similar *basudhārā* was arranged over the roots of a wood-apple (*bel, bilva*) tree, a symbol of Śiva. In that case the water was allowed to flow into the ground and where it watered the tree.

Rāma

In view of the central place of Rāma and Sītā in the religious life of neighboring areas of India, the small role they occupy in the ritual calendar of rural Bengal is noteworthy. In Bengal, temples dedicated to Rāma, or Sītā and Rāma, or Hanumān are uncommon and mostly established by immigrants from northern India. Images of these figures are not found in the gods' rooms of Bengali houses. However, the *Rāmāyaṇa* narrative is quite popular among Bengalis, and was very well known to people in Kelomal, mainly in the Kṛttivāsa Bengali version, which most people did not distinguish from the Vālmiki Sanskrit version. They conflated the *satya yuga* with the era in which Rāma was king (Rāma *rājya*), a time when order and virtue reigned. According to Kṛttivāsa, Rāma worshiped Durgā before invading Lanka to recover Sītā from her abductor Rāvana. In Bengal, this episode is treated as the authority for the "untimely" worship of Durgā in the autumn. Hanumān is often invoked by Bengalis as an exemplar of devotion, valor, and strength.

Despite their evident knowledge and interest, there was only one major *pūjā* to Rāma in one household in Kelomal on the occasion of Rāma *navamī*, Rāma's birthday. The family that held this *pūjā* had lived for some years in Rāmrājtalā, a suburb of Howrah city and a station on the Southeastern Railway line. The town is obviously named for Rāma and, as the name suggests, it is a place where Rāma rules; there is a major celebration of Rāma *navamī* in Rāmrājtalā, but it is one of very few in West Bengal. Bengalis would doubtless have been happy to make a place for Rāma *navamī* in their ritual calendar if it did not occur in the month of Caitra. The ninth day of the bright fortnight in Caitra occurs during a season dominated by distinctively Bengali rituals, often at the same time as Gājan, on the day following Annapūrṇā Pūjā, and in the midst of the three days designated for the spring worship of Durgā. Elsewhere I have reviewed the likely reasons for the congestion in the ritual calendar at this season (Nicholas 2013:59–64).

During the course of my fieldwork there was one exceptional event dedicated to Rāma. I will describe in chapter 5 the elaborate worship of the goddess Śītalā in Dubkalua in 1969. Immediately after the completion of Śītalā Pūjā, the young men of the village collected nearly Rs.100 to pay for an event called *Rāma Rasāyana*, "Essence of Rāma," a recitation and discourse on the *Rāmāyaṇa*. The underlying conception is that hearing the words of the *Rāmāyaṇa* has physical and moral benefits. The same principle applies to the *Bhāgavata Purāṇa*: listening to a recitation of the deeds of Kṛṣṇa is physically and morally beneficial to a person. The reciter was a Vyasokta Brahman, reputed for his knowledge of *Rāmāyaṇa*, who lived in the village of Byabattar about 20 kilometers from Kelomal. He was accompanied by two percussionists, one playing tabla and one the *khañjani*, a kind of frame drum used in Odisha. The recitation, which went on for three hours during each of two evenings, was heard by several hundred people thanks to a battery-powered loudspeaker system. The significance of Rāma's exile, of Sītā's abduction, of the moral model of Lakṣmaṇa, and of the devotion of Hanumān were all well known. The stories illustrating those virtues sounded especially splendid in the cadence of the reciter. The main point is that Rāma was a part of the pantheon of people in Kelomal, but primarily through narrative rather than through ritual.

Satya Nārāyaṇa

Satya Nārāyaṇa, a deity worshiped very commonly in households in Kelomal, is revered in many parts of India; however, Kane (1954:V,437) noted that this god is "very popular in Bengal and Maharashtra." Kane also said that the Satya Nārāyaṇa *vrata* is described in the *Bhāviṣya Purāṇa*; he quoted Hara Prasad Shastri who, in the early twentieth century, wrote that

> the worship of Satya Nārāyaṇa . . . has a Mahomedan origin. It was originally (and even now in many places) called '*Satyapīrer pūjā*.' It occurs in the *Revākhaṇḍa* of the *Skandapurāṇa* (Vangavasi ed.) but does not occur in the Venk. Press edition. Vide also JBORS vol. XVI at p.328 where the same scholar says that the Mahomedan custom of offering 'Sirṇi' to Satyapīr was adopted by Bengal Hindus as worship of Satya Nārāyaṇa.

The addition of *satya* to the name of this deity invokes the quality of veritable existence, one of the three constituent qualities (*guṇas*) of Hindu thought. The others are, *rajas* ("activity") and *tamas* ("entropy"). In Bengal, an active deity—the goddess Durgā is the foremost example—is characterized by a mixture of the *guṇa* of *rajas* with *satya*. Few deities are predominantly *tāmasik*, but *tamas* predominates in the goddess Kālī, whose name refers to *kāla*, "time," the ultimate destroyer of all things. Even without the prefix, Nārāyaṇa possesses the quality of *satya*, but while, as a name of Viṣṇu, Nārāyaṇa evokes the image of the universal ruler, Satya Nārāyaṇa is credited with a lot of less-than-universalistic intervention in worldly affairs. The tales of Satya Nārāyaṇa are like those of many local Bengali deities who assert their need for recognition and worship in a pantheon dominated by better known deities. In Bengal, but not in other parts of India, similar stories are told about Satya Pīr, a legendary Muslim saint. Satya Nārāyaṇa and Satya Pīr are active in the affairs of humans but Nārāyaṇa is not.

The *Skanda Purāṇa* is a text with many late interpolations. One that is included in the Vaṇgavāsi edition, which was published in Kolkata in Bengali script, and not included in the Mumbai Veṇkateśvara Devanagari edition, suggests the obvious: that the conflation of Muslim and Hindu cults took place in Bengal. Satya Pīr and Satya Nārāyaṇa are treated as identical in many Bengali-language works. Rāmeśvara Bhaṭṭācārya, a famous early eighteenth-century author, wrote a work sometimes called *Satya Pīrer Kathā* ("The Story of Satya Pir") and sometimes called *Satya Nārāyaṇer Brata Kathā* ("The Story of the Vow of Satya Nārāyaṇa"), in which the two forms are both described as the "*avatāra* for the *kali yuga*" (Cakrabarti 1964:536). Tony Stewart (1995:578), who has translated some of the Satya Pīr stories, says that they became part of the Satya Nārāyaṇa narrative "in a sophisticated and long-term process of Sanskritization." With the sharpening of the distinction between Hindus and Muslims in the twentieth century, Brahmans who perform Satya Nārāyaṇa *pūjā* became disinclined to suggest the existence of a Muslim *avatāra*. However, in Bengal, the one mandatory offering in the *pūjā* is *sinni*. *Sinni*, the usual Bengali pronunciation of the Persian word *sirni*, is a common offering at the shrine of a sainted Muslim *pīr*. It is a mashed up concoction of bananas, milk, and sweet items. *Sinni* is also offered to other "Muslim deities"; in Kelomal, a Muslim must be invited to offer it at the shrine of Olābibi, goddess of cholera, on behalf of the Hindu villagers. However, Brahmans routinely offer *sinni* to Satya Nārāyaṇa, though it is offered to no other Hindu deity. *Sinni* is often prepared in large quantities so that there is *prasād* for every house in the village.

Syncretism

The term "syncretism" was evidently introduced into English in the seventeenth century to refer to—and to disparage—efforts to harmonize Protestant doctrine with that of the Church of Rome. In Victorian times, Andrew Lang borrowed it to refer to the process in which the gods of cultures in contact with one another are melded into unitary figures. As twentieth-century anthropologists studied the increasing instances of asymmetrical cultural contacts, the term came into common use to refer to many forms of borrowing and reinterpretation. The identification of West African gods with Catholic saints in Brazil and the numerous millennialist renderings of the Book of Revelation in revitalization movements around the world are examples of "syncretistic" phenomena. In this sense, in anthropology "syncretism" belongs to the era of "cultural traits," and not to the concept of culture as a symbolic system.

Systems are integrated, not "shreds and patches" drawn from different sources and stitched together to make a fabric that has no intrinsic unity or coherence. When people adopt novelties from cultural encounters they do so in ways that make sense, that are interpretable, and that they can integrate into their cosmologies. Although it is sometimes thought of as a mechanical process of assembling a part from this system and a part from that, the term "syncretism" could still be useful if it is understood as an intellectual process of symbolic integration or synthesis that produces a new coherent framework, enabling people to make sense of things previously unfamiliar. In unstable times, there are constant challenges to existing worldviews and cosmologies. Human beings crave coherence; they create it where there is none, and they impose spurious order on natural systems that they otherwise cannot understand. The intellectual impulse to incorporate the new into existing cosmologies is a feature of humanity that probably evolved along with language and grammar. It is not the act of borrowing but the act of integrating what is borrowed into what is already there—changing both the old and the new—that characterizes this cultural process. The institution of a "Muslim" food offering for a Hindu deity with an Islamic alter ego seems perfectly sensible to most people. To an anthropologist, it is a cultural borrowing—a syncretism—but it has to be seen in the right light, as a part of making sense of Islam in the context of Hindu polytheism.

Worship

Anthropomorphic images of Satya Nārāyaṇa were occasionally prepared, though it was usual practice to invoke the god in a pot and to forego the expense and more elaborate ritual required for an image. When an image was prepared, it was of a conventional four-armed Viṣṇu, holding a discus, mace, conch, and lotus. He was sometimes given a blue complexion, which indicated the extent to which Satya Nārāyaṇa was identified as Kṛṣṇa, or—perhaps more accurately for the unsophisticated Vaiṣṇava devotees of rural Bengal—the extent to which Kṛṣṇa was seen as the encompassing form of Viṣṇu. In one depiction, a blue four-armed Satya Nārāyaṇa held aloft the conch and discus of Viṣṇu, while holding the flute of Kṛṣṇa with his lower hands.

A century ago Dinesh Chandra Sen wrote, "There is not a village in Bengal where Satya Nārāyaṇ is not worshipped once every week. . . ." (Sen 1914:678). At the time he wrote, there were both Hindus and Muslims in a great many of the villages of both eastern and western Bengal. However, what he said then was still generally true in Kelomal in 1969; there were very numerous occasions on which Satya Nārāyaṇa was worshiped.

Integral to the worship of Satya Nārāyaṇa is listening to the stories that describe his activities among human beings. Middle Bengali literature is a vast store of such narratives, dealing with the gods and goddesses of Bengal, stories called *maṅgal kāvyā*, *pā̃cāli*, *brata kathā*, or simply *kathā*. *Maṅgal kāvyā* are mostly long verse narratives, divided into episodes called *pālā* ("turn"), that are performed—by recitation, singing, and/or acting—over a week or more, with separate segments for day and night. The final episode of a *maṅgal kāvyā* is often called the *jāgaraṇ pālā*. *Jāgaraṇ* is a vigil; one stays awake all night—or, at least, does not lie down in a bed—in observance of a mental commitment to the deity honored in the *maṅgal kāvyā*. A *pā̃cāli* (the term if often translated as "song") is also a verse narrative, though usually not as long as a *maṅgal kāvyā*. As was noted in the previous chapter, *brata* in Bengali has come to refer to a self-denying religious observance, undertaken mostly by women, who worship a particular deity, and listen to the *brata kathā*. Some of these narratives are taken from puranic sources, but most were composed in Bengali. The term *vrata* in Sanskrit has a weightier significance, more akin to ritual. Though I have used "vow stories" to translate *brata katha*, *bratas* are "vows" only in the sense that they entail personal commitments.

A century ago, D. C. Sen said that there were innumerable short manuscripts of Satya Nārāyaṇa stories found everywhere in Bengal villages. Old manuscripts had to be recopied from time to time, with more recent copies sometimes written in school notebooks or on loose sheets of paper. However, hand-written versions have largely been replaced by inexpensive books, printed and bound in the style of Bengali manuscripts, and published under the title *Śrī Śrī Satya Nārāyaṇa Pā̃cāli*. Whether from manuscript, printed book, or memory, these stories are read aloud or recited as essential elements of the worship. The three interconnected stories that constitute the *pā̃cāli* have been elegantly translated by Tony Stewart (1995a:581–96); I will provide only brief summaries here. Narratives of this type are well-known in Bengal: they give accounts of deities who are not yet receiving worship—perhaps not yet even recognized as divinities. They depict the misfortune and grief that come to those who fail to worship them properly, and the benefits that flow to those who discover their divinity and learn to worship them. In the case of the worship of Satya Nārāyaṇa or Satya Pīr, the mandatory offering of *sinni* is described in the manuscripts and printed books, as well as in the *Purohit Darpaṇ*, the Brahmanical manual for domestic priests. *Kā̃cā* (uncooked) *sinni* is made by mixing bananas, flour, milk, spice, and a sweetener, usually molasses (*guṛ*). *Pākā* (cooked) *sinni* is simply *sandeś* (a molded sweet made of milk curds [*chānā*] with added sugar). *Bātāsā*, sugar wafers, are common offerings in many Vaiṣṇava rituals. These are items, particularly *kā̃cā sinni*, that are offered during the *'urs* or death anniversary at the shrine of a Muslim Pīr. In Kelomal, *kā̃cā sinni* is also offered at the shrines of Olābibi. While Muslims are asked to make the offerings to Olābibi on behalf of Hindu villagers, Brahmans offer *sinni* to Satya Nārāyaṇa.

The Story of the Poor Brahman. In Mathurā there was a poor Brahman who got his living by begging from house to house. One day his begging produced nothing; he sat disconsolately beneath a tree and began to cry. Satya Nārāyaṇa appeared before him in the guise of a Muslim fakir and asked the Brahman to tell him why he was crying. When he heard the Brahman's plight, the fakir told him to go home and worship Satya Pīr. When the Brahman said he had only the Nārāyaṇa Śilā (*śālagrāma*) form in which to worship, and that it cannot be used to worship a Muslim (*yavana*), the fakir smiled and said, "There is no difference between the *Puran* and the *Koran*. Ram and Rahim are different names for the same thing." [Stewart's version is different: "The Veda and the Quran derive from a common source."] Then he revealed himself as Nārāyaṇa, with four hands, holding a conch shell, discus, mace, and lotus respectively. When the Brahman worshiped him with an offering of *sinni*, his poverty and sadness were banished.

The second story is very brief.

The Woodcutters' Story. A group of woodcutters, on their way to the forest, stopped at the Brahman's house. They were astounded at his sudden wealth and asked for an explanation. The Brahman told them everything that had happened to him and how to worship Satya Nārāyaṇa with an offering of *sinni*. When the woodcutters worshiped as they were instructed, they also became wealthy.

The third story, much longer than the first two, bears a strong resemblance to a number of middle period Bengali narratives about the adventures of sea-going traders who get into trouble far from home and are saved by the proper worship of a deity who was being wrongly ignored or dishonored.

The Merchant's Story. A trader learned to worship Satya Nārāyaṇa from the woodcutters. His wife delivered a beautiful daughter and the trader promised Satya Nārāyaṇa a *pūjā* with offering of *sinni*. The daughter was, in the course of time, married to a handsome young man who became a partner with his wife's father in a trading venture. There is a description of their journey down the Bhagirathi–Hugli River, with accounts of the famous deities they worshiped along the way. They passed out into the Bay of Bengal and sailed along the coast, past Puri where they ate the *prasād* of Jagannātha. They reached their destination, the city of Hiranyapatana, which appears to be on Sri Lanka. Satya Nārāyaṇa, aggrieved that that the merchant had failed to offer him *sinni*, had the wealth of the king of Hiranyapatana transferred to the merchant's ship, so that it appeared that the men were thieves. They were put in prison.

The merchant's wife languished at home; she had run out of money, and yet had no news from her husband. One day she happened by the house of a pious Brahman who offered *sinni* to Satya Nārāyaṇa every day. Having learned from the Brahman's wife the power of Satya Nārāyaṇa and how to worship him, she performed the *pūjā* herself and promised to do so again when her husband returned.

Satya Nārāyaṇa was satisfied. Appearing to the king in a dream, he told him that the two merchants had been wrongly imprisoned, that they were faithful devotees, and that the king should release them, give them wealth equal to ten times what they brought, and send them home. If he failed to do so, Satya Nārāyaṇa promised to extinguish the king's lineage. The king brought the prisoners to his court, treated them like royal visitors, gave them treasure as instructed, and sent them off.

As the ships sailed up the Hugli, Satya Nārāyaṇa appeared to the trader as a celibate religious student. He asked what they were carrying in their ship, and the trader told him they had only coal. The god turned the cargo into ash. The merchant immediately recognized his error and abjectly threw himself at the feet of the student. Satya Nārāyaṇa lectured him about the error of attempting to deceive a god, and reminded him of his unfulfilled promise of worship with an offering of *sinni*. After an abject apology, the treasure was restored and they were at last able to return home.

When the ship reached the dock, the merchant's daughter was engaged in worshiping Satya Nārāyaṇa. She turned her attention from the god to her husband and, as she dashed toward the ship, she dropped some *sinni* on the ground. Satya Nārāyaṇa was again offended: he sank the ship and drowned her husband. Satya Nārāyaṇa appeared again to the wife, this time disguised as an astrologer. He spoke to the young woman about the dishonor that befell Satya Nārāyaṇa when his *prasād* was dropped, and advised her to retrieve the *sinni* and to eat it reverently. When she did so, the ship was raised and her husband was restored to life.

The merchant organized a great *pūjā* for Satya Nārāyaṇa and offered a vast quantity of *sinni*, so that the entire public could share in the *prasād*. Satya Nārāyaṇa was well pleased that the commitment had been fulfilled, and he gave the merchant much more wealth.

These narratives are very similar to the Sanskrit versions of the *brata kathā* found in the *Skanda Purāṇa*, but the Bengali stories were modified to include Satya Pīr, to specify the offering of *sinni* to the deity, and to locate the merchant's travels in familiar territory. There is no Islamic element in the puranic stories.

The Song of Satya Pīr. An oral version of the narrative that I collected in 1961 compounds elements of the written stories with some features drawn from other Hindu–Muslim hybrids such as Bon Bibi and Dakṣiṇa Rāy. This one was also told by the Paṭuās who told the *Kṛṣṇa Līlā* related above; and, like that story, it was told in rhymed couplets that accompanied colorful scroll pictures. It is particularly appropriate to the Paṭuās with their mixed Muslim–Hindu identities.

> Salutation, Satya Pīr. I take your name.
> Without you there is no virtue.
> The tiger will not devour and the buffalo will not touch
> Those who take the name of Satya Pīr when entering the forest.
>
> One day Satya Pīr thought,
> "I shall go to be worshiped in the land of the King of Sindh."
> Thinking thus, Sāheb Satya Pīr disguised himself as a fakir and departed.
> He presented himself before the king and asked the king to say the words of worship.
> Addressing the fakir, the king promised him an offering of *sinni* worth five annas;
> With sincerity he also offered a cow and a calf.
> After some time a son was born to the king,
> But the promised offering to the Pīr was forgotten.
>
> The king sailed abroad to do trade.
> In the middle of the river his boat was made to sink.

Striking his head, the king cried, "Alas.
What shall I do to recover my sunken boat?
This time, Father Pīr, if I get my boat,
I shall give the promised offering and a milking cow.

Hearing all this, the Pīr changed his mind.
He brought up the sunken boat.

With devotion (*bhakti bhāve*) the king gave an offering of flowers,
And he who had been Satya Pīr became Satya Nārāyaṇa.

On seeing Satya Nārāyaṇa, everyone became joyous,
And they worshiped him with many kinds of offerings.

Here ends the tale of Father Pīr.
Hindus and Muslims together say *sālām*.

The Practice of Satya Nārāyaṇa *Pūjā*

I gathered information on the practice of Satya Nārāyāṇa Pūjā from over a hundred households and lineages in Kelomal. Practices were very diverse, varying widely from one house to the next. Some families treated this *pūjā* as a *nitya karma* (regularly repeated): some held Satya Nārāyaṇa Pūjā on every full-moon night, while others also worshiped him monthly, but on the *saṃkrānti*, the last day of the solar month, the day on which the sun makes the transition from one sign to another. The neighbors of such regular worshipers were just as likely to report that they follow no schedule, treating the worship as a *kāmya pūjā* (performed when desired). Some said that they worshiped Satya Nārāyaṇa only in the month of Baiśākh, for example, or that they worshiped "when devotion comes" (*jakhan bhakti elo*), as one man eloquently put it.

Houses that had clan deities (*kuladevatā*) held daily worship for their god, but they added more elaborate ceremonies—quite often Satya Nārāyaṇa Pūjā—on important dates in the Vaiṣṇava calendar, such as Rāma Navamī, Rās or Dol Pūrṇimā. The Ghosh

Bari, whose Durgā Pūjā I have described (Nicholas 2013), held a Satya Nārāyaṇa Puja immediately after Jay Caṇḍī Pūjā, which is a compact recapitulation of Durgā Pūjā two days after the immersion of the image of the goddess. A nearby Brahman family worshiped Satya Nārāyaṇa two days after that, on Kojāgarī Pūrṇimā, the night of Lakṣmī worship. Yet another Kayastha family in the neighborhood did Satya Nārāyaṇa Pūjā on the night following Kālī Pūjā, a fortnight after Kojāgarī Pūrṇimā. A Mahisya household in the same vicinity held Satya Nārāyaṇa Pūjā once a year, on Akṣay Tṛtīyā, in lunar Baiśākh.

Some families worshiped during daylight, others at night. A few had clay images, many invoked the deity into a pot for worship, and those families that had clan deities embodied in *śālagrām* treated those stones as all-purpose images. It was common for people to make mental commitments (*mānasik, mānat*) to Satya Nārāyaṇa, promising him a *pūjā* after the birth of a child, or at the time of the first rice (*annaprāśana*) rite for a child. A few poor people said that they offered *pūjā* when they had the ingredients for *sinni* available to them. Where the worship was done in conjunction with another Vaiṣṇava ritual, it was customary to invite the local *kīrtan* party to sing, though their songs celebrated Kṛṣṇa and the love of Rādhā for Kṛṣṇa, and said nothing about Satya Nārāyaṇa. When there was *kīrtan*, there was usually also Hari *luṭ* at the conclusion of the songs. A couple of minority castes—the Weavers (formerly Launderers), and the Fishers, held Satya Nārāyaṇa Pūjās for their local caste groups, with clay images and elaborate offerings. Whatever the occasion—small domestic rite or community *pūjā*—the reading aloud of the Satya Nārāyaṇa *pā̃cāli* was considered indispensable. In this respect, Satya Nārāyaṇa Pūjā resembled the practice of a *brata* rite.

Fisher's Satya Nārāyaṇa Pūjā

There was a large, compact neighborhood of the Fisher caste centered in Murarikalua, and including adjacent houses on the north side of Khojār Bheṛi in the villages of Hirapur and Padampur. In 1961 there were 131 members of this caste in Kelomal, and perhaps as many as 200 in the total neighborhood. They reported their caste name as Rajbangsi ("lineage of kings"), but they were commonly called Jāli ("netter') or Tīyar ("hunter"). Many men of this caste relied predominantly on fishing for their livelihoods. There were not many men in Kelomal, regardless of caste, who did not fish occasionally. Spinning line for fish-nets and weaving fish-nets was a spare-time occupation of a great many men of all castes. However, the Fishers caught fish for sale in the market, with the women of the caste generally doing the selling. Mahisyas considered the practice of allowing women to sit in the market and bargain over the price of fish to be undignified, lower-caste behavior. Mahisyas, and people of other castes as well, often disparage Fisher women, whose vocabularies justified the English epithet "fishwife." Sometimes Mahisyas of more devout Vaiṣṇava disposition claimed to disapprove of Fishers' caste occupation since it involved killing fish, though in truth almost everyone in Kelomal killed fish as often as possible. The Fishers lived separately from the Mahisyas and the higher castes and conducted much of their social life in their own extensive neighborhood.

Starting about the time of Indian independence, the Fishers of Kelomal began holding a Satya Nārāyaṇa Pūjā (as well as Sarasvatī Pūjā, mentioned earlier) in their neighborhood. They took subscriptions (*cā̃dā*) from households of their caste to pay for the cost of a clay image of the deity, offerings, decorations, the honorarium of the priest, and entertainment. The incentive for many of the young men who did the organizational work and collected the subscriptions was entertainment. The example of collectively organized Durgā Pūjās, and other community-organized *pūjās*—in contrast to the Durgā Pūjās of the old *zamindār* houses—figured strongly in the establishment of the Fisher's Satya Nārāyaṇa Pūjā. The choice of Satya Nārāyaṇa among all the possible deities was influenced by the facts that none would challenge the right of even a low caste to worship him as they saw fit, and that they had great flexibility with respect to choice of dates for their worship. For this caste, the slack season for fishing—the hot, dry weather before the onset of the monsoon—was the best time for them to organize such an event.

Preparations for the Fishers' Satya Nārāyaṇa Pūjā began on the morning of the full-moon day of Jyaiṣṭha (May/June) in 1969. A young apprentice from the family of the image-maker in Murarikalua came to a small mud-built, open-front, tile-roofed temple in the Fisher neighborhood where an unfinished image of Satya Nārāyaṇa had been placed. He completed work on the image, repairing some cracks, making items such as the discus, lotus, club, and conch shell that Nārāyaṇa holds in his four hands, and painting the whole thing. He completed his work that afternoon. The temperature was about 38°C (100°F), and it did not cool off much in the evening.

I do not know how much money the young men collected. Expenses for the image, the generous offerings, and the Brahman were near Rs.100. They complained that they did not have enough money for a "band party," a group of costumed Dom musicians who drum and play music to accompany dancing by the young men. They said the band party cost Rs.30 to 40. However, they did have the *ḍhāk* (barrel drum), which they regarded as necessary; that cost Rs.4. And there was a *kīrtan dal*, which took its compensation from the food offerings and locally distilled liquor (*deśi mad*). Just how much of the budget went to purchase liquor was never stated, but there were several supplemental solicitations late that night for contributions to purchase additional liquor.

The Brahman who performed rituals for the Fishers lived in a village about 4 kilometers from Kelomal. He had many *jajmāns* to serve on this full-moon day. His first visit to Kelomal was at 4 p.m. At that time he performed a *pūjā* at the Hari Mandir in Murarikalua. After worshiping there, he appeared briefly at the Fishers' temple, then went on to neighborhoods of their caste in other villages. He returned to Kelomal at about 10 p.m. The Fishers planned a *pūjā* in a rather grand style, like Durgā Pūjā in some elements, with a formal procession to immerse a pot and to invoke the deity, the offering of sixteen items (*upācāras*) to the deity, and the flower offerings (*puṣpāñjali*) by the worshipers. In other respects it resembled Kālī Pūjā, with youngsters shooting off firecrackers, painting their faces and dancing wildly, and men drinking a lot. These are not activities normally appropriate for a *sāttvika* deity such as Satya Nārāyaṇa, though no one was surprised that the Fishers behaved in such a manner.

The procession to immerse the deity's pot left the temple at about 10:30 p.m., accompanied by two *ḍhāks* (they had collected additional funds), and a group of *kīrtan* singers who had the double-headed Vaiṣṇava drum (*khol*), two sets of small cymbals (*karatāl*), and a small brass gong (*kā̃si*). The procession went through Murarikalua to the Hari Mandir, where the priest placed the pot—still empty—before the *tulasī* shrine and offered a small platter of rice, fruit, and vegetables. Then it proceeded to the consecrated pond of the Karkun house (the former *zamindārs*). The immersion of a pot to invoke a deity is always conceptually performed in the Ganga. Since that sacred river is far away, Gaṅgā Pūjā is performed to make the water at hand as efficacious as that of the river itself. While such Gaṅgā Pūjās are common and usually quite simple, the priest of the Fishers did something out of the ordinary. He sent two men, who acted on behalf of the Fisher caste group, into the pond to fetch some mud. They constructed a small altar (*bedi*) on the side of the tank, a simple mud platform with three small pillars in a row on top. The Brahman explained the significance in two ways: The pillars stood for the netherworld (*patal*), the earth (*martya*, he said *masti*), and heaven (*svarga*); or for the rivers of the three worlds, the Bhagirathi, the Sarasvati, and the Mandakini. He lit incense sticks on the altar, put a small garland on the central pillar, and placed before it a platter of rice, fruit, and vegetables as an offering to Ganga. The Brahman stood in the pond with the two men representing the Fisher caste facing him, standing on the bank. The Brahman gave them a *mantra* to recite, identifying them as *jajmāns* on behalf of their local caste group. He held a brass pot that had been prepared with sprigs of leaves of five significant trees and marked with a *puttalikā*. Reciting a *mantra*, he immersed the pot, withdrew it from the water—now embodying Satya Nārāyaṇa—and placed it on his head. To the accompaniment of the *ḍhāks*, one of the Fisher men raised an honorific umbrella over the deity.

The procession was led by a man who poured water from a small brass pot to cleanse the path before the passage of the deity.

Figure 10. Fishers' Satya Nārāyaṇa image and pot. The pot representation of the deity was seated on a *yantra*, dressed in a coarse cotton *gāmchā*, and adorned with a *cā̃d mālā* (pith cut-out garland). The image of the deity was a conventional representation of Viṣṇu that did not show anything to distinguish it as Satya Nārāyaṇa. The string surrounding the image defines a sacred space that may not be entered by anyone other than the priest.

The *kīrtan* party was singing, drumming, and clanging their cymbals and gong. At 11:30 p.m. this raucous party stopped at the Karkun house to request permission for their *pūjā*, by 1969 a formality and legacy of the old order. The Brahman remained outside the gate with the deity's pot on his head while the *ḍhāks* and *kīrtan* singers went inside. Both a hurricane lamp and a Petromax lantern were also carried inside, but the Brahman objected, saying that one light should always accompany the deity.

In all, it was a very pompous show for a group of lower caste people to stage. In part, it was a very good imitation of the kind of collectively organized *pūjās* that had come into being with the development of modern publics in other sectors of Bengali society, and in part it was an assertion of the standing of the Fishers as a respectable caste group in the face of a social reality that did not affirm it. Bowing before the former *zamindār* was a way of saying that they were as worthy as other, higher caste *prajās*. But, at the same time, as the vehicle for these assertions they were using a benign deity, one more difficult to offend than Durgā or Kālī.

The procession continued back to the Fisher neighborhood where the Brahman placed the deity's pot before the image, which was by then painted and dressed. Although the setting lacked the grandeur of a high-caste *pūjā maṇḍap*, the arrangement and offerings were intended to mimic a Durgā Pūjā or other regal event. The *naivedya* offerings were gracefully displayed; the *pūjā* equipment for the Brahman was all in place; there were flowers, including a lotus; mango twigs were arranged for a *homa* fire sacrifice; and there was even a mirror placed beneath the image of Satya Nārāyaṇa in imitation of Durgā Pūjā. The difference resided in a large pot of *kā̃cā sinni* that stood on the side of the image. It had been made with five *poās* (about 1.25 kilograms) of wheat flour, five *poās* of cane molasses, five *poās* of raw milk, and 41 (*daś gaṇḍā ekṭā*) bananas. In addition, there was a platter of sugar wafers (*bātāsā*) representing *pākkā sinni*. These were the "Islamic" offerings that distinguished Satya Nārāyaṇa from the other Hindu gods (and from deities named Satya Nārāyaṇa in other parts of India). After it had been offered to the deity, *sinni* would become *prasād* for members of the Fisher community.

The order of activity by the Brahman was somewhat unusual, in that he presented the main offerings to the deity before performing the rituals that were intended to endow the image with sight (*cakṣura dāna*) and breath (*prāṇa pratiṣṭhā*). The deity was fully present in the form of the pot, so theoretically, the image was irrelevant to the worship. Moreover, it was the practice of the

Fishers to allow the image to stand in the temple shed for a full year before immersing it, so the enlivened image played a different role for them than the images of Durgā and the other deities did for the high castes.

Worship began at about midnight, an unusual hour for a Vaiṣṇava *pūjā*. The two men who had represented the caste at the immersion of the pot participated in the *saṃkalpa*, the rite identifying the *jajmān* on whose behalf worship was being carried out. After the *saṃkalpa*, the Brahman began a two-track performance: offering flowers, water, and food to Satya Nārāyaṇa while simultaneously reading his *pā̃cāli* stories. He paused at about 1:20 a.m. to perform the *cakṣura dāna* (giving vision) and *prāṇa pratiṣṭhā* (establishing breath) rituals for the image of the deity. These were done behind a curtain so the worshipers could not see these mysterious acts. When the image had thus been enlivened, he returned to the *pā̃cāli*. He finished reading at about 1:45 a.m. and prepared to light the *homa* fire. One of the men who participated in the *saṃkalpa* touched the Brahman's foot as he poured *ghī* into the fire, physically conveying the benefits of the sacrifice to the *jajmāns*.

The Brahman performed *āratī* (display of lights), accompanied by the *ḍhāk* and gong, then assembled the remaining worshipers to offer *puṣpāñjali*. (Some people had gone off to sleep, and others had gone elsewhere to drink.) The entire worship was not completed until nearly 2:30 a.m. The Brahman had not eaten a meal through the day. He had to cook his own rice after the conclusion of his night's work, as he could not eat food cooked by his own low-caste *jajmāns*. He slept on the verandah of the house adjacent to the temple and returned home the following morning.

The neighborhood of the Weavers (formerly Launderers) also held a collective Satya Nārāyaṇa Pūjā. Their *pūjā* was equally a reflection of the problem of their caste. Launderer (Dhopā) is a low caste. However, they had given up doing other people's laundry and handloom weaving had become a near-universal occupation among them. When asked their caste, they responded "Tanti" (Weaver). However, it was known that other Bengali Tantis did not recognize them as being of the same caste, and would not arrange marriages with them. They arranged marriages with families far from Kelomal who also asserted that they were Weavers. Others in Kelomal continued to call them Dhopa. In other words, this group was working its way out of a stigmatized status, but there was still a distance to travel before it was established in a new position. They held a Satya Nārāyaṇa Pūjā like that of the Fishers, but as it was on the last day of Caitra (March/April), the day of the most intense activities of the Gājan, it was difficult for me to observe how far they had elaborated it and made it resemble the practices of higher-status castes.

Domestic Satya Nārāyaṇa Pūjās

As I have said, there is no typical pattern of Satya Nārāyaṇa worship. Prosperous households that have lineage deities (*kuladevatā*) represented by *śālagrām* stones in domestic temples often hold Satya Nārāyaṇa Pūjās, treating the *śālagrām* as the deity. The service of a Brahman priest is almost always necessary for such worship. In the Karkun house, this practice was followed in their Raghunāth Jiu temple. Besides the usual equipment of worship—flowers, water, incense, brass vessels, a lamp, and a *naivedya* of five *poās* of sun-dried rice—there was an elaborate recipe for *kā̃cā sinni*. In a large basin 25 pairs of bananas were mashed up with five *poās* of milk, five *poās* of wheat flour, five *poās* of cane molasses, camphor, powdered cardamom, raisins, and ground coconut. *Pākā sinni* included both *sandeś* and *bātāsā*. It was customary for women of the house to fast before listening to the Satya Nārāyaṇa *Pā̃cāli* read aloud by the priest, then to break their fast with *sinni*.

Families that held Satya Nārāyaṇa Pūjā on full-moon nights usually combined the observance with Hari *luṭ*. A group of *kīrtan* singers, who performed songs celebrating Rādhā and Kṛṣṇa and displayed their own devotion to Kṛṣṇa, sang for some time outside the house of the worshiper. The priest offered a basket of *bātāsās* to the deity. Since *bātāsās* are equally appropriate offerings to Kṛṣṇa and, as *pākā sinni*, to Satya Nārāyaṇa, they may serve two purposes. After the deity has received them, the wafers were thrown among the people who had assembled around the singers, and a scramble to collect them ensued.

A Karan man from Bhubankalua reported an idiosyncratic practice. On the western edge of Tamluk, where the road leaves town, there is a shrine (*thān*) to Mānik Pīr, a legendary saint known throughout Bengal. It was usual for travelers to toss a small coin toward the shrine on leaving town in hopes of obtaining the *pīr's* protection on the journey. Stating that Mānik Pīr is equivalent to Satya Pir, he bathed in the pond adjacent to Mānik Pīr's shrine, and offered *sinni*, a small coin, and a wooden horse to the *pīr*, considering that this was also worship given to Satya Nārāyaṇa.

• • •

I have used the word "pervasive" to underscore the influence of Vaiṣṇavism in Kelomal, in rural East Medinipur, and throughout West Bengal. The omnipresence of this strand of Hindu practice is due to a very great extent to the influence of Caitanya, and to the personal example of *bhakti* piety he set. From the care of the *tulasī* plant to the processional *kīrtan* parties on *pūrṇimā* nights, devotionalism is the dominant expression of religion among the ordinary people of the villages. But such observances as the cycle of annual rituals for the clan deities of the influential, high-caste houses are less practices of devotional Vaiṣṇavism than of canonical Brahmanism; there is much of Bengal Vaiṣṇavism that predates or is independent of the movement initiated by Caitanya. And, on the other end of the distribution, practices that connect Islam with Hindu divinities and rituals derive from the practical reason of ordinary people. Although some elements of Vaiṣṇava practice in Kelomal are drawn from scriptural authorities and some are creations of illiterate commoners, villagers do not perceive such a great gap, largely because they all share the attitude of *bhakti*. And, in a further step, most people did not seem to find unbridgeable differences between Vaiṣṇava rituals and those devoted to Śiva and Śakti, although some pious Vaiṣṇavas object to animal sacrifices, as do some well-educated "modernizers."

4. Cycles of Lakṣmī Worship

Lakṣmī, the goddess whose name is synonymous with well-being through wealth and prosperity, is worshiped around the year in Kelomal. While Vaiṣṇavism is pervasive, Lakṣmī is ubiquitous. Her worship is very nearly universal among Hindus in these villages among all castes and in poor as well as prosperous families. Lakṣmī is frequently depicted as a beautiful young woman of golden (*gauri*) complexion, seated on a lotus in the midst of an ocean, dressed in an auspicious gold-bordered red sari, ornamented with a golden crown and rich jewels, holding a golden vessel in the crook of her arm, with a lotus on one hand and a sheaf of golden rice in the other.

However, peasants usually encounter her in other forms: in the eyes of village people, freshly threshed rice heaped in large measuring-baskets is one of the most auspicious of her manifestations. Rice being poured into the granary is Lakṣmī entering the house. The most commonly used term for rice—while it is still in the husk and golden in color—is *dhān*, a word derived from *dhan*, which means "wealth." During harvest season, a married woman who has both a living husband and a son—the "Lakṣmī of the house" (*gṛha-lakṣmī*)—often draws *alpanā* designs representing Lakṣmī's footprints leading into the granary.

Lakṣmī's domain of activity is preeminently the individual house; she is worshiped primarily by particular families for their own benefit, not collectively by villages or caste groups. There are four different calendars for the worship of Lakṣmī in the households of Kelomal, corresponding to the four levels of worship discussed in Chapter 2. A small number of families observe all four; almost every family observes one or two. Two calendars, which I refer to as the "ruler" and the "cosmopolitan," conform to practices enjoined in Sanskrit code books (*śāstra*), authorities such as the ritual portions of the *Skanda* and *Liṅga Purāṇas* and the *Tithi Tattva* ("Doctrine of the Lunar Days") by Raghunandana, the sixteenth-century Bengali authority (Kane 1958:V, 199, 209–91).

In Kelomal the "ruler" calendar included two observances, Kojāgarī Lakṣmī Pūjā, on the full-moon night of lunar Āśvina (September/October), and the Alakṣmī and Lakṣmī Pūjās on the following new-moon night in lunar Kārtik (October/November). The "cosmopolitan" calendar of worship, known as Khanda-pālā Lakṣmī Pūjā, was performed during the bright lunar fortnights of Bhādra (August/September), Pauṣa (December/January), and Caitra (March/April). The days on which these observances were held, although placed in lunar months, were solar days. Thursdays were preferred since that is Lakṣmī's day (*Lakṣmībār*). However, if any of these Thursdays was an inauspicious lunar day, then a Sunday or Monday was selected instead. The almanac (see Pañjikā 1970:31 of the front matter) was regularly consulted for guidance as to appropriate days as determined by complicated astrological procedures.

The third calendar of Lakṣmī worship in Kelomal followed "the custom of the country" (*deśācār*) and consisted of Lakṣmī Pūjās done on Thursdays throughout the year, regardless of what lunar day it might be and regardless of planetary or astral conjunction. This calendar culminated in Banāi Pūjā, which was done on the penultimate day of Pauṣa, the last day of Pauṣa, or the first day of Māgha (January/February) by subjects of the former domains of Tamluk, Kashijora, and Mandalghat respectively. Although there is no mention of these observances in Sanskrit authorities, they are commonly discussed in popular Bengali texts (e.g., Bhaṭṭācāryya

1968/9) on proper customary conduct (*sadācār*) and they were carried out in most respectable Kelomal households.

The fourth calendar of Lakṣmī worship in Kelomal followed "popular custom" (*lokācār*): It consisted of the worship of Lakṣmī each Thursday during Agrahāyaṇa (November/December) and Pauṣa, the months during which the principal rice crop ripened, was harvested and threshed. It was marked by a special ceremony on one Thursday (or other auspicious day, according to some people) after threshing had begun, called Golā Pūjā ("granary worship") or Dhānya Sthāpano ("rice depositing"). The days for these observances are not set out in Sanskrit authorities nor do they appear in the Bengali almanac, but they are the most widely observed occasions of Lakṣmī worship in Kelomal.

The "Ruler's" Calendar of Lakṣmī Worship

Kojāgarī Lakṣmī Pūjā

The worship of Lakṣmī by village families or clans whose control over land and wealth was such that other villagers were regarded as their "subjects" (*prajā*)—in other words, roughly, the old *zamindār* class—is an integral part of the worship of the goddesses of power and control, among whom Durgā is foremost. One of the old men of this class referred to Durgā Pūjā as *āmāder sarkāri pūjā*, which might be rendered "our official or governmental worship." The Kojāgarī full-moon night follows five days after the conclusion of Durgā Pūjā. This is a rare occasion on which Lakṣmī is worshiped in the form of an anthropomorphic clay image (*pratimā*), fully dressed and ornamented. Image-makers prepare these images at the same time they are making images of Durgā for families of the former *zamindārs*. Other families who worship Lakṣmī on Kojāgarī *pūrṇimā*—including other Kayasthas, Brahmans, and a few prosperous households of other castes—do so by invoking her in a water pot (*ghaṭ*). There is a considerable difference of scale between the rituals of worship with an image and worship with only the water pot embodiment. A single domestic priest can worship her in pot form on behalf of many different families on that one day. However, to do a full worship of the image requires about four hours of continuous activity for one or two priests. (If there is a second Brahman, he serves as *tantra-dhārak*, "holder of the ritual manual," who reads the procedures and *mantras* to the *pūjak*, the Brahman who performs the worship.)

In the Ghosh Bari of Banamalikalua, in the autumn of 1970, only two servants worked throughout the Kojāgarī Lakṣmī Pūjā, which was much smaller in scale than Durgā Pūjā; one was a Karan who oversaw arrangements, and one was a Weaver who did heavier work and ran errands such as collecting the pith and tinsel ornaments for the image from the Garland-maker's house. The worship was performed by the Ghosh clan priest (*kula-purohita*) without the assistance of a second Brahman (see Nicholas 2013: 132–41 for further details). The Barber who usually attended to the Brahman was ill and sent his twelve year-old son and thirteen year-old daughter in his place. The barrel drum (*ḍhāk*), gongs (*jhā̃j*, *ghaṛi*, *kā̃sar*), and other musical instruments played by Doms that accompany many *pūjās* are excluded from the worship of Lakṣmī. She is thought to favor quiet, restrained voices, and the sweet sound of the conch shell trumpet; her ill-omened elder sister Alakṣmī is said to be attracted by loud noise. Many of the people of the Ghosh Bari who lived away from the village left after the conclusion of Durgā Pūjā, so the number of worshipers in attendance was not large and the amount of food that had to be prepared was greatly reduced.

As is often the case, what is, for men, simply an occasion of worship, is, in addition, a self-denying *brata* for women. Thus, the married women of the clan abstained from cooked food during the day and did not eat anything in the evening until it had first been offered to Lakṣmī, so that it came to them as *prasād*. Lakṣmī was offered only a "cool" (*śītal*), light, easily digested meal in the evening. Preparations were begun about 4 p.m. for this meal, featuring *luci* (bread made of white flour fried in clarified butter into a puffy form), instead of the usual meal that has boiled rice as the staple.

The image of the goddess, complete and clothed, but not yet ornamented or given vision and breath, was seated on the worship platform (*pūjā dālān*) on the spot previously occupied by the image of Durgā. A servant carried the image and adorned it with a tinseled pith crown and various other ornaments (*ḍāker gahanā*). The image used in this rite is comparatively small, only about a meter ("two hands") in height. She has two arms and is in a sitting position, wearing the auspicious red sari, red lac (*āltā*) dye around the edges of her feet, and vermilion (*sindūr*) in the parting of her hair (*sīmanta*) that mark a married woman whose husband is alive. Some images of Lakṣmī for Kojāgarī Pūjā, such as that of the Karkun house, include her distinctive animal conveyance (*vāhana*), the owl, at her feet; but it is not the Ghosh Bari custom (*kulācār*) to do this. The right hand of the image shows the gesture (*mudrā*) of blessing; the left holds a lotus.

When the priest arrived at about 6 p.m., the sun had set. The auspicious procession to immerse Lakṣmī's pot left the pavilion at 6:30. It consisted of two men of the Ghosh clan, their clan priest, two servants (one of whom carried a Petromax lantern, the other an honorific umbrella), and two children from the Barber family to aid the Brahman. A special brass pot that was used only for worship was carried by the priest to the bathing place at the Ghosh's consecrated pond (*pratiṣṭha pukur*). After washing the pot, he immersed it in the pond, allowing water to flow into it as he recited a *mantra* in a near whisper. As he did so, the goddess herself was said to enter the pot, after which no one but the Brahman could touch it. He carried the pot with great care and walked cautiously, to avoid tripping or spilling any of the water. The Barber boy walked at the head of the procession, sprinkling water from a small brass pot to cleanse the path for the goddess. One of the servants held the umbrella over the deity, a Ghosh Bari man fanned the pot with a white yak-tail fly-whisk (*śveta cāmara*), and the Barber girl blew a conch shell—all acts of royal honor to the deity. The priest carried the pot into the pavilion and up the stairs to the worship platform and seated it on a heap of unhusked rice directly in front of the image.

There followed about half an hour of preparations and preliminary rites, performed by the priest, before the *saṃkalpa*, the declaration of the intention to perform the worship of Lakṣmī for the benefit of all of the families of the Kelomal Ghosh Bari. During

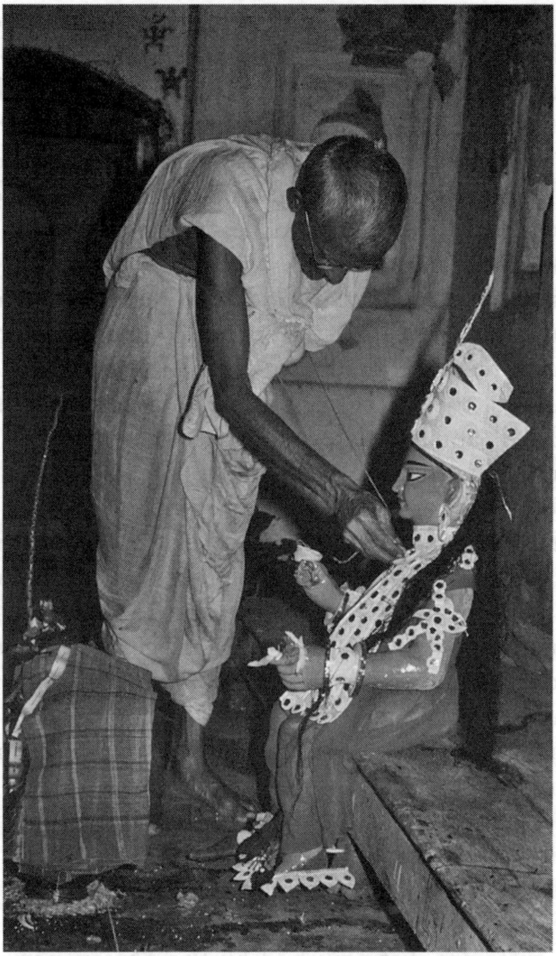

Figure 11. Kojāgarī Lakṣmī, during the *prāṇa pratiṣṭhā* ceremony, seated on the platform where the image of Durga stood earlier. The pot representation is seated before the image dressed in a *gāmchā*.

this preliminary period several married women of the house who were observing the *brata*, came onto the worship platform and, after inquiring whether the immersion of the pot was completed (i.e., whether the goddess was present), bowed before the goddess and addressed personal prayers to her. These prayers (*prārthanā*) were said aloud but in a low voice that was unintelligible except when the syllable "Mā" ("mother") arose in childlike petition. When the *saṃkalpa* was completed, the rituals enlivening the image were performed. At about 7:30 p.m. the worship proper began and continued for two hours, including the making of a complete offering of sixteen elements (*ṣoṛasopacāra*), a fire sacrifice (*homa*), and an *ārāti* display before the goddess at the conclusion, inviting her to take her evening sleep.

It was customary for the goddess to remain invoked in the water pot and in the form of the enlivened image throughout the night and to receive a small *pūjā* on the following day. Then in the evening of the second day she was obsequiously invited to take her leave, and bade farewell in the rite of *visarjana*. This rite has two parts: in one, the priest invites the goddess to abandon her residence by uttering a tantric *mantra* and shaking both the water pot and the image; in the second, the pot and the image are returned to the water. Because the procession to the water, the tossing of the image into the water, and the splashing around of the water auspiciously touched by the image are such prominent features of this rite, *visarjana* has become in Bengali practically synonymous with "immersion"; thus, the concluding rite is the complementary opposite of the initial rite of the "immersion of the water pot."

Although a *ṣoṛasopacāra pūjā* is elaborate, there is nothing unusual about the rites of worshiping Lakṣmī on Kojāgarī *pūrṇimā* so far as the work of the priest or the men of the worshiping clan are concerned. However, the rites of the women who take Kojāgarī Lakṣmī's *brata* are distinguished by the observance of a vigil (*jāgaraṇa*) on this night as an indication of their faithful devotion (*niṣṭhā bhakti*) to the goddess. The name of the day is generally said to be derived from *ko jāgara*, "who remains awake." The *brata kathās* of Lakṣmī, like the more elaborate *maṅgala kāvyas*, relate basic problems of human existence to failure to worship a particular deity and show how the institution and regular observance of proper worship resolve the problem. The act of listening attentively to the *brata* story—and with one's mind fixed upon the deity—is an intrinsic, result-producing part of the worship. Although there are oral versions of many *brata kathā*, they were usually read from inexpensive printed books or from the almanac.

Lakṣmī is synonymous with prosperity; her *brata* stories all deal with the lack or loss of prosperity and its consequences for the well-being (*maṅgal, kalyāṇa*) of a family—emphasizing the primarily domestic focus of the worship of Lakṣmī, even in the "ruler" calendar. Some other features of Lakṣmī's *brata* stories will emerge from comparisons among them. The story of Lakṣmī for the Kojāgarī full-moon night is:

Kojāgarī Lakṣmī *Brata Kathā*

In certain land there was a good king with many happy subjects. According to his decree, any goods that remained unsold in the market of his country would be purchased by the royal treasury. One day a Blacksmith from another kingdom brought an iron image of a maiden for sale. When no one in the market wanted to purchase the image, he began walking through the footpaths crying. "*Ogo*, who wants to buy Alakṣmī." No one came to purchase Alakṣmī and when the king heard the Blacksmith's cry, he called him in and explained his rule. He purchased the image and had it put in his house.

In the evening the king was on his way to perform his customary worship in the domestic shrine of his house when he heard what seemed to be a young woman crying aloud. In the gods' room he found a girl of such exceptional beauty that she illuminated the entire room; she was sitting with her face in her hands and crying. She said she was the Lakṣmī of his kingdom (*Rāj-lakṣmī*) and that she had dwelt there for a long time. Now she would have to leave because Alakṣmī had come into his house. He implored her to stay but she said it was impossible. However, she granted him the ability to understand the language of worms, insects, animals, and birds, before she disappeared, which he was required to keep secret.

On the next evening he saw a beautiful maiden leaving his palace. She was the Lakṣmī of his good fortune (*Bhāgya-lakṣmī*) and she too could not remain in the house with Alakṣmī. The king could not sleep that night, so he got up and went outside very late and met the Lakṣmī of his renown (*Yaśa-lakṣmī*) departing through the main gate. It was not possible for her to stay in the same place with Alakṣmī.

On the third night he saw the forms of a god and a goddess leaving his palace. The goddess said she was the Lakṣmī of his clan (*Kula-lakṣmī*) and that she could not dwell with Alakṣmī. The god said, "I am Dharma-rāj. I cannot remain here any longer because you have given Alakṣmī a place in your house. Why did you bring Alakṣmī into your house?"

The king said, "Dharma-rāj, you know all about this and you know that there was no sin in my mind. I pledged to buy whatever remained unsold in the markets of my kingdom. It was in support of that pledge that I purchased Alakṣmī. I would have fallen from my dharma if I had failed to keep that pledge, Dharma-rāj. Should I have done that? Raj-lakṣmī, Bhāgya-lakṣmī, and Yaśa-lakṣmī have deserted me. I did not stand in their way. Now Kula-lakṣmī is also leaving and I shall not prevent her. But I shall not let you go. Dharma-rāj, you are the bestower of the dharma that I am only maintaining. That which I have done was only for the sake of dharma. By what logic can you desert me?"

Dharma-rāj acknowledged defeat at the logic of the king. He was in truth the protector of dharma. To abandon him for an act that was done in the protection of dharma would be an extreme injustice. So Dharma-rāj could not leave the kingdom, but Kula-lakṣmī departed.

As the days passed, the king's circumstances worsened. The queen began to worry a great deal. Then a new problem appeared. The queen used to sit to feed the king. For several days she noticed that when the king sat to eat a company of black ants swarmed around his plate. Nothing tasted good to him any longer. One day while he was eating he asked the queen to tell the cook to leave the *ghī* out of his food. Then in the evening when he was eating, with the queen at his side fanning him, the ants began swarming around his plate as usual. The largest of the ants said,

"Look, brother, at this affair! How poor the king has become since he purchased Alakṣmī. How difficult is this life! He cannot afford even a spot of *ghī* in his food."

Through Rāj-lakṣmī's boon the king could understand their language and when he heard the ant talking he began to smile. The queen was very curious and asked him why he had suddenly begun to smile. He said, "If I tell the reason to anyone, I shall die." This only increased the queen's curiosity. She thought he was lying for the sake of some joke. She asked him again. The king said, "Very well, if you no longer want me, if you will be happy to see me die, then we shall go to the bank of the Ganges and I will explain it to you there." The queen still disbelieved him, so that very evening they went to the side of the Ganges. Again the queen said, "Now tell me, Mahārāj. I shall have no peace until I hear the reason."

The king said in a somewhat haughty voice, "Oh, I understand. Your knowing the reason for my smiling is more valuable to you than my life."

The queen replied, "Stop all these puzzles, Mahārāj. Just tell me why you smiled all of a sudden."

There was a dense jungle next to the river. A pair of goats emerged from that jungle just in time to hear this conversation. Then an attractive bunch of grass happened to float past them and the female goat said, "Look at that beautiful bunch of grass floating in the water of the Ganges. Please get it for me dear. I have a great desire to eat it."

The male goat said, "You're out of your mind! I should drown in the middle of the Ganges so you can eat some grass? Am I a fool like the king to sacrifice my life for a woman's whim?"

It was as if the king were awakened from a sleep by these words. He thought, "That's right. The queen is a frightening woman. Her husband's life is nothing compared to her whim. What can women not do? I have come here to sacrifice my life beguiled by this wicked woman!" As his loathing mounted, he resolved that he would no longer live with this sort of woman. He abandoned her in the midst of that jungle and returned alone to his capital. The queen wandered crying through the jungle.

One day the queen heard the sound of a conch shell and cymbals in the midst of the jungle. Following the sound she came upon many girls, daughters of the forest sages, making images of Lakṣmī from rice-flour paste, coloring them, decorating them beautifully, and worshiping them with *naivedya* offerings. Besides the *naivedya* there were parched rice, green coconut water, the soft interior of palmyra fruits, and cakes of molasses. The queen asked them why they were performing this worship. The girls were astounded at her ignorance. They said, "You see all this and you don't understand? Today is the Kojāgarī full-moon day in the month of Āśvina. Did you not know that Lakṣmī is to be worshiped on this day?"

The queen asked what fruits were obtained by this worship and the girls said, "If you offer this worship before Lakṣmī you can have whatever boon you want. Alakṣmī is banished and Lakṣmī becomes gracious."

The queen then took some of the rice flour from the girls and made a Lakṣmī image of her own. Together with the girls she devotedly worshiped Lakṣmī with offerings of flowers and sandalwood paste. Then she ate some of the parched rice, coconut water, palmyra fruit, other fruits, and uncooked vegetables that had been offered to the goddess. She observed a vigil throughout the night with the girls.

As a result of the queen's worship and observance of this *brata*, Alakṣmī was banished from the royal palace. Conditions there immediately began to return to their former prosperity. When the king awoke in the morning he was astounded and wondered what had brought about this miraculous change. Dharma-rāj appeared before him and told him that Alakṣmī had finally departed. He explained that this was the result of the worship, *brata*, and vigil performed by the queen in the jungle with the daughters of the sages.

The king saluted Dharma-rāj with devotion. Thinking that he had given his wife enough hardship, he took a troop of men and searched the jungle. When she was found they returned to the capital. From that time onward the queen performed the Kojāgarī worship of Lakṣmī with great splendor. Their former happiness returned to them. One by one Rāj-lakṣmī, Bhāgya-lakṣmī, Yaśa-lakṣmī, and Kula-lakṣmī all returned. And from this event the Kojāgarī worship of Lakṣmī became known throughout the world. (Bhaṭṭācārya n.d.:29–37, cf. Nag 1998, McDaniel: 2003:68–71).

The most obvious lesson in this story is that the maintenance of one's dharma occasionally demands difficult, self-abnegating actions that may lead to grief. The dharma of kings (*rāj-dharma*) is particularly demanding since it requires the ruler to undertake self-sacrificing actions not merely to maintain his own family, but to maintain his entire kingdom, since all of his subjects are equally his dependents. Thus, when his own wife interferes with his selfless action, he casts her off in a jungle and returns alone to his palace. The bodily relationship between wife and husband means that her worship, even far from home, redounds to his benefit. There are other messages in this story that will become apparent with the further examination of Lakṣmī worship and the associated stories.

The distinctive feature of the worship of Lakṣmī described in this story—the making of images of the goddess from rice flour paste (*pituli*)—was, in Kelomal, usually done in connection with the worship of Lakṣmī on the dark new-moon night of Kārtik following the Kojāgarī *pūrṇimā* in Āśvina. A great number of observances are clustered around the new-moon night of Kārtik, which is known in North India as Dīvālī (*dīpāvalī*), with its picturesque "row of lamps" ritual that leaves small flickering lights along the edges of roofs, railings, sometimes every flat surface on which a small earthenware oil lamp can be made to stand (see Kane 1958:V, 194–206 for all of the observances that take place at this time). Nowadays, strings of small electrical lights are used in many houses.

Some Bengali families do such illuminations in connection with the worship of Lakṣmī on this night. However, the new-moon night of Kārtik is known preeminently in Bengal as Kālī Pūjā. In those houses where Kālī is worshiped—which in Kelomal was most prosperous Brahman and Kayastha houses that are not "rulers," that is, who were not the former *zamindārs* who performed Durgā Pūjā—the worship of Lakṣmī as well as Alakṣmī constituted preliminary rites to Kālī Pūjā. In some Brahman and Kayastha houses where Kālī Pūjā was not done, women worshiped *gaṛā* ("constructed," "built up") Lakṣmī, with images formed of rice flour paste, colored with four or five dyes, like the images described in the *brata* story. However, where Kālī was worshiped, both Lakṣmī and Alakṣmī were worshiped in a different form. The things that delight Kālī are the opposite of those that give pleasure to Lakṣmī. Thus, not only is Kālī's worship accompanied by loud drums and gongs, but it is also the occasion on which fireworks are particularly appropriate because they frighten away the fearsome ghouls who accompany Kālī. While there are some skyrockets and aerial displays, the favorite fireworks are simply explosives, from ordinary firecrackers to small bombs. Such a boisterous and noisy celebration on the occasion of Lakṣmī worship repels Lakṣmī and attracts Alakṣmī.

On the new-moon night of Kārtik in 1970, my wife and I were guests in the house of Mohan Lal Ghosh of Banamalikalua. He was not related to the Kelomal Ghosh Bari but a descendant of the Sarkar clan through his father's mother. Although not a wealthy man—his house was made of earth rather than brick—he was well respected by other villagers as hard-working and honest; he was elected president of the statutory village *pañcāyat* in the first election to that council. (There is an account of his Kālī Pūjā in *The Night of the Gods*, Nicholas 2013:142–57.) The worship of Lakṣmī and Alakṣmī took place between about 7:15 and 7:45 that evening. A domestic priest from Banamalikalua performed Alakṣmī and Lakṣmī Pūjās, then hurriedly cycled away to worship elsewhere on this busy night. (Kālī Pūjā was presided over by two other Brahmans.)

The images of Lakṣmī and Alakṣmī were prepared before the priest arrived. They were made by the women of the house, including Mohan Babu's wife, the wife of his father's elder brother's son who lived in an adjacent house, their daughters, and Mohan Babu's widowed mother. (Also living in a room of Mohan Babu's house at that time was a recently widowed Rarhi Brahman man, originally from East Bengal, and his two daughters; the girls joined energetically in the preparations.) A single layer of tissue from the trunk of a banana plant was cut into sections about 30 centimeters long, forming a shallow gutter. One section was gracefully decorated with lumps of delicious pastes made of papaya, apple, pomelo, and a special sweet made from grated coconut and molasses (*nārkel-nāṛu*); this would be Lakṣmī. It was placed on a low stool over an auspicious *ālpanā* diagram drawn by Mohan Babu's mother in a downstairs room of the house. A second section was prepared with useless garbage:

a couple of lumps of bull's dung, a banana peel, pomelo rind, and a wad of loose hair pulled from a woman's comb. This would become Alakṣmī; it was placed on a window ledge outside the house. On a third section were placed ten small oil lamps of the type used for illuminating houses on this night. This was kept with the ritual apparatus for worshiping inside the room.

When the priest arrived he carried Alakṣmī's image inside the room and quickly worshiped her with a recitation of her contemplation verse (*dhyāna mantra*):

> Alakṣmī—black in color, wrathful and quarrelsome; wearing black clothes and ornamented with iron; sitting on a broken seat, with two arms and skin abraded by gritty sandalwood paste; with a broom and broken winnowing fan; with an oily body, mounted on an ass—I salute you.

Then, with water from a brass pot, he rinsed his left foot over Alakṣmī, allowing the water to fall from his foot onto the image—an extremely demeaning gesture. To signify that this was indeed a living deity, he lit a candle, placed it on the banana stalk, and handed it over to the children. From the candle they lit torches made of fist-sized bundles of jute stalks, then ran around the house and through the neighborhood carrying the image and chanting:

> Go away, ruined Lakṣmī!
> Good Lakṣmī, come into the house.

After they all had turns carrying the image and had burnt a good number of torches, they tossed Alakṣmī into a ditch just outside the neighborhood, where youngsters were accustomed to defecating. Giving this unpropitious goddess as many gross insults as possible was, of course, intended to make her feel extremely unwelcome.

Meanwhile, the priest continued with the worship of Lakṣmī inside the house, making a small offering of five elements (*pāñcopacāra*) to her. The women of this house were preoccupied with the preparation for Kālī worship and did not have time to listen to the *brata* story for the new-moon night of Kārtik. However, in the Brahman and Kayastha houses where rice flour paste images of Lakṣmī were made (and where the useless and inauspicious items of Alakṣmī were assembled on a broken winnowing fan), the following *brata* story was read. Like the other *brata kathā* of the "ruler" calendar, this one is said to be about a king, but it is not about kingship or rule. In fact, this king is apparently a Brahman and not a Ksatriya.

Kārtik Lakṣmī Brata

The king of a certain country had five daughters. One day he called everyone in the house together and asked, "By whose good fortune (*bhāgya*) do you eat?" To please the king they all said, "Mahārāj, we eat by your good fortune." Only one of them gave a different answer, the king's youngest daughter. She said, "I do not believe that father. Mother Lakṣmī gives food to everyone, and each one lives by the strength of his own good fortune."

The king, deeply offended by the words of his youngest daughter, said to the queen, "Do you hear this precocious girl?" He told the girl, "I am going to give you in marriage to him whose face I first see tomorrow morning. Then we shall see by whose good fortune you eat."

The queen tried to avert this calamity by secretly sending men through the town to order people to stay off the streets. However, in an adjacent kingdom, a poor Brahman heard the king's decree and saw in it an auspicious conjunction. After all, this was a wealthy king. He would not simply give away his daughter; he would certainly give the bridegroom some money as a dowry (*yautuka*). Thinking this, he took his son to the king's gate and told him to stay there until he returned.

In the morning when the king arose, after he had saluted the sun, he went outside. He saw the boy and asked him what he was doing there. The poor Brahman returned at that moment and reminded the king of his decree. The king gave his daughter in marriage to the poor Brahman's son and he gave the boy some money as a dowry. Then, with mortifying cruelty, he told his daughter, "Now go and eat by your own fortune. Let's see how Lakṣmī will feed you!" The girl made no reply but simply saluted her father and mother respectfully and went off with her husband and his father to the other kingdom. Her husband's mother was delighted to see her and welcomed her into the house with the proper ceremony.

Daily the princess arose early, before anyone else. She cleaned the house thoroughly and cooked the meal. She fed her husband's father, his mother, her husband, and last of all she herself ate that which was left, usually just the leavings on her husband's plate. Thus she spent her days, enduring much hardship.

One day she told her husband and his father, "Look here. You should never come home empty-handed. If you don't get anything else, pick up a piece of straw and bring it home." So father and son both began to bring home something or other every day. One day the princess's husband had found nothing to bring. Finally, he saw a dead cobra lying on the path and, there being nothing else, he picked it up and brought it home to his wife. She was not at all angry and said, "You did well. Put it on the shelf."

A few days later the son of the king [the brother of the virtuous princess] fell seriously ill. Various physicians attended him but the illness did not abate. At last one physician said that he could treat the case if he had the head of a dead cobra. The king immediately announced by beat of drum throughout the kingdom that whoever could supply the head of a dead cobra could name his own reward. When the princess heard the announcement she asked her husband's father to take the snake to the royal palace. She gave him one instruction: "If the king offers you money, do not accept it. Only say that on the new-moon night of the month of Kārtik, no one in the palace nor in any of the houses of the king's subjects should light any lamps."

The man delivered the snake and the prince's illness abated. The king called the Brahman before him and asked him what riches he wished. The Brahman related the girl's request and the king immediately sent a proclamation banning the lighting of lamps on the new-moon night of Kārtik. That night came and it was time for the worship of Lakṣmī, but throughout the kingdom not a flicker of light was to be seen. The princess had cleaned the house, drawn auspicious diagrams, prepared a pot, and worshiped

Mother Lakṣmī properly with offerings of flowers and sandalwood paste. There were lamps lit on the four sides of the goddess's pot; the princess, who had fasted throughout the day, now sat waiting for Mother Lakṣmī.

Mother Lakṣmī, riding on the back of her owl, had toured the entire kingdom but, not seeing even a trace of light, told the owl to leave that kingdom. Just at that moment the owl spied a light in a small cottage in the woods and he took Mother Lakṣmī there. The princess reverently covered the back of her neck with the end of her sari and prostrated herself in salutation. Filled with devotion, she seated Mother Lakṣmī and worshiped her. When she had finished reading the words of worship she said, "Please don't take offense mother, but we are terribly poor."

Mother Lakṣmī said, "I am made very happy by your devotion (*bhakti*) and firm faith (*niṣṭhā*). You people shall have no more sorrows. I am going to leave my anklets with you. You shall worship me regularly in the months of Bhādra, Kārtik, Pauṣa, and Caitra. Do not rush around, but walk sedately; do not be quarrelsome; never steal even a straw; never complain about there not being enough at home; and always observe pure conduct. Then you shall suffer from no more grief." With this advice, Mother Lakṣmī departed.

By the grace of Mother Lakṣmī the princess received everything. Their little cottage was transformed into a palace. They had wealth, servants, elephants, and horses—all the things one needs for a happy life. The princess happily attended to the housekeeping.

One day the princess suggested to her husband's father that if he were to consecrate a pond, it would provide an occasion for a grand feast for all of the villagers. The Brahman did as she suggested and invited everyone in the village to a sumptuous feast. Rich and poor, high and low, everyone ate and praised them.

Meanwhile, the princess's father, who had been king of the adjacent kingdom, was, on the day of the feast, walking the roads begging as a result of his contempt for Lakṣmī. He got hardly anything to eat, and, having heard of a great feast in this house, went with the hope of getting a good meal. When the princess saw her father, she asked her husband's father to fetch him. She arranged for him to wash and clean up, gave him new clothes, sat him on a silver stool, and gave him his meal on a golden plate. Still, he did not recognize his daughter. He would glance toward her, then stuff his mouth with rice again. Tears began dripping on his chest. Seeing her father cry, the girl could not prevent herself from crying also. When he asked her why she was crying, she said, "For the same reason you are." Then he said, "Mā, I was once also a king. I had a daughter exactly like you. I was so merciless toward her that I gave her in marriage to the son of a poor Brahman just to get her out of the house. I do not know whether she is even alive any longer."

Crying heavily, the princess said, "I am that unfortunate girl, father—the one you sent to test her own fortune. Now do you believe that it is Mother Lakṣmī who gives us all what we eat?"

Inwardly, he felt a mortal wound; he felt like an insignificant particle mixed in the earth. He said, "Don't shame (*lajjā*) me more, Mā, I am extremely wicked. Today my eyes of knowledge have been opened." Then he began to cry.

The girl told him her whole story, then sang the praises of Mother Lakṣmī and asked her father to worship this goddess. He returned to his kingdom and told his wife what had happened. She quickly arranged to bring her daughter and the girl's husband. The mother and daughter cried a great deal when they met, and they related many events of happiness and sorrow.

The king and queen began the prescribed worship of Lakṣmī. Their daughter taught them all the rules and procedures. By the grace of Lakṣmī their former wealth was restored. After reigning for a while longer they gave the kingdom to the daughter and her husband and went to heaven. The daughter and her husband enjoyed the kingdom for a long time, then they taught their children how to worship Lakṣmī and told them to teach others how to do this. Then they went to heaven. From that the story of the worship of Lakṣmī has spread throughout the world. (Vidyāratna n.d.:77–81)

The "ruler" calendar of Lakṣmī worship is confined to two occasions that occur within the framework of the autumn worship of goddesses. The other goddesses worshiped during this period are the powerful Durgā, the dangerous Kālī, and the regal Jagaddhātrī.

In general, the worship of these goddesses is done in the houses of high-caste people who in the past dominated the area and ruled over dependents. Both of these *brata* stories for the "ruler" calendar are ostensibly about kings, although the Kārtik Lakṣmī *brata kathā* is not about kingship but about families, the good conduct of women, and the necessity of worshiping Lakṣmī for prosperity. And, indeed, the women of the houses in which the powerful goddesses are worshiped are unfailingly attentive to Lakṣmī throughout the autumn sequence of worship beginning with Durgā, progressing to Kālī, and concluding with Jagaddhātrī.

The bright full-moon night is a time for the living and for the auspicious Lakṣmī; the dark new-moon night is a time for the dead and for the inauspicious Alakṣmī. Thus, the worship of the unpropitious, black Alakṣmī is appropriate to the moonless night, on which she accompanies Kālī's dangerous minions. Alakṣmī is represented as the inverse of Lakṣmī, as made up of worthless refuse suitable to be thrown away in an inauspicious place by children. The winnowing fan, often used to represent Lakṣmī, is a common household implement that separates grain from chaff; it both symbolizes and enacts the retention of what is valuable while disposing of valueless waste. A broken winnowing fan no longer capable of doing its work is thus suitable as a representation of Alakṣmī, whose presence is repulsive to all forms of Lakṣmī (prosperity).

Even though these two occasions of Lakṣmī worship are associated with rulership, the burden of worship falls more heavily on the women than the men of the house, both in the *pūjās* and in the accompanying *brata* stories. Lakṣmī is the model wife; a virtuous wife is the living presence of Lakṣmī in the house. She brings prosperity through modest, quiet, good conduct.

The "Cosmopolitan" Calendar of Lakṣmī Worship

Khanda Pālā Lakṣmī Pūjā

The principal crop in the Kelomal area is "winter" (*āman*, *haimantika*) rice, harvested in Agrahāyaṇa and Pauṣa. Until the introduction of high-yielding rice varieties, winter rice was the only food-grain crop in this locality. However, in Bengal as a whole there are three rice crops: *āuś*, planted broadcast in fields that can be plowed in the hot months of Caitra and Baiśākh, which is harvested in the rainy season; *āman*; and *boro*, a transplanted crop grown in low-lying fields after the *āman* harvest, and harvested in Caitra and Baiśākh. Thus, although in Kelomal there is only one rice harvest in a year, throughout Bengal there are three such auspicious occasions, and the calendar of Lakṣmī worship connected with the agricultural cycle takes account of all three. I have described this calendar as "cosmopolitan" because of its all-Bengal character, in contrast to the more parochial character of the remaining two calendars. As was discussed in Chapter 2, these *pūjās* are described as *śiṣṭācār*, "the custom of refined people" or "the practice of polite society." The dates for the "cosmopolitan" calendar are given in the almanac and observed by most Brahman and Kayastha families, but by almost no one else.

The *pūjās* of Lakṣmī in Bhādra (for the *āuś* rice harvest), in Pauṣa (for the *āman* harvest), and in Caitra (for the *boro* harvest), are known as *Khanda-pālā* Lakṣmī *pūjās*. *Khanda-pālā* Lakṣmī is the form of the goddess who dwells in the crops; it is principally in the form of rice that she is worshiped on these occasions. There is variation in the observance of this *pūjā* in different clans (*kulācār*). I describe here the practices of the Karkun house in Kelomal.

Before the designated day of worship in Pauṣa an amount of newly threshed rice was sorted out and only the whitest and finest grains were selected. These were to amount to "seventeen *khubis* and seventeen *muṭhos*." A *khubi* is a measuring basket made of cane (*bet*) which, when filled, holds a *seer* (about a kilogram); a *muṭho* is an extra fistful added to the filled basket, representing overflowing abundance. The number seventeen is conventional—it was explained as being the "rule" (*niyam*) for this worship—and belongs to a set of such numbers (sixteen for Maṅgal Caṇḍī, thirteen for Tārinī) appropriate for goddesses of the household. Being one more than the number of completeness—there are sixteen annas in a Rupee, and sixteen segments in a full moon—seventeen, like the extra fistful of rice in each measure, stood for plenty. The

Figure 12. Threshing rice in the month of Pauṣa (December/January). The straw is beaten against a loosely woven bamboo frame. The grain falls through the frame and is swept up in heaps on the threshing floor.

representation of Lakṣmī in this form signified a copious yield, and the abundance of the best and finest. The measured-out rice was heaped up on a large brass platter. Seventeen unripe areca nuts were placed on the pile of rice. The presentation of an areca nut is an honorific gesture; in this form of Lakṣmī it had the additional effect of representing seventeen small heads, in much the same way as the green coconut placed over the mouth of a deity's pot makes a kind of head for the deity.

During worship, seventeen cotton wicks soaked in oil were placed around the edge of the platter and lighted to indicate the existence of life in the heap of rice. The goddess was also represented in an auspicious rice-flour *ālpanā* drawing done on the verandah of the house by one of the women. Seventeen grains of fine, white, husked rice were sprinkled over this. In addition, a bowl called the "treasury bowl" (*bhā̃ṛārer bāṭī*), filled to overflowing with rice that was been husked after parboiling (*siddha cāul*), was worshiped. Since there would be no new rice for the Caitra and

Bhādra Khanda-pālā Lakṣmī *pūjās*, the rice used in Pauṣa was saved for them.

Except for the form in which the goddess appears—that is, as a heap of new rice—the procedures of worship were ordinary. Fifteen of the sixteen elements of worship were the same on each occasion; one seasonal substitution was made: radishes in Pauṣa, mangoes in Caitra, and palmyra fruits in Bhādra. However, the *naivedya* offering, which in the Karkun house was one and a quarter *seers* (about 1.15 kg) of *ātap cāul*, rice not parboiled before husking, was kept for the house rather than becoming part of the priest's entitlement (*pāonā*). Since this offering was the very presence of the Lakṣmī of the house, it was cooked and eaten in the house. One seer of parboiled rice was given to the Brahman in its place.

There was a separate story told with Lakṣmī's *brata* on each of the three *Khanda-pālās*, in Pauṣa, Caitra, and Bhādra.

Pauṣa Lakṣmī *Brata Kathā*

There was a poor Brahman woman who had five sons and a daughter. Her husband had died when she was carrying the youngest son, and since that time her life had been very difficult. One day her daughter, who was the oldest of her children, suggested that she ask her wealthy brother for help. Carrying her youngest son with her, she went to her brother's house, where she found his wife at home. She told the woman her sad story, but the brother's wife was not sympathetic. Finally, she said she could do one thing: if the widow came daily to the house and cleaned the rice and lentils, she might keep whatever broken grains she found. In addition, if she did other housework, the brother's wife would give her a little rice, lentils, oil, and salt. After she had done the work for a while the widow began receiving just a little broken rice and rice powder. One day she asked for a few of the dried-up ends of a squash vine that grew in the courtyard. The brother's wife denied her even these on the pretext that she had to get her husband's permission first. After three days' wait, when the widow was about to leave, her brother's wife said sweetly, "Why don't you wait a bit? I have some whole squash leaves for you. My head is burning up with lice. Just pick them for me and I'll give you the leaves."

The widow said that it was Lakṣmībār (Thursday) and she would not kill even a louse on this day. Anyway, her children had practically nothing to eat, so she was in a hurry to take the broken rice grains home. The brother's wife flew into a rage and struck the widow. The broken rice tied in the end of her sari were scattered over the courtyard. The woman was screaming at her as the widow left the house, crying silently. As she walked empty-handed she determined to take whatever she found on the path and cook it.

The first thing she saw was a large cobra lying dead at the side of the road. She thought, "How much longer could we carry on like this? If I cook this and we all eat it, we will all fall dead together." She tied the snake in the end of her sari and went home. She said nothing to her children but went to the kitchen and cut the snake into pieces. She put them into a pot of salt water and set it on the hearth to cook. Then something amazing happened. As she added wood to the fire and the pot began to boil, golden foam began to spill from the pot. The kitchen was soon immersed in gold. With great joy, she took a bit of the gold and, forgetting her hunger entirely, want to the market with all her children.

Since it was Lakṣmī's day, when they returned from marketing, the Brahmani quickly bathed and purified herself. She prepared the seat for Lakṣmī by drawing auspicious diagrams in rice powder and scattering new rice over it. She made *pāyes* and cakes of rice powder. She engaged a proper Brahman to worship Lakṣmī on her behalf. She invited twelve Brahmans to eat and presented each of them with *dakṣinā*. She personally delivered some of Lakṣmī's *prasād* to each house in the neighborhood. Then she fed her children and, last of all, she herself ate the Mother's *prasād*.

There was so much gold from the snake that within six months her house had become like that of a king. Workers, male and female servants, a Brahman cook and serving women, elephants and horses, guards—nothing was missing. The Brahmani's daughter was of marriageable age and the great king of an adjacent kingdom asked for her to be given to his son. The marriage was done with great pomp and the girl went to her husband's father's house as a royal bride. Within a short time three of her sons were married to daughters of three great houses; they brought three brides like Lakṣmī to illuminate her house.

Meanwhile, her brother's wife wondered in amazement at what had happened. She decided that her husband's sister had gotten some secret magical spell (*mantra-gupti*). One day she invited the widow to visit, together with her sons and their wives. The widow fed everyone very well. They put on jewelry with diamonds and pearls and expensive clothes. Then they all went to the brother's wife's house in palanquins. The woman greeted them obsequiously and took the widow and her sons' wives into the house, where she laid out fine sitting mats and offered them fifty kinds of delicate food.

Instead of sitting down, the wives took off some of their jewelry and put it on the sitting mats. They recited a verse, as if in worship: "Golden ornaments, diamonds, and pearls, we honor you, for whose auspiciousness we have today been invited." Then they sat down with their hands folded. The brother's wife did not understand their meaning and asked the widow to explain.

The Brahmani said, "In the days of our sadness it never crossed your mind to look for us. You spilled the few grains of broken rice I had collected and could not part with a couple of squash leaves to preserve our lives. Now our condition has improved, so you issued an invitation to our golden ornaments, diamonds, and pearls. That is why they have put down their ornaments and said these words."

The brother's wife was ashamed and she acknowledged her fault. Still the wives would not touch her food. The Brahmani took her sons and their wives home. She lived happily in her family for many years. When she was old she taught her sons' wives all the rules and laws for worshiping Lakṣmī, then she went to heaven. The wives began to worship Lakṣmī each year, filled with devotion, just as their husbands' mother had done. From their observance the story of this worship in time spread from country to country. (Bhaṭṭācāryya n.d.:51–6)

Caitra Lakṣmī Brata Kathā

Nārāyaṇa was about to take a turn around the world of humans in his flower chariot when Lakṣmī appeared and insisted on going with him. He tried to persuade her not to go by telling her that the human world was very hot in the month of Caitra, but she pressed her demand with affectionate childish unreasonableness until he consented. However, he made it a condition that she not get out of the chariot on earth. When they reached the human world, before he got out of the chariot, he specified further that she should not look toward the north. She sat a long time and saw all that she could in other directions before she gave in to temptation and looked to the north. There she saw a beautiful sesame (*til*) field covered with white blossoms. The beauty of the sight made her forget her promise and she got out of the chariot and plucked sesame flowers. She put some in her hair, some around her throat, and wrapped a bunch in the end of her sari before returning to the chariot.

When Nārāyaṇa returned and saw what Lakṣmī had done, he said that the only way she could recompense the owner of the sesame field was through twelve years of service. Disguised as aged Brahmans, they went to the small cottage of the owner, where Nārāyaṇa explained why his wife would have to serve him. Specifying only that they should not feed her rice left on the plate of another, make her sweep the house, or dress her in discarded clothing.

The family consisted of an old Brahman and his wife, three sons and their wives, and two daughters. The old woman clapped her head in amazement, saying that they had only two fistfuls of rice for a day's food. "How will we feed yet another person on that? What a disaster!" Lakṣmī asked her when people would bathe and prepare for a meal. The old Brahmani told her of their poverty; there would be nothing to eat until her three sons returned from begging. Lakṣmī said that everything they wanted was already prepared. The woman, her sons' wives, and their daughters were amazed at what they saw and thought that some goddess had come to live with them. Soon everyone in the family loved Lakṣmī—except the wife of the middle son, who was of an envious nature.

She often offered Lakṣmī food that had been touched by another; this the goddess buried at the foot of a pomegranate tree, where it was transformed into gold and jewels.

At the beginning of the thirteenth year came an astrological conjunction during which bathing in the Ganges was prescribed. Lakṣmī said that she would not attend the festival and gave the old Brahmani some money with which to worship the goddess Gaṅgā. At the riverside Gaṅgā suddenly appeared and received the offering personally. Then everyone knew that it was the offering of a goddess and they rushed home to find Lakṣmī ready to depart with Nārāyaṇa. They implored her to stay, but she said that she could not remain. However, if they worshiped her in the months of Bhādra, Kārtik, Pauṣa, and Caitra, she would not desert them. She said they would find great riches buried beneath the tree. As soon as the gods departed, the middle son's wife dashed to the tree to dig up the buried wealth. A cobra appeared and bit her; she died at the foot of the tree. The others lived like a royal family, worshiping Lakṣmī four times each year. In this way the *brata* of Lakṣmī was spread through their country and others. (Bhaṭṭācāryya n.d.:56–9).

Bhādra Lakṣmī Brata Kathā

A certain Brahman widow dwelt in great poverty with her son. Near their little cottage at the edge of a pond stood a pipal (*asvattha*) tree beneath which the boy played. One day a cowherd passed there selling *kṣīr* (a confection made of thickened milk). The boy asked his mother for one pice to buy some *kṣīr*; she told him she had nothing. He cried and wheedled until she found four cowries (a fifth of a pice), which the boy took to the cowherd. When the cowherd would not give him any of the sweet for so little money he began crying again until the cowherd gave him a small vessel of *kṣīr*. The boy sat down beneath the tree to enjoy this rare treat when the two fledglings of the pair of owls who nested in the tree began crying from hunger. The parents had been out hunting for food all day and had not yet returned. When he heard their cries, the young Brahman climbed up to the hollow, brought them to the ground and fed them some of his *kṣīr*. When they were satisfied he returned them to their nest and finished what remained of the sweet.

When the owls returned at night the young ones told them of the generosity of this poor Brahman boy. Thereafter, the boy made a regular practice of sharing whatever he got to eat with the owlets. When Thursday in the bright lunar fortnight of Bhādra came, the widow worshiped Lakṣmī and the boy gave some of Lakṣmī's *prasād* to the young birds. When their parents returned the owlets began to insist that they do something to help these poor people who were so generous to them. The owls promised to do something. As the conveyance of Lakṣmī they used to go daily to the garden of the goddess. They asked the youngsters to call them on the following morning when the Brahman boy climbed up to the hollow.

The female owl instructed the boy to sit on her back with his eyes closed, holding on to her neck. She would carry him to a certain place where he was to get down and open his eyes. If anyone were to offer him money, he should refuse it and say, "I want a *til-dhūbṛī* [small bundle of sesame seeds]." Then he would be taken to a place prepared for worshiping a deity, with arrow shafts planted at the corners [to demarcate a deity's place], auspicious figures drawn in rice powder, and, facing the deity's pot, on a low stool, a small bundle (*putuli*). He should just take that bundle and return to the owl, who would take him back home. If mother and son would worship before that small bundle every day, they need never worry about money again. Everything happened just as the owl had said, and Mother Lakṣmī gave the boy the *til-dhūbṛī*.

With regular, daily, devoted worship of Lakṣmī the boy and mother soon had the wealth and mastery of a king. When the news of their fortune reached the ears of the king he became anxious that his position might be challenged. He sent some of his men to loot the house and bring back the *til-dhūbṛī*. Lakṣmī left the house; the widow and her son were soon reduced to poverty again. The female owl agreed to take the boy back to Lakṣmī again and she gave him another *til-dhūbṛī*, with a warning not to lose this one. Mother and son worshiped the little bundle daily and locked it away with great care. Good fortune quickly returned.

This time the king decided that he was not dealing with ordinary people and that it would be best for him to have them as relatives (*kuṭumba*). Accordingly, he gave his daughter in marriage to the Brahman boy, together with a lavish dowry (*yautukā*).

Finally, one day, when the chariot of Bhagavān came to fetch the old Brahmani to heaven, she called her son's wife and instructed her: "Understand *bau-ma*, that in the months of Bhādra, Kārtik, Pauṣa, and Caitra you must worship Mother Lakṣmī. And do not discontinue the worship of the *til-dhūbṛī* for even a single day. Twice daily sweep out the house, and sprinkle Ganges water and spread the smoke of incense throughout. Never sleep after sunrise. Never speak in a loud voice. And in the evening show the evening lamp throughout the house."

The wife followed the old woman's instructions exactly and the son performed her *śrāddha* and *tarpaṇ* in fullest form. They lived a happy and contented life and their children and grandchildren perpetuated the worship of Lakṣmī. From then the story of Lakṣmī's *brata* became known throughout the world. (Bhaṭṭācāryya n.d.:22–8)

In view of the agricultural character of the worship of Lakṣmī in the "cosmopolitan" calendar, the *brata* stories are remarkable for their lack of concern with rice crops. Instead, these stories deal with the well-being of the individual family. The Brahman and Kayastha women who know these stories in fact have little to do with agriculture. Although Brahman and Kayastha householders (*gṛhastha*) owned agricultural land, they did not engage in agricultural work—plowing, planting, weeding, harvesting and threshing. That work was done by people of other castes, either under the supervision of the landowner or as sharecroppers. As the providers for the household, Brahman and Kayastha men are responsible for bringing agricultural products—meaning rice, first and foremost—into the house. Once these items are inside the house, they become the responsibility of the women. Thus, within the house, it is the actions of women that conduce to well being through prosperity or Lakṣmī.

Prosperity within the house is not simply a matter of sound "management" or "home economics," although watchfulness over expenditures and care of storerooms and granaries are marks of a good house-mistress (*ginni, gṛhinī*). Everything about the conduct of women is thought to influence the prosperity of the house. In Bengali cultural stereotypes (though rarely in reality), women are characterized as lacking in self-control and, as a result, prone to expressing selfish impulses (like the brother's wife in the Pauṣa story), forgetfulness of their husbands' commands (like Lakṣmī herself in the Caitra story), enviousness of one another's advantages (like the middle son's wife in the Caitra story), and slothfulness (against which the mother warns her son's wife in the Bhādra story). These "natural" feminine proclivities are repulsive to Lakṣmī and drive her from the house. Their opposites, self-abnegation, obedience to the husband's commands, selflessly feeding others and satisfying oneself with what is left after others have eaten, and ceaseless work while the sun shines, are shown in these stories to be conducive to prosperity.

Each story begins with human protagonists in extreme poverty from which they are elevated in exaggerated terms by devotion to Lakṣmī and observance of the self-denying code for conduct that she teaches. These stories, as well as the "ruler" stories, emphasize the observances of women and their worship of Lakṣmī. The Bhādra story, with a boy as the actor who gains Lakṣmī's favor may seem out of place in this set. However, in it, a self-denying woman indulges her son with her last pitiful cowries. It is considered proper for a woman to show her love for her child, especially a son, by occasionally accepting his insistent demands. The danger is that a child who is thus indulged will become selfish and the mother's self-denial will bear rotten fruit. This story, then, conveys the added message that the virtues of selflessness must be imparted to one's children or they will be of little benefit.

There are two features of these stories that are also quite common in *brata* stories related to deities other than Lakṣmī: The human actors are Brahman, and two of them are widows. Brahmans, kings, and wealthy merchants make up a triad in a great many Bengali myths. *Brata* stories are more "exemplary" or "cautionary tales" than are the myths. Proper relations among Brahmans, kings, and wealthy merchants are not ignored in these stories, but such relations are not their principal subject matter. Rather, proper conduct—particularly of women, and the worship of the gods by women—is what is emphasized in *brata* stories. Brahmans are treated as innately superior to persons of other *varnas* in their natural capacities. So it is relatively easy for a Brahman to demonstrate good conduct to persons of any caste, but relatively difficult for a Sudra to demonstrate good conduct to a Brahman. Thus, in *brata* stories, Brahmans generally speak for everyone in society, while Sudras speak only for themselves.

Widowhood is a constant source of anxiety for a married Hindu woman. A wife should be younger than her husband; women who survive the childbearing years have longer life-expectancy than men, and every Hindu village has numerous widows to attest to the statistics. They are easy to identify in their plain white garments, devoid of ornaments and of the auspicious vermilion in the parting of their hair, the marks of married women whose husbands are alive. They are forbidden to remarry and young widows who manage to establish themselves with men are called concubines (*rā̃ṛh*), not wives; for such a woman to bear a child is a misfortune, in sharp contrast to the significance of childbearing among married women. *Satī-dāha*, "the immolation of a faithful wife" on her husband's funeral pyre, or, as it is also called, *saha-maraṇa*, "dying together with" one's husband, is forbidden by law and is, in any event, considered a particularly difficult way to die, for which only a few exceptional women were ever qualified. Most widows are destined to live out the remainder of their years according to whatever fate may bring them. Many have to forage for themselves, neglected by their sons' wives. To become a menial maidservant (*jhi*) under the command of a brother's wife is the usual lot of a widow who returns to her brother's house. Thus, stories of poverty-stricken and abused widows arouse deep and well-placed fears in the hearts of Bengali women, and remind them of how to treat their sons' wives. A great many *bratas* promise that women who observe them carefully will never be widows.

The Calendar of Lakṣmī Worship According to the Custom of the Country

Thursday, Lakṣmī's Day

In many Kelomal households, as well as elsewhere in West Bengal, Lakṣmī is worshiped on every Thursday throughout the year. This practice is mentioned in the *brata* story for Pauṣa related earlier, which also implicitly says that when a person is able he/she should have this worship done by a Brahman priest. Worship performed by a priest is regarded as intrinsically more effective than worship done by oneself; the deity is more honored and the offering is more easily accept if a twice-born man does the worship in one's name. Nevertheless, all of the many inexpensive manuals of Lakṣmī worship contain directions for worshiping this goddess without mediation, and usually contain specific instructions that "women, Sudras, and the like" will not pronounce the powerful syllable *Om*, but will substitute *namaḥ* ("salutation") in its place. Women often worship Lakṣmī by themselves, and most worship that is offered on ordinary Thursdays throughout the year is done by married women in their husbands' houses. This practice is not confined to any caste or social stratum; it is a "custom of the country" (*deśācār*).

There are permanent images or representations of Lakṣmī in almost all Hindu homes. Common in both rich and poor families are small, unglazed pottery bowls with a small pedestal base and the face of the goddess crudely molded on one side. Another very ordinary representation is "Lakṣmī's basket" (*Lakṣmīr jhā̃pi*), a standard one-*poā* (approx. 500 gram) rice-measuring basket, covered in red cloth, emblematic of a married woman, on which are stitched cowry shells, signifying wealth. Such baskets usually contain miniature items of a married woman's toilet: a comb, mirror, packet of vermilion, receptacle for eye-liner, and red-bordered sari. A special tall, round wooden box painted with red lacquer, used to hold powdered vermilion (*sindūr kauṭā*) also represents Lakṣmī. Vermilion symbolizes a married woman whose husband is alive, identifies her as *gṛhalakṣmī*, the "Lakṣmī of the house" who is responsible for its prosperity. Many people also have inexpensive unbaked, painted clay images and/or polychrome lithograph pictures of Lakṣmī as her visible presence in the home. Well-to-do families—almost all of them Brahmans and Kayasthas—have brass images of her, which are kept in the temples of the clan deity (*kuladevatā*) or in the "gods' rooms" (*ṭhākur ghar*) of their houses. The usual practice is for a Brahman domestic priest (*purohit*) to worship daily all of the deities in a clan temple or *ṭhākur ghar*. Prosperous families, even those who are not Brahmans or Kayasthas, sometimes receive weekly visits from their domestic priests for Lakṣmī worship.

The worship of Lakṣmī on ordinary Thursdays is usually a simple matter, whether it is done by a priest or by the women of the house. Only five items need to be offered: flowers (*phul*), scent (*gandha*, usually white sandalwood paste), incense (*dhup*), a lamp (*dīp*), and a *naivedya* offering of a small measure of rice. In addition, seasonal "fruits and roots" (*phal-mūl*)—fresh fruits and root vegetables that can be eaten without cooking—are cut into small pieces and arranged in attractive mounds on polished brass plates to be offered to the goddess. Once this has been given to her it becomes remnants of her food and is eaten as the *prasād* of Lakṣmī by everyone in the house. There is a *brata* story for the worship of Lakṣmī on ordinary Thursdays, which includes the directions for the special feature of this occasion, the exchange of vermilion marks among married women.

The Story of Lakṣmī for Thursdays

Lakṣmī was properly seated at the left hand of her husband Nārāyaṇa and they were engaged in pleasant conversation. The sage Nārada approached with a question for the goddess: why did she move so erratically from the house of one human being to another, leaving behind such extreme want (*bhīṣaṇ durbhikṣa*) and starvation when she departed. She explained:

"Listen attentively and I shall tell you how I got the name 'Fickle' (Cañcalā). Sleeping during the day and bad practices, anger and selfishness, sloth, quarrels, and falsehood pervade the family (*saṃsāra*, a term that also refers to the world, or all that moves). Women laugh loudly and shout. They go to bed at night quarreling with one another. They go here and there just as they fancy, abandoning grace, affection, modesty, and the like. They indulge in fads such as coloring their cheeks and forget to perform the evening rites. At dawn no one polishes the floor with cow-dung and water because the odor might taint her chemise.

"Women were created in the image of Lakṣmī. I sent them to earth for the sake of happiness. With a little happiness they forget me, and nowadays they live a luxurious life, doing no work or bad work. They are not worshipful toward their husbands' fathers and mothers; they shower them ceaselessly with harsh language. They do not indulge their husbands' relatives and they always want to remain independent. Those qualities that are the ornaments of a woman, of which modesty is foremost, have one by one been banished from their hearts.

"If they see a guest coming they can only think of the trouble it will entail, and many of them even eat before their husbands. They are contemptuous of their husbands and do not listen to their words; they have given up housework and cooking. They waste their time in masculine amusements; none of them can tell anything but lies. They constantly make me angry; that is why I am fickle and turn away from house after house. Human hearts are full of envy, hatred, and malice; human minds are twisted by their inability to witness the good fortune of others. They are devoid of devotion to the gods and Brahmans, they treat elders abusively, and seek only their own happiness. To satisfy their tastes they eat what is prohibited, and as a result suffer much grief and early death. How can I remain steady in a house of such sinful character? But if a woman abandons all such faults and become an observer of good practices, I shall dwell steadily with her day and night."

Nārada then praised the goddess as "Full of Grace" (*Dayāmayī*) and "She Who Gave Birth to the World" (*Jagat-prasūti*). He asked her how humans could live without misery when she withheld her mercy. She thought on this question and asked Nārāyaṇa what she should do. Her directed her to go to the human world and teach the Lakṣmī *brata*.

The goddess's first dismaying encounter among human beings occurred in the family of the rich Dhanapati ["Lord of Wealth"] Rāy in the city of Avanti. His wife, seven sons, and sons' wives lived in a golden family devoid of malice and envy until Dhanapati died. Then the sons' wives cast a "net of deception" over their husbands and within a short time they had separated their cooking and eating arrangements (*pṛthak-anna*). Lakṣmī abandoned these families and the wives began to treat their husbands' mother abusively. The old woman was about to commit suicide when Lakṣmī appeared before her in disguise. The goddess listened to the old woman's sad tale and told her that suicide was a great sin. She advised her to return to her house and to observe the Lakṣmī *brata* following these procedures:

"On Thursday (*Gurubār*) evening all of the women [of the house] will gather with the common resolution of observing Lakṣmī's *brata*. Put a spot of vermilion on a pot filled with water and place a perfect sprig of mango leaves on its mouth. Arrange a sitting place and on it put a betel leaf prepared with areca nut, then mix up some vermilion; these are the rules of this *brata*. Around the edges place lighted incense sticks and a lamp, then sit and hear the story while holding some *dūrbā* grass in your hand. Thinking of the image of Lakṣmī, listen attentively to the story of this *brata*. At the end of the story ululate and reverently salute; after that, all of the married women whose husbands are alive will take some vermilion."

The goddess then told the old woman the various fruits of the devoted observance of Lakṣmī's *brata*: not only wealth but also the total well-being of the family, including freedom from debilitating illnesses that render husbands unable to earn for their families. She revealed herself in her true form to Dhanapati's widow and directed her to return to her house and to call together her sons' wives to perform the worship. The old woman followed Lakṣmī's instruction and soon her family was reunited, happy, and prosperous again. Lakṣmī's *brata* was soon done in every house in the city of Avanti.

A wealthy merchant's son from Srinagar happened to visit the house of a man in Avanti at the time the women were observing the *brata*. He inquired about the purpose of the worship and they told him that it was for the prosperity and well-being of the family. The merchant committed the "fault of egoism" (*ahaṃkāra doṣa*) by declaring that if one were not fated to have wealth (*kapāle nā thāke*) then Lakṣmī certainly would not give it to him. For that fault, the goddess immediately abandoned him. As he was departing on a trading voyage his seven boats sank in the middle of the water, and his brick house and buildings were destroyed by a stroke of lightning. Brotherly affection (*bhrātṛbhāva*) deserted his family, and they separated their cooking and eating arrangements. The merchant was quickly reduced to begging from door to door. One day his wandering brought him back to Avanti, where all the women were observing Lakṣmī's *brata*. Suddenly he realized that Lakṣmī had abandoned him because of his egoism. Filled with devotion, he praised the goddess in an elaborate hymn celebrating her various forms: among them, in the Dvāpara age, Rādhā, beloved of Lord Kṛṣṇa; in the kingdom, Rājalakṣmī, the prosperity of the king; and in the family, Gṛhalakṣmī, the married women of the house. He hastened back to Srinagar where he established Lakṣmī's *brata*. She mercifully removed the impediments he had encountered and even re-floated his sunken boats.

The story of the *brata kathā* concludes with a reminder that those married women who observe it will have wealth, sons, and when they die, heaven. They are instructed again to color the parting of one another's hair with the vermilion of the worship and to make the auspicious *ulu* sound. (Bhaṭṭācaryya 1968/9:4–15)

The married women of a joint family originally belonged to other families; they are brought together, often from diverse backgrounds, and made into women of their husbands' family by marriage. It takes serious ritual work to effect a translation of this magnitude, and the marriage rites are quite long and complicated. An important symbolic and substantive element in the marriage is the placing of a vermilion mark (*sindūra-dānā*) in the parting of the bride's hair (*sĩthi, sīmanta*) by the groom. It is customary to use a small rice measuring-basket (*poā*)—one of the symbols of Lakṣmī—to make that first vermilion mark. Vermilion symbolizes blood, thought to be the contribution of a woman to reproduction; she wears the mark continuously so long as her husband is alive. When the groom has made the first vermilion mark, he is supposed to pull the end of the bride's sari (*ghomṭā*) over her head, an indication of "modesty" (*lajjā*), a complex concept that includes the capacity to feel shame when it is appropriate, chastity, and obedience to her husband, as well as to those whom he obeys (Inden and Nicholas 1977:49–50).

When a young bride enters a large family there are many people whom she is expected to obey—the wives of her husbands' elder brothers, for example, and most particularly the senior wife—usually her husband's mother—who is the mistress of the house. Bengalis know that the lot of a young wife is often hard. The mistress of the house may direct her to do a great deal of work and give her the most disagreeable tasks. Unity among the wives of brothers is difficult to obtain; jealousy sparks quarrels among them and each seeks to better her position at the expense of the others. They are given to scheming about ways to become independent so that they need no longer take orders from senior wives. In such circumstances, women may fall short of the ideal for wives of the same family. Their weekly ritual renewal of one another's vermilion marks in the presence of Laksmi, who herself displays all of the auspicious marks of a married woman, is intended to bring about their unity by enacting what they have in common.

The first episode of the Thursday Lakṣmī *brata* story includes both the goddess's list of faults to which women are said to be prone, and her own virtuous example in asking her husband to direct her actions. The second episode shows that disunity among wives leads to the destruction of the family, which in turn leads to the loss of prosperity and to the maltreatment of widows. The third episode identifies a further danger to the unity and prosperity of a family: egoism. Egoism or selfishness is a danger to the family because anything other than equal sharing, any favoritism, gives rise to envy and malice. The egoism of the merchant destroyed fraternal affection in his family and led to its ruin. This episode also underscores one of the most significant elements of the *brata* story for Kārtik; it is not one's fate or good fortune that is responsible for prosperity or its lack; rather it is constant, unswerving observance of the code for conduct that is conducive to Lakṣmī. The weekly ritual acts as a restorative in an environment of unceasing pressure.

This story, in the usual exaggerated terms, illustrates a common experience for most people outside the poorest and lowest castes: A family that is prosperous in one generation may be ruined in the next by the quarrels and vindictiveness that attend the partition of joint property. While the jealousy of sons' wives toward one another is often publicly blamed for the division of property and families—beginning with and symbolized by the separation of cooking and eating arrangements within the house—it is usually the egoism of men that is responsible for their seeking revenge, often through prolonged and ruinous litigation that finally destroys their inheritance.

Banāi Puja

The most important occasion of Lakṣmī worship following the custom of the country is called Banāi Pūjā. The term *banāi* is derived from *bandhan*, "binding," and refers to tying Lakṣmī to the house. This *puja* is done sometime around the final day of Pauṣa (December/January), which is the nominal winter solstice and the occasion of a great many observances that vary considerably from one part of Bengal to another. This is the end of the main rice harvest; new rice is eaten on this day in the form of *piṭhā*, a sweet cake made of rice flour, from which it gets the name *piṭhā-pārvaṇa*, "*piṭhā* festival." Also known as Makar Saṃkrānti, the last day of Pauṣa is the day on which the sun moves into the sign of the *makar*. An imaginary aquatic animal conceived of as having the body of a dolphin, the scales of a fish, and the trunk of an elephant, the *makar* is the special conveyance (*vāhana*) of the goddess Gaṅgā. In some families a special preparation called *makar*, made of cut-up uncooked fruits and vegetables mixed with milk and molasses, is offered to the gods on this day. It is the day on which bathing in the Ganges at the point of its confluence with the sea is thought to confer the greatest benefit. Thousands of pilgrims go by boat to Sagar Island to bathe and to enjoy the great fair—the Gaṅgā Sāgar Melā—that is held in conjunction with this rite.

Figure 13. Pauṣa Vāruṇī at the Barga Bhīmā temple in Tamluk. Women who want to become pregnant bathe and tie stones or bits of brick to the leafless tree in the foreground.

In Tamluk it is a day for the special worship of the goddess of the kingdom, Barga Bhīmā, a form of Kālī whose stone temple overlooking the Rupnarayan River was constructed or reconstructed in the eleventh century. According to the astrologers, the astral conjunction on the thirteenth day of the dark lunar fortnight in Caitra is the Vāruṇī day on which bathing in the Ganges brings the benefits of several hundred baths in the Ganges during solar eclipses. According to the custom of the country in Tamluk, the last day of Pauṣa is called Pauṣa Vāruṇī; and several thousand pilgrims come to bathe in the river (in fact now just a canal that flows into the Rupnarayan River), to offer their worship to Barga Bhīmā, and to purchase household effects at the fair. On this day women may observe a special rite to overcome barrenness. Beside the Barga Bhīmā temple is a pond where they bathe and in which they find small stones or broken pieces of brick. They come directly from the bathing place, wearing their wet garments, up the steps to the temple compound where one of the priests directs them to circumambulate a particular tree, embrace it, and to tie their stones to the branches of the tree with torn pieces of cloth. Because of all these special events in Tamluk it is the custom of that kingdom to begin the Banāi Pūjā of Lakṣmī on the penultimate day of Pauṣa. However, in the adjacent *parganās* of Kashijora and Moyna the custom is to perform Banāi beginning on the last day of Pauṣa, and people who originated from these kingdoms usually continued this practice for three or four generations after settling in Kelomal. The custom in Mandalghat Pargana is to begin Banāi on the first day of Māgha, which corresponds to the special bathing festival there, and many families perpetuated this practice though they lived in Tamluk Pargana.

There are significant differences among these little kingdoms in the procedures by which Lakṣmī is worshiped in the Banāi Pūjā, and these are compounded by the differences among castes and even between clans of the same caste. The common elements among these various forms of worship are:

(1) On the first evening of worship, Lakṣmī, in the form of new unhusked rice and/or whole heads of rice (*dhān-śiṣ*), is brought into the courtyard or the area immediately outside the house. This worship is sometimes called *bāhir* (outside) or *uṭhāne* (in the courtyard) Lakṣmī Pūjā.

(2) Arrangements are made to tie Lakṣmī to the "substances of the house" (*gharer dravya*)—agricultural implements, storage boxes, the granary, etc.—connected by means of a rope of braided rice straw (*bāuni*, from which the term Banāi is said to be derived).

(3) The householder awaits the first cry of the jackal—and in some cases two, five, or seven other nocturnal creatures—and then requests the domestic priest to carry out the worship of Lakṣmī.

(4) Arrangements are made to protect Lakṣmī while she remains out of doors overnight.

(5) The second day of worship is known as Lakṣmī's rest (*biśrāma*); she remains outside throughout the day and night.

(6) Early on the third day the rice is picked up and placed in the granary, and any other forms of Lakṣmī kept outside are ceremoniously returned to the house.

The great variety of ways in which Lakṣmī is represented and in which these steps are carried out in Banāi Pūjā, with striking variation in the practices even between adjacent houses, is testimony to the fact that the individual house is the cosmos of Lakṣmī; this is preeminently true at the culmination of the rice harvest. A close look at the elements of this worship demonstrates that the abundance of rice represents the well-being of the household, rather than that of the clan, caste, village, or kingdom.

(1) **Lakṣmī is taken out of the house.** In the kingdom of Tamluk it was customary to take the goddess outside on the evening before the last day of Pauṣa. The object of most Lakṣmī worship is to keep the goddess dwelling steadily in one's house, and yet she must reenter the house afresh after each rice harvest. There is some danger that she might fail to return, once she has left; so families take various precautions to see to it that she does not desert them. Thus, it is usual to establish her outside but within the courtyard of the house, or—if entirely outside the house—on the threshing floor where bundles of rice awaiting threshing are stacked, or near the granary, which are considered to be her natural dwelling places. Representations of Lakṣmī are established on auspicious *ālpanā* diagrams, drawn with rice flour, depicting rice, agricultural implements, and the goddess herself. The representations of the goddess are quite varied: new unhusked rice spread on the ground, a substantial heap of new rice (sometimes more than 50 kilograms), the first bundle of rice cut in the harvest (*moṭe-biṛā*), five whole rice heads inserted in a lump of pure cow dung (usually fitted with a five-leafed mango twig and a vermilion-daubed areca nut, indicating the presence of a living being, held fast to the ground by a bamboo pole), a measuring basket filled to overflowing with new unhusked rice, and the brass or pottery images of the goddess kept in the house or the family *pūjā* room. Lakṣmī is often present in three or four forms; some families purposely keep more than one inside the house to protect against the desertion of this fickle goddess.

(2) **Lakṣmī is tied to the substances of the house.** The rules for braiding the rope (*bāuni*) to be used to tie the goddess to

the house are almost as varied as her representations. It may be braided from new rice straw (*bicāli*), straw mixed with jute, coconut, or other fibers, or just from the heads of new rice. Some families use a new cotton thread, from which an auspicious mango leaf is suspended, to entirely surround the house. Whatever the procedure, it is usual to link the goddess to those things within the house that are regarded as the repositories of abundance: boxes in which valuables are kept, the room in which dried and preserved foods are stored, the granary, and the plow and other agricultural implements. Sometimes these symbols of prosperity are drawn in *ālpanā* figures near a drawing of Lakṣmī and enclosed by the drawing of a rope; sometimes the footsteps of the goddess are drawn extending from the outside the house leading inward toward the granary or storage boxes. The principal objective of Banāi Pūjā is to bind Lakṣmī to the things within the house that are conducive to prosperity, the places where she abides in a well-ordered family.

(3) **The hearing of the initial sounds.** Banāi Pūjā follows the solar calendar, rather than the luni-solar or weekly calendars that determine the days on which she is otherwise worshiped. There are no astrologically propitious or unpropitious times for this worship. Instead of the almanac, omens are used to determine the right time for worship. Known as "getting the cry" or "getting the sound" (*ḍāk/sāṛ-dharā*), these omens are the calls of various animals and/or birds. There is nearly universal agreement that the first cry of the jackals (which usually occur just after sunset) must be heard before worship can begin, but some families say that three, five, or seven additional animals or birds must be heard. Lists of these cries are very heterogeneous: cat, cow, gecko, Lakṣmī's owl, numerous other birds. Auspicious and inauspicious animals, wild and domestic ones, carnivores, herbivores, and carrion-eaters are variously strung together according to the conventions of different families. But almost everyone agrees that some such sign or signs of this class is/are essential before Lakṣmī worship can be performed. The work of the domestic priest on this occasion is

generic. Banāi Pūjā does not appear in the *śāstras*; Brahmans seem to have inserted themselves into a domestic rite where their services are not actually necessary.

(4) **Lakṣmī is protected during her stay out of doors.** Again, families follow very different procedures for making the goddess's abiding outside the house as comfortable as possible. She may be covered with new straw and provided with an umbrella to protect her from the dew (*śiśir*) that "falls" in this season. Cane measuring baskets of various sizes are placed over heaps of new grain to provide them with protection. Praying that she not depart, the householder and his family then retire for the night.

(5) **Lakṣmī rests on the second day.** Although the goddess is "free from work" (*biśrām*) on the second day of Banāi Pūjā, families following the Tamluk calendar may have a busy day. A household with sufficient means and a good harvest "sends worship" (*pūjā pāṭhāno*) to the principal deities of its own village and all of the surrounding villages. It is considered good practice, as well, to send worship to the goddess Śītalā of Maisali village, the most powerful mother of any village in the vicinity (see chapter 5). And if some people of the household attend the *melā* in Tamluk, they also take an offering to Barga Bhīmā. "Sending worship" consists of preparing a plate or a banana-leaf packet of food—new sun-dried, husked rice, some fresh fruits and vegetables, often some of the *piṭhā* cakes and *makar* prepared on this day—to the temple of the deity. The priests who attend these various temples remain in them throughout the morning to present the offering to the deities, for which they receive a *dakṣiṇa* offering (in 1969, usually five pice) and the food left uneaten by the deity.

Meanwhile, houses receive visits from people who provide services to them throughout the year. The Hari caste women from Darja village who are the midwives in Kelomal, the Garland-maker who has provided flowers for the worship of Lakṣmī during Agrahāyaṇa and Pauṣa, the Barber or his wife or mother, the Launderer—all who provide regular services to a household during the year—

visit for "begged rice" (*māgan cāul*) on this day. Families gave them from a quarter of a seer (approximately 250 grams) to a seer (approximately a kilogram) of new parboiled rice, according to the donors' means.

(6) The return of Lakṣmī to the house. Banāi Pūjā ends on the morning of the third day. Permanent representations of Lakṣmī—metal and ceramic sculptures, pictures, Lakṣmī's *jhā̃pi*, etc.—are carried back to their usual places inside the house. Rice used in this worship must be carefully swept up and put into measuring baskets. Some families pour this rice into the granaries that hold their general stock. However, others have the custom of not eating this rice, but rather storing it in the measuring baskets inside the granary until the next harvest, feeding it to cows, or sun-drying then husking it for offering to other gods throughout the year (in which case it is eventually consumed in the houses of the domestic priests). The picking up of the grain from the place of worship outside the house marks the end of Banāi Puja. This worship is not a *brata* and there is no story that accompanies it.

The Calendar of Lakṣmī Worship According to Popular Custom

Concern over the yield of rice in Kelomal is most strongly focused in the harvest months of Agrahāyaṇa and Pauṣa. As lifelong cultivators, most men in Kelomal are quite adept at estimating yields of standing crops. But they also know that it is not wise to plan on a prosperous year before the threshed grain is safe in the granary. Disasters such as late autumn cyclones can carry away everything in a single stroke. For ordinary farmers, the season for worshiping Lakṣmī most intensively is the months of the harvest. Well-to-do families that observe the popular custom (*lokācār*) of worshiping Lakṣmī on every Thursday throughout the year arrange for especially splendid worship on the Thursdays of Agrahāyaṇa and Pauṣa: The Garland-maker provides additional flowers, and the variety and size of food offerings is increased. In the somewhat less prosperous families where Thursday Lakṣmī worship is carried out by the women of the house, the domestic priest is usually engaged to make the offerings on Thursdays during the harvest months. And even the poorest families, which worship Lakṣmī only occasionally during most of the year, offer a *pūjā* every Thursday in Agrahāyaṇa and Pauṣa, usually performed by the women of the house, but almost always at least once by the domestic priest.

Although the domestic priests who serve the Brahmans, Kayasthas, and Navaśākha castes are not markedly more busy than usual in this season, the Vyasokta Brahmans of the Mahisyas, and the Orissan Brahmans who are domestic priests of the Karans have extraordinarily busy Thursdays. During the harvest season, as one Brahman explained, everyone should worship Lakṣmī with the "attitude of a cowherd" (*rākhāliya mate*). His reference was to the *brata* story sometimes called the "Tale of the Cowherd" (*Rākhāler Upākhyāna*) or the "*Brata* Story of the Goddess of the Fields" (*Kṣetra-devīr Brata Kathā*), which is told on a Thursday of Agrahāyaṇa.

Brata Story for Agrahāyaṇa

[Instruction] The *brata* story of the Goddess of the Fields (*Kṣetra devī*) is to be told after the worship of Lakṣmī on a Thursday during the bright lunar fortnight in Agrahāyaṇa.

A poor Brahman died, leaving behind his widow and a five-year-old son named Viṣṇu. The widow sought refuge in her brother's house, where her brother's wife made her into a menial maidservant and Viṣṇu into a cowherd. They had a hard life with little to eat and a constant hectoring from the brother's wife. When Viṣṇu grew big enough, his mother's brother declared that henceforth his work would be agriculture. He bought a plow and oxen and sent Viṣṇu to the fields, where he labored all day long, in sun and rain, without any increase in his diet. He did not return to the house at noon [as is usual for Bengali farmers] because his mother's brother and his wife would chide him for failure to do sufficient work. His mother worried constantly about him and gathered up whatever leftovers she could find—puffed, parched, or fried rice, fruits, and so on—and carried them to her son in the field. Viṣṇu invariably washed his hands and face and offered the food to the Goddess of the Fields before eating; thus, he ate only the *prasād* of the Goddess.

One day Viṣṇu's mother could find nothing to take him except the dried grains of rice stuck to old banana-leaf plates. Seeing that he could not even swallow this stuff, she went in search of something that would moisten it. Milk was being boiled in the house; she took the skin that had formed on the surface and put it on the leaf. Just then her brother's wife appeared and began abusing her. That night she filled her husband's ears with accusations about his sister's bad conduct and theft, until he was burning with rage. On the next morning he angrily expelled them from his house.

It was a Thursday during the bright lunar fortnight in the month of Agrahāyaṇa. Mother and son wandered, crying from hunger throughout the day. They finally sat down under a tree at the edge of a field. The Goddess of the Fields saw their troubles; she appeared before Viṣṇu in the guise of an old Brahman woman and said: "Why are you crying dear son? You have nothing to fear. From now on your troubles will be banished. Take this rice. Trade half of it with a grocer for some parched and puffed rice and molasses to eat. You will find a small cottage beside the marshy land next to that distant field; you two will sleep there tonight. Tomorrow morning when you wake up, take the remaining half of the rice and scatter it all over that marshy land and also here and there in that field. If you do this, you will have no more trouble." Then she departed.

The grocer was extremely pleased with the quality of the seeds Viṣṇu had to trade and gave him a good variety of prepared food. Mother and son reached the cottage just before evening and set about cleaning it. Then they divided their food in two, put half aside, and offered the other half to the Goddess of the Fields before eating. They arose before dawn, bathed, and sowed the seeds as directed. Then they took their remaining food, divided it in halves again, offered it to the Goddess and ate happily. On the next morning those fields were a wonderful sight: they were covered with ripe rice plants bearing measure after measure of golden grain.

Some of the farmers of that country went to their landlord, Dayalu Jamidar, and told him about the golden rice sprung up overnight. He went to see for himself, met Viṣṇu and his mother, and heard their story. He immediately felt a great affection for them and took them to his house. He arranged for the sacrificial thread ceremony for Viṣṇu and then gave him his own beautiful daughter in marriage. As a part of the dowry (*yautuka*) Viṣṇu received the field in which the golden rice stood.

Then Viṣṇu and his mother returned to the little cottage. With the help of his wife's father's cultivators he harvested the rice and stored it in the cottage. He sold a little bit of it in the market and got enough money to begin constructing a grand house. Masons began to arrive from this country and others and they set to work.

Meanwhile, Viṣṇu's mother's brother and his wife had fallen upon hard times after their departure. Their cattle died and they lost their land; finally they were not getting even one meal a day. They were searching for work in other countries when they heard the rumor that a great landlord was building a large house and many people were getting work there. When they arrive the mother's brother's wife got a job carrying bricks and crushing stone. Viṣṇu happened to catch sight of them and told his mother, who sent a servant woman to fetch them. When they saw Viṣṇu and his mother they began crying. Viṣṇu respectfully saluted them by taking dust from their feet. They were bathed and oiled and given fine new clothes. They remained throughout the next year and when a Thursday in the bright lunar fortnight of Agrahāyaṇa came again, Viṣṇu showed his mother's brother and his wife how to observe the *brata* of the Goddess of the Fields. Viṣṇu said, "*Māmā*, if you observe this *brata* every year no trouble will befall you." He then gave them plenty of money and sent them back to their house. There, observing the *brata* of the Goddess of the Fields regularly, their condition quickly improved and they became wealthy.

After living happily for a few years, Viṣṇu's mother taught her son's wife the *brata* of the Goddess of the Fields and she went to heaven. In this way the *brata* became known in country after country. (Bhaṭṭācāryya n.d.:45–51)

Alone in the cycle of Lakṣmī *bratas*, this story deals with a farmer. While he is presented in the guise of a poor Brahman widow's son, he is unmistakably a cultivator. The story contains elements of the Pauṣa story—the poor widow treated oppressively by the brother's wife—and the Bhādra story—the poor widow's son who wins the favor of the goddess. But here the goddess's reward is not a wish-fulfilling *til-dhūbṛī* nor a kitchen full of gold, but rather an excellent crop. At this season of the year, no one could wish more fervently for anything than this as a reward for months of hard work and uncertainty. This concern is equally present in the families of farmers and of higher caste landowners who do not themselves plow, plant, and harvest. Even people who do not depend primarily on agriculture for their livelihoods, but "eat purchased rice" (*cāul kine khāe*), think that the quality of the rice harvest will determine the well-being of their families for the coming year. Therefore, the worship of Lakṣmī in this season was the most widely observed in the annual cycle of household *pūjās* in Kelomal.

Granary Worship

The culmination of Lakṣmī worship according to popular custom was the rite known colloquially as Golā Pūjā, "Granary Worship," or somewhat more formally as "Depositing the Rice" (*dhānya sthāpāno*). Like Banāi Pūjā, this *pūjā* was observed in different ways by people of different castes, clans, families, and kingdoms. In some families, mostly of Mahisya and Karan castes, it was considered to be identical with the conclusion of the Banāi Puja, when the rice of Lakṣmī was deposited in the granary. Some of these families performed a rite preliminary to the Banāi called "Increasing the Field (or Yield)" (*khet bāṛāno*), in which rice plants still standing in the field were worshiped by men of the house, following the example of the protagonist of the story of the Goddess of the Fields.

Many families considered the right time for the Granary Worship to be just before the first of the newly threshed rice was poured into it, normally in Agrahāyaṇa. Brahmans and Kayasthas generally consulted the almanac to find an auspicious day for the ceremony, while Mahisyas and Karans included it in the worship of Lakṣmī on a Thursday, when the domestic priest would prform regular Lakṣmī Pūjā. Representations of Lakṣmī in the form of a basket filled to overflowing with new rice, rice still in the head, or the first bundle of rice taken in the harvest were especially

Figure 14. A granary with images of Lakṣmī's footprints leading to the door through which newly threshed rice is poured.

worshiped on this occasion, although the goddess was sometimes also invoked in a pot in the usual way. *Ālpanā* diagrams of the footsteps of the goddess, showing her as entering the granary and not leaving it, were sometimes drawn as a part of this worship. When the domestic priest was finished worshiping, the first large measuring basket full of newly threshed rice was poured into the granary by the head of the house or, in a Brahman or Kayastha house, by a servant. The basket filled with new rice that was used in the worship of Lakṣmī might also be placed in the granary to remain through the year. Like the Banāi Pūjā, of which it was sometimes a part, Granary Worship or Depositing the Rice was not regarded as a *brata* and there was no special story connected with it.

Lakṣmī is Never Ignored

Durgā Pūjā, which was the most important ritual of the year for the formerly ruling families, is also an occasion for Lakṣmī worship. Images of the four deities whom Bengalis regard as the children of Durgā—Kārtik, Gaṇeśa, Sarasvatī, and Lakṣmī—stood together with Durgā on the platform. The worship of the children was subordinated to that of Durgā, but they all received ritual attention during this prolonged ceremony. However, there was another representation of Lakṣmī present on the stage. A winnowing fan (Nicholas 2013:127–28) was brought out from the house. The winnowing fan (*kulo*) is a symbol drawn from the repertoire of women's daily work—an everyday, utilitarian instrument that separates grain from chaff. Importance is placed on the fact that the *kulo* retains the valuable grain while discharging the chaff; it

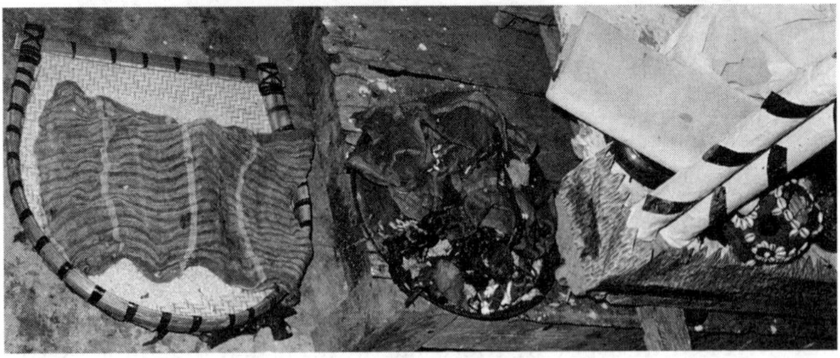

Figure 15. Lakṣmī *bod* on the winnowing fan at the left. Lakṣmī's basket, ornamented with cowrie shells, is on the platform next to the post at the right. Between these two objects is a platter of offerings.

is the opposite of the strainer (*cālani*), which allows the valuable stuff to pass through it and retains what is to be discarded. The winnowing fan used to represent Lakṣmī, called a *bod*, was filled with sun-dried rice, a whole turmeric root, an areca nut, a cowrie shell, and a model boat, all covered with a new *gāmchā*. These are all auspicious items; the boat, I was told, represents success in trade (*bāṇijya*). The *bod* was also a presence of Lakṣmī during Jagaddhātrī Pūjā. It was brought out from the house for the final worship and placed on the platform alongside the image of the goddess. At the same time, one of the women also brought another typical domestic object, Lakṣmī's basket (*jhā̃pi*). This goddess, who controls prosperity, was on people's minds all the time. She is fickle (*cañcalā*) and she was known to have deserted many people.

Sarasvatī

Sarasvatī, the beautiful sister of Lakṣmī, is very widely worshiped, most commonly in schools, quite often in individual houses where there are students, and less commonly with the kind of community *pūjā* described in Chapter 1, the Fisher neighborhood festival. She is depicted as a lovely woman with a serene expression, holding a *vīṇā* (she is the goddess of musicians) and a book (she is the goddess of learning), accompanied by her graceful *vāhana*, the swan. Her *pūjā* is held on the fifth day of the bright fortnight of Māgha (January/February), which is called Śrī Pañcamī, Śrī being a name of Lakṣmī. Learned opinion calls for worship of Lakṣmī as well as Sarasvatī, but Lakṣmī is eclipsed by Sarasvatī on this occasion. Alone among the many household and neighborhood *pūjās* on Śrī Pañcamī in 1969 was one held in a prosperous Mahisya house in Balikalua, where, according to the family tradition (*prathā*), Lakṣmī, Nārāyaṇa, and Sarasvatī were worshiped jointly.

In Kelomal there were Sarasvatī *pūjās* in the schools, where images of the goddess were prepared, and in a dozen houses, some of which also had images of the goddess made by the local image-makers. Students brought their books, pens, and inkwells, which were deposited as the feet of the goddess; owners of musical instruments also brought them for her blessing. Praying to the goddess for success in studies was considered mandatory for students. In view of the importance placed on widely feared examinations in career choices and opportunities for higher education, the petitions of many young worshipers were undoubtedly heartfelt. However, for the most part, Sarasvatī Pūjā in Kelomal was a party for school children, a day away from studies, with special treats for all and happy reminiscences by the elders and teachers.

Figure 16. Preparing for the worship of Lakṣmī, Nārāyaṇa, and Sarasvatī in the Bhuñya household in Balikalua. Sarasvatī is on the left side of Nārāyaṇa, giving precedence to Lakṣmī even on the occasion of Sarasvatī Pūjā. The decorative enclosure is made of locally woven cotton fabrics.

Figure 17. Students at the Kelomal Primary School received a special feast for Sarasvatī Pūjā.

5. Dangerous Goddesses

All goddesses are "dangerous" in some sense, but there are important differences among them. If Lakṣmī abandons a person, she brings great misfortune; yet she is never said to be terrifying. Nor did I hear anyone express fear of Sarasvatī, although most had a difficult time with school examinations. Lakṣmī and Sarasvatī are quite different from Śītalā and Manasā, whose powers are quite frightening—infectious diseases and the bites of poisonous snakes. Kālī is the archetypal terrifying goddess for Bengali Hindus. She is usually represented holding a sacrificial blade in one hand and a severed human head dripping blood in another of her four hands; in addition, she wears a necklace of severed heads and a girdle of human limbs. She dances on the cremation ground, with anthropophagous female demons and jackals as companions. She is addressed as "Mother"; and she is implored to care for her devotees, who assume the role of abandoned children. Śītalā and Manasā—also invariably entreated as "Mother"—borrow some of their frightening aspects from Kālī.

Śītalā

From the perspective of the ordinary people of Kelomal—the farmers, fishers, and artisans who constituted the majority of people in the community—Śītalā was the most important goddess in the pantheon. Because of her importance I have previously written much about this goddess (Nicholas 2003:62–77, 166–211), including work written in collaboration with Aditi Nath Sarkar (Nicholas 2003:105–65). For the Brahmans and Kayasthas, Durga held the foremost position among goddesses and among all of the divinities; she represented sovereignty and legitimized their dominant position. But for Mahisyas and other non-dominant groups Śītalā was "the mother of our village" (*āmāder grāmer mā*). For the Brahmans and Kayasthas the wider community of Kelomal was the principal social unit, though everyone knew which individual village was his or her abode. But the identity of Kelomal as a social unit became secondary when Śītalā was worshiped: Then the eight constituent villages—each with clear boundaries—were distinguished from one another. And for the Mahisyas and other middle and lower castes, the individual village, each with its own Mahisya head (*mukhya* or *āmin*) and its own mother goddess, was their primary identification.

Learning how Śītalā came to occupy such an important position for people in Kelomal, and for people throughout the region, opens a door on the social history of rural Bengal. Certain parts of that history, dealing with invasions, rulers, and economic affairs, can be obtained from written sources. But testimony about the experience of ordinary people is hard to find. Tracing the rise to prominence of Śītalā, and of her companion the Fever Demon Jvarāsura, provides evidence about an influential part of that experience.

Most acts of worship contain statements, explicit or implicit, about who is to benefit, who is to receive the fruits of worship. In many *pūjās*, including the great autumnal worship of Durgā, Kālī, and Jagaddhātrī, there is a formal *saṃkalpa*, a kind of dedication in which the names of those offering worship are recited, with their *gotra* identifications, giving the *saṃkalpa* a veneer of Vedic authority. There are *saṃkalpa* recitations at less momentous *pūjās*, but there are also many occasions—as when worship is done within a house or a cluster of related houses—where the beneficiaries are only implicitly identified. When an individual makes a mental commitment to a particular deity (*mānasik*, *mānat*) it is almost always done for an explicitly stated beneficiary and benefit, often the curing of an ailment or birth of a son.

As noted earlier, some of the most important *pūjās* are done for the sake of the "country" (*deś*), not for a single household or clan. The identification of one's *deś* depends on who is asking and in what context. If a person from Kelomal were asked in Kolkata, "What is your *deś*?" the answer might well be "Purba Medinipur," the name of the home district. However, asked by someone from Purba Medinipur, the same person would respond with "Kelomal." Within Kelomal the name of the person's village would be the appropriate reply, though such a question would not often be asked among neighbors. India is a *deś*, as is West Bengal, and as is each district and individual village. The Gājan, the preeminent "rite of spring" in Kelomal and throughout West Bengal, treated *deś* in a very comprehensive fashion. The *deś* that received the benefits of the sacrifices of the ascetics who performed the Gājan was very broad and not distinctly bounded. Participants came from several villages; the fields and ponds that were fertilized by their ritual belonged to their villages and to others beyond them. This was *deś* in a very extensive and not clearly defined sense.

By contrast, Śītalā *pūjā* (also known as *śayalā*, or *śayalā pūjā*) defined *deś* very explicitly; it corresponded to the boundaries of the village (*grām*) that the inhabitants recognized as a community. In densely settled continuous strings of habitation these boundaries were often not obvious. There were other village deities that were also possessions of their communities, some of them puranic gods and some parochial; some of them were worshiped at the same time as Śītalā. However, Śītalā *pūjā* was the common village ritual, and it demarcated the limits of the village. Villages were sometimes defined by the roster of households included among those obligated to contribute to the cost of worship, or by who was made to pay the entire cost in the form of a fine assessed by other villagers for some infraction, or by physically marking the boundaries of the village, or a combination of these. The head of each socially recognized village was a Mahisya, regardless of the presence of the dominant Kayasthas. It was as if the village belonged to the Mahisyas even when the land belonged to wealthy high-caste households. Kayasthas and Brahmans contributed to the cost of the Śītalā *pūjās*, but they did so as fellow villagers rather than as superiors.

Factionalism kept the villages of Kelomal in low-grade turmoil much of the time. Personal rivalries and disputes between prominent leaders aligned families on one side or the other. Political parties seeking support drew on factional alignments to mobilize votes, exacerbating the cleavages in the community. Against these fissiparous forces, the strongly felt necessity of coming together for the collective worship of Śītalā was the principal force unifying or reunifying fractured villages. The ritual itself was a source of pleasure; most people were happy at the prospect. At the same time, many people spoke about the dire consequences they feared if they failed to perform it. The effort to collect the funds for the *pūjā* brought rivals together and created at least temporary unity.

The principal cost of a Śītalā Pūjā was hiring a "traveling song party" (*śayāl gān dāl*), a group of singers and musicians who perform the narrative of the goddess's activities among mortals, the deeds that led to her being recognized as a deity and receiving worship. The performers were specialists from other villages who traveled to the locations of worship. Their song, the *Śītalā Maṅgal*, or *Śītalār Jāgāraṇ Pālā* ("Śītalā's Vigil Drama"), is a *maṅgal kāvya*, one of the Bengali mythological narrative poems discussed in Chapter 2. Most of these poems exist in several versions, each composed by a different author. However, the root narrative or narratives (There are sometimes three or four stories in a single *mangal kavya*.) are similar among the variants, suggesting that they were drawn from a common oral tradition. While the *maṅgal kāvyas* about different deities are quite different from one another, most have a common element: A deity appears among mortals who fail to recognize the importance and power of that deity. The god demonstrates his or her special power, often with calamitous consequences for humans; their eyes opened, the humans begin worshiping, whereupon their world gets set right again.

Śītalā Maṅgals

The choice of Śītalā for mother of the village seems a strange one. Although there is a bit of late Sanskrit verse depicting her as possibly an attractive woman, she is usually represented in Bengali verse as an ancient hag, dressed as a widow. Some images of the goddess in temples show the pustules of smallpox adorning her face. It seems evident that the disease itself played an important part in her attainment of such an exalted position. Smallpox (*variola major*) was recognized in India around the seventh century CE. The earliest known images of Śītalā, or a goddess with her distinguishing features, date from the eleventh and twelfth centuries. Indian medical texts offer treatments for smallpox—called either *masūrikā* or Śītalā—from the sixteenth century. The first known example of Bengali literature celebrating this goddess dates from 1690. There is a sudden efflorescence of *Śītalā Maṅgal* compositions in the middle of the eighteenth century (Nicholas 2003:166–91). The middle of the eighteenth century was a time of trouble in Bengal: There were raids by Maratha bandits, European colonial powers were doing business up and down the Hugli River, the British rose to effective control over Bengal, and there was a devastating famine in 1770.

In the absence of an effective campaign of immunization (which finally led to the total elimination of the disease in 1979) smallpox persists only in a relatively large human population, a group large enough and dense enough to sustain an infection in at least one person somewhere in its midst at all times. There is no animal reservoir for the virus and normally it does not live long outside a human host. A case of smallpox confers lifelong immunity to survivors. Case fatality rates range from 20 to 40 percent of those infected; in immune-compromised populations the rate may go to 50 percent. Malnutrition is a leading cause of lowered levels of immunity among poor people. Thus, conditions for a devastating epidemic came together in Bengal in the late eighteenth century.

When an epidemic occurred, almost everyone who was not immune contracted the disease. Before the introduction of the Jenner vaccine variolation (giving a person a bit of the virus from an active case in an effort to induce a mild case) was widely practiced in Bengal. Although the procedure provided protection against a second infection, it did not guarantee a mild case and it did not prevent the infected person from communicating the disease to others. Moreover, the largest share of the non-immune population consisted of youngsters born since the last epidemic. Before

Figure 18. There were two images of Śītalā in Banamalikalua. The new brass image on the left, with a serene visage, is adorned with a silver repoussé crown and a delicate garment. The original image, a shapeless piece of laterite, had acquired faint, unattractive facial features, a vermilion complexion, and a garment of locally woven cloth. The goddess had also been invoked into the pot on the left, considered necessary for the village *pūjā*, though not for daily worship.

vaccination, epidemics in Bengal tended to occur about every seven years, a period during which there was a gradual increase in the population of young children. Thus, epidemics disproportionately affected children; and the death rate was particularly high among poorly nourished children. The *Śītalā Maṅgal* narrative emphasizes the deaths of children and the devastation of families.

Smallpox epidemiology in Bengal was also influenced by the weather. The virus is usually transmitted from one person to another through the air. The hot dry months of spring (*basanta*)—Caitra, Baiśākh, and Jyaiṣṭha—(mid-March to mid-June) were most conducive to the airborne transmission of the smallpox virus. When the monsoon rain began in June, smallpox transmission dropped off very rapidly. In fact, the usual Bengali name of smallpox is *basanta* or *basanta rog*, "disease of spring." This is the period during which individual villages sought to organize the worship of their village goddess. An epidemic was a community calamity, and the prudent community got itself together to show this goddess its devotion with the prayer that they would not collectively share the affliction.

Smallpox is a terrible disease—the eruptions that give it its name appear all over the body, leaving permanent scars on those who survive. Yet the villagers called it *māer dayā*, "mother's mercy." And, though one of the major symptoms is a very high fever, the name of the goddess herself, Śītalā, means "the cool one." This obvious effort at reversing values, at least in words, was still evident when I did fieldwork, even though smallpox was nearly eradicated by that time, thanks to the global vaccination campaign mounted by the World Health Organization in the 1960s and early '70s. (The eradication of smallpox was not an established fact for villagers, besides which Śītalā was said to be responsible for other cutaneous diseases; her worship was unaffected by epidemiological data. For more details see Nicholas 2003:166–91)

Śītalā Maṅgal poems are like others of the class: a goddess who is unknown and not respected by humans obtains worship by demonstrating her powers in ways that are mostly quite distressing. Aditi Nath Sarkar and I have written about the Śītalā narratives, and we have translated some of them (Nicholas 2003:105–65). In summary, Śītalā is unrecognized by people, from simple people like the king's toll collector to the king himself. She is a ragged crone with bags of pulses (*dāl*) that she brings to sell in the market. (In Ayurvedic texts smallpox is called *masūrikā*, a word derived from *masūr*, a common variety of pulse that resembles smallpox pustules.) Like all deities, she has a conveyance, but hers is an unpropitious ass, which, in the *maṅgal* poem, becomes the pack animal for her bags of pulses. Everyone who eats her pulses falls ill with smallpox. She destroys families and entire kingdoms; the stories emphasize the excessive death rates among children. In some episodes she is accompanied by a serving woman, Raktābatī, "Possessor of the Blood"; but her constant companion, whom she treats as a son, is Jvarāsura, the Fever Demon. Although these texts describe the prodromal fever that afflicts smallpox victims shortly before the eruptions appear on the skin, they also describe other fevers, particularly malaria, which swept through deltaic Bengal in the nineteenth century. It seems to be malaria that gave Javarāsura his place in these stories. As in other *maṅgal kāvyas*, when people understand the source of their difficulty and begin to worship Śītalā with proper devotion and sacrifices, she restores the lives of the victims.

The *Śītalā Maṅgal* performances I have seen were based on the version composed by Nityānanda Cakravartī, a courtier of Rajnarayan, Raja of Kashijora (r. 1756–1770), a small estate

Figure 19. A costumed performance of the *Śītalā Maṅgal* in Dubkalua. The King of Virāṭa, whose subjects have fallen victim to smallpox, worships the goddess, portrayed by a male performer.

adjacent to Kelomal that had its headquarters in the nearby town of Raghunathbari. Some performers had the texts written in school notebooks (although published copies were available), but they did not follow the script very closely. The episodes that they performed carried the story line of Nityānanda's text but the performers interspersed local references and made occasional excursions into the narratives of Caṇḍī and the snake goddess Manasā. Most groups were prepared to expand their performances to extend over several nights. (The great *Caṇḍī Maṅgal* of Mukunda Cakravarti, which was a model for many other compositions, is arranged to extend over eight days, with a separate section for each day- and night-time performance.) However, when I was doing fieldwork, few villages were willing to spend the money to maintain a *śayāl gān dāl* for more than a day. The members of a group had to be fed and housed as well as paid; and, since their season is only about three months in duration, their services were in great demand. In 1969 we saw only one two-day performance in Kelomal; the others were one day and night. These performances were considered great events; people enjoyed them and felt that they contributed to their lives beyond the obvious religious benefits. And the performances were intrinsic elements of the worship of the goddess, as important as the offerings and sacrifices; they were not only mythic narratives but also constituents of the ritual.

The companies of performers were quite varied in composition. The company organized by Bisnupada Mandal of Pakuria village, not far from Kelomal, which performed in Dubkalua, was made up of thirteen men from Pakuria and four other nearby villages. All of the members of this group were Mahisyas, except for one caste Vaiṣṇava. There were two *khols*, the two-headed drums that are used in Vaiṣṇava *kīrtans*, a pair of *karatāls* (small brass cymbals also used in *kīrtans*), a bamboo flute, a harmonium, and a cornet, an instrument rarely found in *śayāl gān*. All the members of this group sang or played instruments. While most groups sang the story, with different singers taking the roles of different characters, the Pakuria company performed in costume, *yātrā* style. One man even dressed as Śītalā's *vāhana*, the ass. Whether it was persuasive acting or the willing suspension of disbelief, many women carrying young children rushed forward to touch the feet of the young man who played the part of Śītalā.

The fourteen-member party from Ilka, a village in Mahishadal Thana about twenty kilometers from Kelomal, performed in Murarikalua. The Ilka group included two *khols*, *karatāls*, and a harmonium. This group, organized by a Vyaskota Brahman, included five Brahmans, six Mahisyas, and three Vaisnavas. The *śayāl gān dāl* from Udaychak village, which performed in Satkalua, was quite large, with 25 performers, all of whom were Mahisyas. There were two *khols*, a harmonium, *karatāls*, and drummer who played both *ḍhol* and *tablā*; other members of this group took separate parts in the drama. The party from Amgachia village was quite small by contrast, consisting only of two *khols*, two pairs of *karatāls*, a harmonium, and a singer, an Utkal Sreni Brahman who was the group's leader.

The core of every performance is the large central section of the *Śītalā Maṅgal* called the *Virāṭa Pālā* or *Śītalār Jāgāraṇ Pālā*, the story of Śītalā's arrival in the kingdom of Virāṭa (a location borrowed from the Mahabhārata), which is also called "Śītalā's Vigil Drama," that is, the drama for which one stays awake all night to honor the goddess. It is preceded by several *vandanās* (salutations of other deities), and, in the case of a prolonged performance, one of the preliminary *pālās* of *Śītalā Maṅgal*. However, what everyone looks forward to is the episode in which Śītalā forces the king of Virāṭa and his subjects to recognize her as a goddess and to offer her suitable worship.

The *Virāṭa Pala* begins with the goddess dressed in rags, driving her ass, laden with bags of pulses, toward Virāṭa. Entrance to the kingdom is controlled by a toll collector named Nimā Jagati—a familiar type, a greedy bureaucrat prepared to take as much as he can. In this case he helps himself to a generous share of her load of pulses; he feeds them to his sons, who soon fall ill and die of smallpox.

The story of the goddess's obtaining worship in Virāṭa was modeled after an older story in *Manasā Maṅgal*, where that goddess has control over poisonous serpents (see below). Here, the king fails to worship Śītalā, and his sons fall victim to smallpox. The kingdom is ruined by the disease; nine lakhs of subjects die. Throughout the calamity, the queen and the wife of her youngest son remain steadfast worshipers of Śītalā. At last the king offers her worship, and she is worshiped with blood sacrifices in every house in the kingdom. Śītalā restores life to all who had perished, including the sons of the toll collector; and her worship among mortals is established forever.

Other *pālās* in Nityānanda's text, and in the works of other *Śītalā Maṅgal* authors, are also quite interesting. In one, Śītalā introduces her worship in Gokul, where Kṛṣṇa and Balarām are persuaded of her powers; in another *pālā* she gives smallpox to Lava and Kuśa, the sons of Rāma and Sītā who appear in some *Rāmāyaṇas*. The general thrust is always the same: People do not know Śītalā, they do not understand her power, and they fail to worship her. She gives them smallpox; then they understand and worship her. When she is worshiped, she is merciful. The performers embroider on these stories, they intersperse *kīrtans*, drawn from the Vaiṣṇava repertoire that they think suit the mood of the story; and they make reference to prominent local people and events. The effect of the performance is to bring the mythical realm close to the community, or vice versa. It often seemed as if the events described occurred in the village where the performance was taking place.

Śītalā Pūjā

Worship of Śītalā varied quite a lot from one village to another, in each case following a distinct customary path believed to be very old. In five of the villages there were permanent images of the goddess. In some places she was worshiped in her temple, in others she was brought out to a public area, or to the verandah of the headman's house. In a village that did not have a permanent image, the goddess was invoked in a pot, which was worshiped on the verandah of the headman's house. In one village there were many occasions throughout the year when the goddess was worshiped with animal sacrifices by people who had made *mānasiks*; however, when the village performed collective worship she received only a fish and no other animal sacrifice. In another village she received only one animal sacrifice in a year, on the occasion of the collective village worship.

In one village there was a procession that went through the village, tracing every footpath to the point where it left the village, planting a flagpole at each boundary. (People there said that when there was an outbreak of cholera they took a *kīrtan* procession [*beṛā kīrtan*] singing Vaiṣṇava devotional songs around the village, visiting the same boundary markers.) No Kelomal village created a temporary image of Śītalā, but some other nearby villages did so. While temporary images of deities are customarily immersed in ponds or rivers after worship, the usual practice for Śītalā is to carry the image outside the boundaries of the village and leave it, usually in some other village, to be degraded by the weather. While the elements of the *pūjā* performed by the Brahman remained very much the same, the personalities of the goddess and forms of worship considered appropriate to each were quite different from one village to another. At the same time, the commonly expressed belief was that Śītalā is a single deity; all of the various forms are representations of one goddess.

Olābibi

The description of diseases controlled by Śītalā is very extensive, and it includes a range of diseases with cutaneous symptoms (e.g., measles and chickenpox) that goes far beyond smallpox. In addition, there are fevers that appear to be forms of malaria. Śītalā's constant companion, Jvarāsura, is the Fever Demon whose province seems to be mainly malaria. While smallpox and malaria undoubtedly did not originate in Bengal, it appears that cholera did. Vibrio organisms live freely in the water of Bengal's innumerable ponds. Most vibrio organisms are not dangerous, or cause only minor gastroenteritis. However, the free-living vibrio is prone to mutation; one mutant, Vibrio cholerae, multiplies in the small intestine and secretes a toxin that draws fluids and electrolytes from the body. These fluids are very rapidly excreted in a stream of slightly milky fluid called "rice-water stool," and also by vomiting. If the fluids and electrolytes are not replaced quickly, an infected person may die within a few hours of the onset. Moreover, the copious rice-water stool can quickly contaminate a water supply, and pass the infection on to others. It is likely that cholera was a transient disease localized in deltaic Bengal before 1817, when it was first distinguished from other diarrheal diseases. The increase in worldwide communications that was taking place at that time, augmented by large numbers of pilgrims from India making the *haj* to Mecca, led to an outbreak that spread around the world in what became the first cholera pandemic (1817–1824).

People in deltaic Bengal say gastrointestinal disease is not Śītalā's province. Olābibi—a goddess with a Muslim identity—is responsible for cholera and for other forms of diarrheal diseases, which are not always distinguished from cholera by villagers. Persistent diarrhea in infants is a frequent cause of mortality and, as with smallpox, the deaths of children are sources of particular grief for parents. In most villages in the area, the worship of Olābibi took place at the same time as Śītalā. The songs narrating the appearance of Olābibi and cholera were sung by the same groups that performed the *Śītalā Maṅgal*. However, in Kelomal, the offerings made at the Olābibi shrine were presented by a Muslim on behalf of the Hindu villagers. How cholera became identified with Muslims is not clear. Historical accounts of the beginning of the 1817 pandemic place it in a Muslim village in lower Bengal, and it is known that Muslims traveling to Mecca carried the disease with them, contaminating water supplies along the way. However, in rural Bengal, cholera did not discriminate in its choice of victims.

In 1969 I recorded two versions of *Olābibir Gān* that are quite different from one another (Nicholas 2003:202–06). In one, Olābibi is born to the daughter of the Badshah. The girl was impregnated by Nārāyaṇa (i.e., Viṣṇu) when she inhaled the scent of a flower. The Badshah banishes his apparently sinful daughter to the jungle, where she is protected by Olābibi (perhaps a borrowing from a story of Bonbibi, the Islamic goddess of the jungle). Meanwhile, Olābibi kills the son of the Badshah's minister with cholera. She asks the minister for *śinni* (the Islamic offering described in Chapter 3); when she is worshiped, she restores the child to life. The minister attempts to get the Badshah to worship Olābibi; but the Badshah

Figure 20. Offerings at the shrine of Olābibi are made by a Muslim woman on behalf of Dubkalua village. The singers who are performing the Olābibi song in the background are Hindu, as are all the curious children.

is contemptuous, saying that Olābibi is a *devī* of "Bengalis and beggars" (*bāṅgāli-kāṅgāli*). He challenges the goddess to show him a miracle by bringing him the immovable black stone, the Ka'aba, from Mecca, which she immediately does. When Olābibi reveals herself as the child of his daughter, the Badshah worships her and all is set right.

The second version I recorded involves Kṛṣṇa rather than Nārāyaṇa. Kṛṣṇa is confronted by a *rākṣasī*, an anthropophagous demoness, who has transformed herself into four sisters: Olā (diarrhea), Uṭhā (vomit), Hasan (smile), and Campak (a flower). They declare that their task is to kill humans. Keeping Hasan and Campak with him, Kṛṣṇa allows Olā and Uṭhā to go to the mortal world—but only to places where the name of the Lord (*Hari nām*) is not heard. Olā and Uṭhā have to wait for three ages; but with the arrival of the present degraded *kali yuga*, they find employment. As a demonstration of their power, they kill the sons of a cowherd, then offer to restore them to life if the Badshah will worship Olābibi. When he does so, Olābibi restores the boys to life.

Since I did this fieldwork, there has been new research on Olābibi. In his unpublished M.Phil. thesis Shubhankar Ghosh studied the prominent Olābibi temple in Shibpur, Haora, just across the Hugli River from Kolkata, and also several temples of Olābibi and other hybrid Hindu-Muslim deities in South 24 Parganas District, an area especially rich in such deities. In South 24 Parganas there are both Hindu and Muslim performers who sing the *Olābibi Pālā Gān*; in the Kelomal area, all of the performers were Hindus. A study of the songs of Olābibi (and some of the other Bibis) performed in South 24 Parganas District lists three episodes (*pālā*): *Bīrsiṅgha Rājār Pālā*, *Ichapbādsāh bā Putradān Pālā*, and *Sultānchabir Pālā* (Naskar 1999:373–84). The stories are similar to those summarized here. For example, the *pālā* of Raja Birsingha tells of the deaths of the king's sons from cholera, the queen's worship of Olābibi, and the restoration to life of the sons by Olābibi. The Olābibi narrative has clearly not been standardized to the same extent as *Śītalā Maṅgal*; but the conventions are distinctive in that the goddess shows her power by killing children, humans recognize her as a deity and worship her, after which she restores the children to life. While I never met anyone who expected deceased children to be brought back to life, their reverence for the deity did not seem to be diminished by their realistic perspective.

While there are very elaborate temples for Olābibi in South 24 Parganas, the shrines (*thān*) for the goddess in East Medinipur were much more modest. In Kelomal, the shrine was commonly constructed of about nine courses of brick laid in three steps. Three mounds were constructed on the top step. From a distance one could visualize a miniature mosque with three domes. (In one village there were four mounds.) The interpretation of the shrine was also not standardized, and people commonly assigned different names to the mounds. Olābibi or Olāuṭhā was always among the identities.

The Olābibi *thāns* in Kelomal were outdoors, usually near a village Śītalā temple. They often needed repair, due to the weather; repairs and painting were usually done just before worship, that is, when preparations for Śītalā Pūjā were being made. The shrines were often decorated with streamers prepared by the Garland Maker; and the domes that were said to represent female figures were daubed liberally with vermilion (*sindūr*), which is usually a marker for a Hindu rather than a Muslim woman.

Keeping cholera away from the community was the object of performing worship. Offerings of rice, fruits, and sweets were similar to those offered to a Hindu deity, but *śinni*—considered a Muslim item, and bearing a Persian name—was the obligatory offering, as it was for Satya Pīr/Satya Nārāyaṇa. And it was thought necessary for the offerings to be presented by a Muslim. Several people from the village of Kumorganj, which is adjacent to Kelomal and has a large Muslim population, performed these rites in various Kelomal villages. In Banamalikalua in 1969 the offering was made by the widow of the man who had performed that role in previous years (see Fig. 18).

A Visit from the Mother of Maisāli

The *pūjās* of Śītalā and Olābibi are usually done on behalf of an entire community. However, there are also occasions when Śītalā is worshiped as a domestic ritual, on behalf of a single household, often as a result of a *mānasik*. Maisāli village is about three kilometers from Kelomal. The Śītalā of that village, known as "Maisali Mā," was said to be the most "conscious" (*jāgratā*) goddess in the vicinity. Most unusually, she frequently traveled to other villages and her visits were considered to be very propitious. She had her own palanquin, which was carried by men from the village that invited her to visit. Her priest was a Vyasokta Brahman and she was invited almost exclusively to the houses of Mahisyas, although the priest said that she could visit Brahmans and Kayasthas, and Fishers as well. Like many other indigenous deities, the Śītalā of Maisali emerged from the earth—or in this case, the water of a stream that flowed near the village. The original form of the goddess (spoken of as the *āsal mā*, "original mother") was said to be a stone, which had become completely hidden, encased in a body that had been built up in gradual stages by the contributions of her beneficiaries: a large brass face daubed heavily with vermilion and dotted with silver pox pustules, fitted with three silver eyes, a nose, and a mouth from which a tongue protruded like that of Kālī. She wore a silver repoussé crown and a gold filigree necklace over a silver breastplate, behind which the original stone was said to reside. She had small silver hands and legs that were not in proportion to her very large head, and was dressed in a red-bordered sari, mark of a married Bengali woman. (See Figure 21.) All of these additions to the original body of the goddess were reflections of her power and the donations it attracted.

The occasion for her visit to Kelomal in 1969 was the marriage of the son of a prosperous Mahisya farmer in Murarikalua. The principal part of the wedding had been done, as is customary, on the previous day at the house of the bride's father. This was a rite of the second day, on which the bride arrived at her marital house. The presence of Maisali Ma conferred multiple blessings on the newlyweds, upstaged the bride's family a bit, and provided a wedding feast that was her *prasād*. The fee for bringing Maisali Mā to Kelomal was Rs.25, a very substantial sum at the time. In addition there was an unusually high payment of Rs.2 to the Dom who played the *ḍhāk*, plus *dakṣiṇā* of Rs.2 to the Brahman *pūjāri* who cooked Śītalā's meal, and Rs.2 to the *beśkāri*, the Brahman who adorned the goddess for worship, in this case a young Vyasokta Brahman who accompanied her from her temple. When the goddess arrived, she was greeted with a *praṇāmī* consisting of five prepared betel leaves (*pān*), five areca nuts (*supāri*), and five coins (*siki*; that is five 4-anna coins, or Rs.1.25).

The food offering itself was a full meal, called a *bhog* or feast, including a dish made from an expensive large fish, suitable for

Figure 21. Maisali Śītalā. The original rock is concealed somewhere beneath her face, which is a brass plate covered with silver pox pustules and smeared with vermilion. The face, body, and decorations have all been added piecemeal over a period of years by donations. The brass umbrella and attendant were the most recent additions.

a wedding feast. One of the Vyasokta Brahmans from Kelomal cooked the *bhog* on this occasion, though he found the role of cook, though referred to as *pūjāri*, to be somewhat undignified. The goddess manifested her liveliness in connection with her *bhog*, which she received every day. She was said to prefer to eat in the kitchen; and if she did not want to leave she would make herself too heavy to lift. The only way to persuade her to return to her temple was to insult her with abusive language, calling her a "slut" (*māgi*) or a "lewd woman" (*khaccar māgi*). Since no one else could eat until she left the kitchen, persuading her to "lighten up" was urgent work. It was said that she also became very heavy when passing in front of sweet shops. Her *pūjā* was done while the meal was being cooked. After the formal worship, with offerings of raw fruits and vegetables, the cooked food was offered to the goddess. At the same time a company of Vaiṣṇava singers performed Kṛṣṇa *kīrtan* in the shade of a temporary shed that had been prepared to shelter them from the sun. The idea that there is something in the Vaiṣṇava repertoire suitable for every occasion is very common among Mahisyas and other Vaiṣṇava-oriented villagers.

When news of Maisali Mā's visit reached the neighborhood, a Mahisya man in Hirapur village, neighboring Kelomal, undertook arrangements for her palanquin to be brought to his house. The man worked as an agricultural laborer, although he also operated a tea stall in Radhamani Hat on market days. He said he could not afford the expense of bringing the goddess to his house on his own; he took advantage of an opportunity largely paid for by someone else. He said that his son, who was four or five years old at the time, had been a sickly infant. He had made a *mānasik* to Maisali Mā, promising her a *pūjā* if his son were to thrive. The boy had become well and he resolved to fulfill his promise, but had waited for several years for the opportunity to do so. There was at least one other visit to a Mahisya house in the locality before Maisali Mā returned to her village.

The idea that different manifestations of the same goddess possess quite different powers and personalities is very widespread in Bengal. Tārakeśvara Śiva is the most powerful Śiva in West Bengal. Whether Kalighat Kālī, who is senior, is more powerful, or the Kālī of Dakṣiṇeśvara, who was so lively for Ramakrishna, is debatable, but they clearly outrank many hundreds of others throughout Bengal. The concept that myriad forms with distinct characteristics are nevertheless the same thing in reality is a significant manifestation of the non-dualistic mode of thought.

Manasā

Manasā, goddess of snakes, was worshiped by almost all Hindu households in Kelomal. There were a few occasions on which she was treated as a community deity; but, although snakes are deadly and although they are feared, they do not afflict the whole community like an infectious disease. Her worship was overwhelmingly done on behalf of individual families. Manasā is a Bengali goddess; although her worship has now spread to areas beyond the borders of Bengal, she first appears in narratives written in Bengali in about the fifteenth century, and it is most likely that she was well known to people long before her story began to be recorded in written form. Manasā's story has been retold by more writers than that of any of the other deities about whom *maṅgal kāvya* were composed. D.C. Sen (1954:229–63) identified 58 authors of *Manasā Maṅgals*; Āśutoṣ Bhaṭṭācāryya (1962) has edited 22 different versions.

While there are differences among the written versions, the great popularity of *Manasā Maṅgal* is based on two narratives that are known to virtually everyone. These stories—which, like others of the genre, are about how an unknown deity establishes her worship among mortals—are included in all versions of the myth. A portion of the much longer poem, composed by the seventeenth century author Ketaka Dāsa, has been translated into English by Edward Dimock (1963:209–94). W. L. Smith (1980) has done a detailed comparison of versions of the Manasā myth composed in eastern and western Bengal, as well as those from Assam and Bihar. The entire fifteenth-century text of Vipradāsa has been translated into French by France Bhattacharya (2007). These are the common elements:

1. Cānd Sadāgar, or Cāndo, a wealthy trader, is a devout worshiper of Śiva who refuses to worship Manasā; he breaks the pots with which the women of his house attempt to worship her. While Cāndo is on a trading voyage Manasā sinks his ships and causes him to suffer severe hardships. However, she keeps him alive because, until he worships her, she will not be accepted as a goddess. He returns home, destitute and unrecognizable

by his servants, who take him for a vagrant until—almost too late—he is able to identify himself.

2. Cāndo had six handsome sons, each of whom was well married. Manasā, "Goddess of Poison" (Biṣaharī), poisoned all six of them. Cāndo was unwilling to cremate their bodies, saying that the smoke from their pyres would represent the triumph of Manasā. Their bodies were floated down a river on rafts. A seventh son, Lakhindar, is born to Cāndo, and in due course is married to Behulā. Each of the newly-weds had a heavenly antecedent; both are fated to undergo an earthly trial. Manasā manages to get a poisonous snake into the wedding chamber, and Lakhindar dies of snakebite. Behulā places his corpse on a raft and she floats, alongside his decomposing body, down a river in search of a means of restoring Lakhindar's life. After several dangerous encounters, Behulā sees the washerwoman Neto at a *ghāṭ* washing clothes on a stone. Behulā observes that Neto—in fact Manasā's ally—solves her child-care problem by killing her children so they don't bother her while she does the laundry, then restores them to life when she is done. Seeing this, Behulā asks Neto for the secret. Neto sends Behulā to the gods, where she performs for Śiva a captivating dance she had learned in her previous heavenly life. Śiva—and Behulā's unflagging devotion—persuade Manasā to remove the poison from Lakhindar's decomposed corpse, restoring his life. When Lakhindar and Behulā return to Cāndo's house, the merchant is finally persuaded that he has to worship Manasā. He does so grudgingly, making an offering to the goddess with his left hand and with his back turned to her. She accepts this reluctant offering, restores the other sons to life, and rescues Cāndo's ships from the ocean, together with their crews and cargos.

The story is very dramatic, and the personalities are strongly drawn. Behulā's devotion is presented as a model of Bengali womanhood. There are places where performance or recitation of *Manasā Maṅgal* is an intrinsic part of the worship of this goddess (Bhattacharyya 1977:230–45), but I did not encounter any in Kelomal or the surrounding villages, where the role of village tutelary goddess is occupied by Śītalā.

Figure 22. A Paṭuā tells the story of Manasā from a scroll painting (*paṭ*). The goddess is the large figure crowned with snakes. The merchant Cāndo and his wife are beside her. The sons and their wives are depicted below the goddess. The faithful Behulā is shown seated inside a separate chamber.

Nevertheless, Manasā's story was well known; it was often told by itinerant Paṭuās, who recited the story of Behulā and Lakhindar accompanied by scroll paintings depicting the dramatic moments. David McCutchion and Suhrid Bhowmick (1999:49–54) describe the Behulā-Lakhindar story as the most popular among all Paṭuā presentations. They provide a translation of one of the performed versions of the story, and they reproduce a panel from one of the scrolls. Performers usually locate the events of the story in familiar places: in eastern Medinipur District, the river down which Behulā traveled is said to be the local Rupnarayan, and the *ghāṭ* where the washerwoman Neto was working is identified as an actual *dhopā-ghāṭ* in Tamluk. This kind of local contextualization is common throughout Bengal; the texts of *maṅgal kāvyas* are set in identifiable places, and performers add their own localizing elements. Thus, the sacred landscape is all around; the activities of the gods take place close to home.

While the worship of Manasā reaches down to the level of the local and the familiar, it has also acquired a Brahmanical legitimacy, represented by the inclusion of this goddess in some of the late Sanskrit *purāṇas*. The process by which Brahmans took charge of indigenous deities and provided them with Sanskrit clothing has been lucidly analyzed by Kunal Chakrabarti (2001:196–201). The narrative concerning the birth and career of Manasā is told in nearly identical form in the *Devī Bhāgavata Purāṇa* (Book 9:48) and the *Brahma Vaivarta Purāṇa* (Chapter 46). However, these passages lack all of the incidents known from the *Manasā Maṅgals* in which she seeks to establish her worship among humans. They present her, and some other important Bengali village goddesses, as constituents or manifestations of the *mūlaprakṛtī*, the original nature of the mother goddess. Likewise, the procedures laid out for worshiping Manasā in the priestly handbook, the *Purohita Darpaṇa* (Bhaṭṭācārya 1973/4:I, 220–21), are mostly quite standard tantric modes of worship. Maity (1966:212–16) collected seven *dhyāna mantras* meant to describe the goddess to the worshiper so that she comes into existence in his mind. Such a *mantra* is often the guide to the iconography of a deity. In West Bengal the most frequently used verse is:

I adore the goddess, the mother of snakes, whose face is like the moon, who is graceful in appearance, the bountiful, who rides on a swan, the noble one, who wears a red garment, who always gives boons of all kinds, who has a smiling face, who is adorned with gold, gems, and various other beautiful jewels (obtained) from snakes, who is accompanied by eight snakes, who has prominent breasts, who is a yoginī and who can take any form at will. (Maity 1966:212)

The pleasant visage described here is a far cry from the terrifying form that is her true appearance according to the *Maṅgal Kāvyas*. A bountiful giver of boons does not sound much like the frightening mistress of snakes who is worshiped in rural Bengal. The eight *nāgas* are also part of her Brahmanization. The snakes that appear in the *Mahābhārata* and various *Purāṇas* are all brought together and worshiped at the same time as Manasā. These mythical serpents are all treated as her responsibility, though they do not figure in the *Manasā Maṅgal* narratives.

Stone sculptures of a snake goddess, some from as early as the ninth century, have been collected from many parts of Bengal. Images of a goddess seated on a lotus surrounded by an array of cobras with their hoods expanded appear somewhat later. This later image is most commonly depicted in drawings. There were two temple images of the goddess in Kelomal. The Murarikalua Pañcānan temple contained an image of Manasā that was a bust of unglazed clay (Figure 26), dressed and ornamented very much like the image of Śītalā, who was also present in the temple, together with a *śālagrām* representation of Visnu, and two small images of Lakṣmī. This is the kind of array of deities that is often found in domestic shrines. The Dubkalua Śītalā temple had a well-made brass image of Manasā, with a hooded cobra on each side of her head. She occupied the position to the left of Śītalā in a three-sectioned throne. Śītalā was in the center and the niche to her right was unoccupied. Elsewhere, the only permanent images were simply brass pots that had been ceremonially established (*sthāpana*) after invoking the goddess into them. However, when she was worshiped on the special occasions of Manasā Puja, she was always represented by a particular tree. The Sanskrit *pūjā paddhati* calls it the *snuhi vṛkṣa*; Bengali texts call it *sij gāch*; botanically it is *Euphorbia neriifolia*, commonly known as Indian spurge. It belongs to a category of plants classified by Bengalis as "Manasā trees." These are cactus-like plants that exude an irritating, poisonous, milky sap when cut. The particular euphorbia that is used in the worship of the goddess of snakes is called, in vernacular Bengali, *phaṇī manasā*. *Phaṇā* is the hood of a cobra; the leaves of this plant resemble the expanded hood of the cobra. A branch of a *phaṇī manasā* was used as a representation of the goddess during worship; with its snake's hood and toxic secretion, it is a symbol drawn from nature.

Manasā Pūjā

The monsoon rains in Bengal usually begin during the first part of June. The welcome downpour on the flat delta land quickly floods the agricultural fields, which became parched and cracked during the preceding hot dry weather. During the rice harvest the fields are frequented by rats, which excavate burrows and fill nests with heads of mature rice. Snakes enter the burrows in pursuit of the rats, and find a steady supply of prey until the rains come. When the fields flood, both rats and snakes seek higher ground; in the densely settled Bengal countryside, there is little high ground that is not inhabited by humans. Thus, the rainy season is also the season in which encounters with snakes are most common, and most often serious or fatal. Thus, the onset of the rainy season is also the time of Manasā worship.

For deities who reside in temples daily worship is obligatory, and if one of the deities in a temple is worshiped, the others must be worshiped at the same time. Thus Manasā receives daily service and offerings (usually modest ones) in village temples. However, for most people there are six occasions on which Manasā is the foremost deity worshiped, though no family observes all six of them: (1) Daśaharā, the tenth day of the bright lunar fortnight of Jyaiṣṭha (May/June); (2) Sthāpana Saṃkrānti, the final day of solar Jyaiṣṭha; (3) Ambubācī, the period at the beginning of the rains when the earth is said to menstruate for three days, beginning on the full-moon day of lunar Jyaiṣṭha; (4) Nāg ("Snake") Pañcamī, the fifth day of the dark lunar fortnight of Āṣāṛha (June/July); (5) Ṣaṭ Pañcamī (which is often also called Nāg Pañcamī), the fifth day of the bright fortnight of Śrāvaṇa (July/August); and (6) Bhādra Saṃkrānti, the final day of solar Bhādra (August/September).

Figure 23. Offerings to Manasā, who is represented, on the left in the photograph, by a sprig from a *phaṇī manasā* plant. The speckles are ground sandalwood, sprinkled by the priest during worship. This was a domestic *pūjā*, performed beside the granary of a Mahisya agricultural household. Granaries attract rats; rats attract snakes.

Offerings: Manasā *pūjās* in Kelomal were almost all domestic rites, carried out in individual households for their protection and as a demonstration of their devotion. The offerings consisted of food, which became *prasād*, consumed by family and those close to them. While individual families and clans had very different practices with regard to the offerings, they were usually mindful of their own past practices with respect to items and quantities, which they referred to as "our rule" or "our custom" (*āmāder niyam*). The offerings made on the Daśaharā day by a Langla Kayet ("Ploughing

Kayastha") household were representative of the offerings at *pūjās* other than the "no cooking" (*arandhan*) *pūjā*. The *pūjā* was performed by a Vyasokta Brahman; the Langla Kayets had not yet made the transition to full Kayastha status (which would have been acknowledged if a Madhya Sreni Brahman had performed the worship). There was a *phaṇī manasā* plant growing in the front of the house, and it was treated as the presence of Manasā. (This is shown in Fig. 2.) In other cases a branch of a *phaṇī manasā* represented the goddess.

First the Brahman received a copper platter containing leaves and flowers. Leaves of the Indian jujube (*śītala kul*) were considered essential; the flowers—water lily and small yellow *kalke* flowers—were used because they most easily available. The platter also contained a *harītakī* (emblic myrobalan), the representative "fruit of worship," and vermilion specially prepared with mustard oil, rather than the commercial powder commonly used. The Brahman was given the special grinding stone used to prepare sandalwood paste, and a stick of sandalwood, which he ground to create the fragrance (*gandha*) to be added to the flowers before they were offered to the goddess.

The food offering (*naivedya*) consisted of five *chaṭāks* (about 250 grams) of *ātap cāul*, and a variety of fruits: dates (*khejur*), plums (*jām*), coconut, mango, cucumber (*śaśā*), orange (*kamalā-lebu*), and three varieties of soaked, uncooked lentils. On a separate platter were two varieties of fried lentils.

All of these offerings are ordinary ones that might be presented to almost any deity. The distinctive offering to Manasā was *muṛki*, parched rice coated with molasses—in this case, molasses made from the sap of the date palm (*khejurer guṛ*), which is more expensive and more delicious than the common molasses made from the palmyra palm (*tāler guṛ*). A large basket containing two and a half seers (about 2.5 kilograms) of *muṛki* was prepared in the house for this *pūjā*. I encountered a few instances in which families excused themselves from worshiping Manasā because they did not have enough rice suitable for making *muṛki*.

The Brahman received the rice, some of the fruit, and a small basket (*dālā*) of *muṛki*. He also received *dakṣiṇā* of four annas (25 paise). The *muṛki* was distributed among neighbors and relatives, who shared in the goddess's *prasād*; most of the remaining offerings were consumed within the household.

Arandhan. "No cooking" (*arandhan*) is a ritual peculiar to the worship of Manasā. According to the Bengali authorities, the day for this observance is the last day (*saṃkrānti*) of Bhādra, and that is when most families in Kelomal observed it. However, it is also the day of Viśvakarmā Pūjā; families who worshiped Viśvakarmā observed *arandhan* on a different day. A few did not cook on the first day of Ambubācī, and some on Daśaharā day. A few people said that, formerly, the ruler of the *parganā* chose the day for *arandhan*, a custom they continued, like the custom concerning Banāi Pūjā. It was considered permissible to choose a different day in Bhādra for this observance, a practice called *icchārandhan* ("not-cooking choice"). *Arandhan* means that a fire is not lit in the hearth (*unān*)

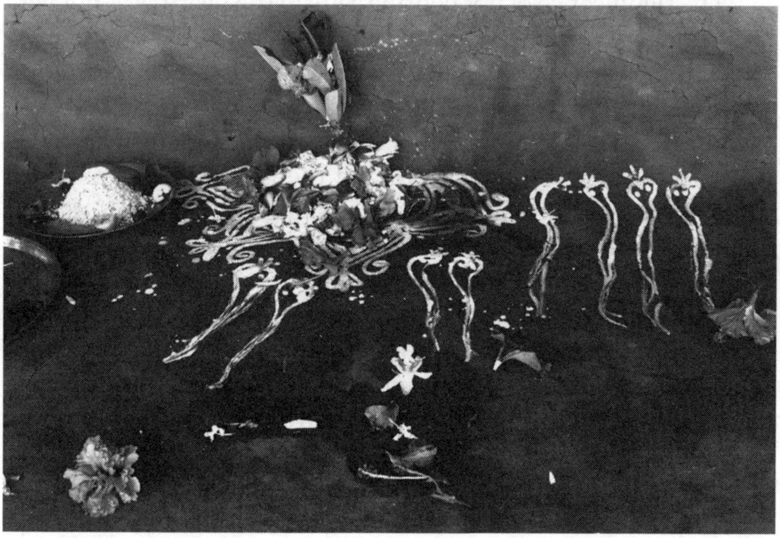

Figure 24. *Aṣṭa Nāg Pūjā.* Pictures of the "eight snakes" are drawn in rice flour near the hearth, which is filled with flowers instead of fuel. A twig from the *phaṇī manasā* plant represents the goddess. A rice offering is on the platter at the left.

on that day. All cooking was done on the previous day; cooked food was saved overnight, then offered to Manasā before being eaten on the following day. Generally, these were rather elaborate meals. One menu included: (1) Rice cooked on the previous day and allowed to soak in water overnight, creating a preparation called *pāntā bhāt*, in which fermentation has just begun. (*Pāntā bhāt* is a common breakfast item in households of sufficient means to have left-over rice.) (2) A variety of fried vegetables including okra, several cucurbits, and a green leafy vegetable. (3) A spiced dish of coconut and squash (*nārikel kumṛo tarkāri*), and *keśarī dal* were offered. (4) The final item was special: *ambal* made with an entire hilsa fish. *Ambal* is the term for a sour (*ṭak*) dish, eaten last in a Bengali meal. Hilsa (*iliś*) is an anadromous fish, similar to shad, which comes into the rivers to spawn when the rains bring a surge of fresh water out into the Bay of Bengal. It is valued highly by Bengalis and commands a premium price on the market; offering a whole *iliś* is a measure of the importance of this goddess.

The significance of not lighting a fire in the hearth was not very clear to many people. Some said that it related to a snake being accidentally burned by a careless young wife, but that interpretation was not widely shared and there was nothing about it in the Manasā mythology. A branch of a *phaṇī manasā* plant was placed down in the hearth on this day, and the goddess was worshiped there. Learned opinion is that not cooking is a sacrifice (*utsarga*) to Manasā (Bandyopadhyaya 1979:I, 68), but that does not explain the particular form of this sacrifice. However it is interpreted, a meal without freshly cooked food is considered a hardship. In some houses, it is a hardship that is endured by everyone. But in some it is borne only by married women, in which case cooking for men may be done on temporary hearths while women eat only the leftover (*bāsi*) food cooked on the previous day.

Aṣṭa Nāg Pūjā. As noted above, worship of the "Eight Snakes" (*aṣṭa nāg*) is apparently a Brahmanical addition to Manasā Pūjā. The *Mahābhārata* and the *Purāṇas* have roles for several great serpents. Some were quite well known, such as Ananta, the thousand-headed serpent on which Viṣṇu sleeps, and Vāsuki, who served along with

Ananta as the churning rope when the gods churned the ocean in search of the elixir of life (*amṛta*). Others—Padmā, Mahāpadmā, Takṣaka, Kulīra, Karkaṭa, and Śaṅkha—are more obscure. But some learned person or persons assembled the full roster of divine snakes in an effort to improve Manasā's status among the gods, an effort that has been largely successful. In conjunction with Manasā Pūjā, when the goddess was represented by a branch of *phaṇī manasā*, *ālpanā* designs of eight snakes were drawn. When *arandhan* was observed, the *phaṇī manasā* branch was placed down in the hearth, and the eight great snakes are shown as emerging from the hearth. The hearth is usually a hole in the floor of the room in which cooking is done. Snakes are thought to live in holes in the earth. In these cases, at least, the connection between not lighting the hearth and propitiating the snake goddess appears to lie in the subterranean residence of the snakes.

Vitality of the tradition. Earlier I mentioned that the narrative of Behulā and Lakhindar was still the most popular story told by Paṭuās, traveling from village to village with scroll paintings illustrating episodes from the narrative. Elsewhere (Nicholas 2013:156–57), I briefly reported an unexpected encounter with the same story on the night of Kālī Pūjā in Kelomal in 1970. Local boys had created a miniature moving diorama of the voyage of Behulā with her husband's corpse on a pond. They made a small raft and small images of Behulā and Lakhindar, which they towed across the pond with a long rope and pulley. Standing on the bank was a miniature figure of a man with a fishing pole in hand. This figure represented a lecherous fisherman who propositioned Behulā, for which he was punished with a case of filariasis. Although Manasā does not have as large a place as Śītalā or Durgā in the annual cycle of Kelomal, her significance is clear and few Hindu households fail to worship her at least once during the rainy season.

6. Śiva, Sūrya, and Dharma

Śiva, Sūrya, and Dharma are distinct male deities with distinct attributes and modes of worship. Yet in Kelomal and elsewhere in rural Bengal they are partially merged into one another and worshiped in ways that add to the confusion. Śiva and Sūrya are well-established puranic gods, while Dharma—as a deity rather than code for conduct—is hardly known outside of Bengal. However, Śiva and Sūrya also have distinctively Bengali identities and these three gods are closely connected in Bengal. I have discussed the worship of these deities in Kelomal in an earlier work (Nicholas 2008b) and I want to avoid repeating myself here. However, they can hardly be ignored in a consideration of the village pantheon, and there are features of their relationship to one another that may be seen more clearly here than in the detailed analysis of the Gājan, where they all engaged.

Śiva

Śiva is found everywhere in India—quite often in temples dedicated to him in which he is represented by a stone image of an erect phallus (*liṅga*) seated in a representation of the external female genitalia (*yoni*), which Bengalis often called *Gaurī-paṭṭa*, "Gaurī seat" (Gaurī is a common appellation of Durgā or Śakti, the powerful goddess who is the spouse of Śiva). Although hundreds of Western visitors to India have found this iconography titillating, Hindu visitors to such temples seem to look right through the obvious to see the god (and, implicitly, his consort at the same time). A more direct representation of generativity is difficult to imagine. Learned people often explain that the union of the male and the female are necessary to maintain creation. The relationship is expressed concisely in the epigram *Śiva śaktihīna śava*, "Śiva without Śakti is a corpse"; that is, the energetic part of a person is due to the feminine constituents. Yet at the same time Śiva has a destructive side that is perhaps derived from the fact that he has absorbed the identities of the dangerous Vedic god Rudra and of the terrifying Bhairava.

Śiva is one of the deities usually found in domestic shrines in Kelomal, whether in dedicated "gods' rooms" within the house, or in small temples. Such shrines were common in the houses of Brahmans and Kayasthas, but they were also found in many Mahisya houses. The images of the deity in such shrines were usually small black stone *bāṇliṅga* (erect phallus) Śivas.

There were several nineteenth-century Śiva temples in Kelomal. The Ghosh Bari alone maintained 12 Śiva temples with daily *pūjās*. They were a familiar type of brick structure with doors on the east side that opened directly on the black stone *yoni-liṅga* inside. Such temples were built by the major landholding houses when they were dominant and they continued to receive regular service from Brahman priests even in less prosperous times. The priests received modest honoraria and some customary entitlements from the descendants of the temples' founder.

There were two temples that were quite different from those built by the landlords: the temple of Rudreśvara in Banamalikalua, which was the site of the Gājan (Nicholas 2008b), and the temple of Pañcānan or Pañcānanda in Murarikalua. Pañcānan ("Five-faces") is an appellation of Śiva; however, it is also a sanskritized form of Pañcu Ṭhākur, the name of a parochial Bengali god often said to be a form of Śiva. Both Rudreśvara and Pañcānan were deities that belonged collectively to Kelomal, and not to the

Figure 25. Daily *pūjā* in one of the Śiva temples of the Ghosh Bari in Banamalikalua.

particular villages in which they were located. While Pañcānan was an inward-looking god whose province was restricted to Kelomal, Rudreśvara was amazingly universal in compass. In Chapter 2 I pointed out that the Gājan was intended to influence fertility over a large and undefined "country" (*deś*). One of the curious features of the Gājan ritual was a ceremony held late at night at which the evening meal (*bhoga*) was offered to Śiva to the accompaniment of a recitation of the *Bhoga Ḍākibār Bai*, an old manuscript copied into a school exercise book (Nicholas 2008b:87–90). While this curious composite text is a salutation of Śiva, it also lays out the geography of all of India in terms of pilgrimage places never seen by anyone in the village, and also great shrines, including Kedārnāth in the Himalayas and Viśvanāth in Banaras among many others. The Gājan is a Bengali ritual carried out by common people and unattested in the *Purāṇas* or elsewhere in Sanskrit texts, yet it encompasses an extensive land. Although the Brahmans and Kayasthas did not take part as ascetics in the Gājan, they nevertheless participated by donating *bhoga* meals to Rudreśvara, and they received the blessing of their houses by the ascetics when they did so. Conversely, the higher castes turned toward the parochial Pañcānan at the end of their most Sanskritic rite: During the ceremonies of Vijayā Daśamī, the conclusion of Durgā Pūjā, after the prescribed shastric rituals were finished, the men of the Ghosh Bari and their servants went together to the Pañcānan temple where each of them drank a drop of the deity's bath water, an affirmation of their common condition as people of the village (Nicholas 2013:130).

Mānasik Pūjā to Pañcānan

Pañcānan of Murarikalua was reputed to be an "alert" (*jāgratā*) deity, that is, a god who is responsive to prayers or to promises made in hopes of gaining his favor. People made mental resolutions (*mānasik, mānat*) to this god, often for the welfare of children. Boys whose health was frail in infancy often went around the village until they were four or five years old with a lock of uncut hair behind the left ear. This was an indication of a promise to Pañcānan; it was cut off when the promise was fulfilled at the temple. In the case of a young girl who was very ill when she was about four years old, her father, a Mahisya cultivator, promised Pañcānan a goat sacrifice if she recovered. He claimed that "the doctors" had given her no chance of survival (though what "doctors" he actually consulted is unclear). He believed that his *mānasik* to Pañcānan was responsible for her return to health. At the time he made the *mānasik*, the priest gave the girl a pair of iron bangles, called "shackles" (*beṛi*), which she was to wear until the vow was completed. When the girl was about seven years of age her father fulfilled his *mānasik* with a *pūjā* at the temple. He said that he was proud that he never used lack of money as an excuse to avoid his commitment to the god, implicitly comparing himself with others who sought divine intervention in a time of trouble but retreated behind poverty when the problem was over. He said he spent Rs.7 on the ceremony, and that he had raised the sacrificial goat himself. Most male goats are castrated at birth, making them gain weight faster and also easier to handle. However, a goat for sacrifice must be an unblemished male, so fulfillment of his vow to Pañcānan was evidently on his mind for some time. The *pūjā* was a family event, with neighbors and close friends also participating. A Dom and his grandson came to provide the drum and gong accompaniment to the sacrifice.

In a society where most people are poor, it is not surprising to see some apparently strict rules violated where income is involved. *Pūjās* for Mahisyas were normally performed by Vyasokta Brahmans. However, the temple of Pañcānan was the possession of Madhya Śreṇī Brahmans. (The men from the Ghosh Bari would not have accepted a drink of the god's bath water from a Vyasokta Brahman.) An honorarium and a share of the *prasād*, including meat, were attractive; and the servant of Pañcānan did not renounce them in the name of caste propriety. The priest finessed the caste issue by allowing the offering from the Mahisya to be made at the same time as the daily *pūjā* to Pañcānan and the other deities resident in the temple, Śītalā and Manasā. The regular food offerings were the usual mixture of raw fruits and vegetables and *ātap* rice, with one platter for Pañcānan and a second for the other deities. There was a bit of cannabis, in recognition of the identity between Pañcānan and Śiva, and some honorific prepared betel leaves.

After the vegetarian offerings were made, the priest asked the girl's father to take off the iron bangles, an act he called "opening the shackles" (*beṛi kholā*). She had been symbolically in bondage to Pañcānan until her father's commitment was fulfilled. After the father had given the bangles to the Brahman, the father rubbed his nose and ears, then bowed to the ground in front of Pañcānan so

Figure 26. Temple of Pañcānan. Pañcānan is the image in the center of the throne (*siṁhāsana*); the goddess Manasā is on his right and the goddess Śītalā is on his left. The inscription carved at the top of the throne says "Śrī Śrī Śītalā," suggesting that the throne was repurposed. The wrap (*uttariya*) the Brahman is wearing is entirely printed with Vaiṣṇava verses. The sacrificial blade is in the foreground. White spots are bits are sandalwood paste sprinkled during worship.

Figure 27. *Kharga*, the sacrificial blade, saluted by the man who will use it to make the sacrifice to Pañcānan. The man is a Mahisya; he is saluting it with a "nose–ear–rubbing *praṇām*."

that his forehead touched the ground. He said this was a "nose–ear–rubbing salutation" (*nāk–kān–malā kheye praṇām*)." The Brahman laid the bangles in front of the deity.

Ritual procedures for the animal sacrifice are elaborate and well-known among villagers. The man who beheads the sacrificial animal must bathe and salute the *kharga*, the sacrificial blade, with a "nose-ear-rubbing *praṇām*." The *kharga* was brought into the temple and placed on a banana leaf, where the Brahman put vermilion and flowers on it, and consecrated it to its purpose. The goat was brought into the temple by the sacrificer and untied at the direction of the Brahman, who put vermilion on its horns and anointed it with water, flowers, leaves of the wood-apple tree (*bel*, the leaves of which resemble Śiva's trident), and a few grains of rice. He whispered a *mantra* into the ear of the animal, including the name of the girl whose return to health was responsible for the sacrifice. He performed a symbolic immolation, touching the *kharga* to the neck of the goat. The Brahman then went outside and consecrated the sacrificial post. He returned to the temple; the sacrificer, his relatives, and the wielder of the *kharga* took the goat outside, where it was clamped in the post and its neck severed. A shallow pottery bowl was filled with blood from the still-pulsing arteries of the goat, a small piece of flesh was placed in it, and it was presented to Pañcānan together with the head of the goat. The Brahman put an oil-soaked cotton wick in the middle of the severed head and lit it. When the sacrifice had been presented, the Brahman proceeded to the *āratī*, the honorific display of a lighted lamp and other ceremonial objects before the images of the gods.

After the *pūjā* was completed, the priest asked the girl to come into the temple. He gave her a handful of flowers and wood-apple leaves, and told her to keep them. He placed a spot of red powder (*ābāṭā*) on her forehead. Meanwhile, the men outside were cleaning up the sacrificial area and butchering the sacrificial goat. All of the participants received some meat, as did the owner of the *kharga*, several houses of relatives, and people who lived in the neighborhood of the sacrificer.

Sūrya

The worship of the sun as a god is a very ancient practice in India. Known in the *Ṛg Veda*, Sūrya is not later submerged into the identity of another god. He is depicted as handsome and masculine, driving his chariot, the sun, across the sky. After the arrival of the Kushans in the first century BCE he began to be represented in Central Asian dress, including boots. The Kushans appear to have been Zoroastrians, so the Indo-European traditions of sun worship may have been merged during this period. Sūrya temples were very widespread across northern India, from Modhera in Gujarat to Konarak in Odisha. Saying a prayer to the sun, with an offering of water while bathing, is still customary in Bengal. Numerous images of Sūrya from pre-Muslim times have been found in Bengal, but today there are no Sūrya temples in the region. In general, in India, worship of Sūrya is confined to those who observe Vedic rituals, especially the *saṃskāra* life-cycle rites; it is not a usual part of what might be thought of as peasant religion. In contrast to the Hindu peasants of Bengal, the Mundari-speaking tribes of the Chota Nagpur region just west of Bengal treat the sun as their highest god. However, the Munda sun god, known as Sing Boṅgā, bears no resemblance to the chariot-driving Vedic Sūrya.

Among Bengalis there is a minor ritual called Itu *pūjā* that was performed in some high-caste Kelomal households. Itu is apparently a shortening of Mitra, the Vedic name of the sun god. The worship of Itu, which is done without an icon, salutes him as Sūrya in a chariot drawn by seven horses. Itu *pūjā* was done throughout the month of Kārtik (October/November) in the Karkun Bari temple of their *kuladevatā*, Raghunāth. A small pot embodying Itu was established with rice and arum plants accompanying it. Offerings were simple: rice and sugar wafers (*bātāsā*). The Brahman who performed the daily service of Raghunāth presented the offerings to the deity. There is a *brata kathā*, about the faithful daughters of a stingy Brahman who bring him prosperity—despite his weak character—by observing a fast and worshiping Itu. However, the fast was not observed by anyone I know of. Though Sūrya was quite important in the Gājan, Itu was not a significant deity in Kelomal.

The offerings made to the sun (*Sūryārghya*) by the ascetics during the Gājan in Kelomal were quite distinctive. I have described them elsewhere (Nicholas 2008b:68–71) and I will not repeat the details here. Most unusually, these offerings—done in the late afternoon as the sun was setting—were made on an altar (*vedi*) that was modeled after the external female genitalia. There was no image of the deity, only the visible sun. Offerings consisted of a sticky fluid called *pañcāmṛta*, which resembled semen, to which was added an unripened fruit containing a prominent seed, usually either a green date or a green mango. Each ascetic poured his or her offering on a mound at the top of the altar, and it flowed into a cavity that extended down into the earth. In other words, the earth

Figure 28. Surya *vedi*, the altar of the sun god. The ascetics in the Gājan make their offerings, pouring them onto the small mound at the top of the altar. The offerings flow into the cavity at the bottom, which extends into the earth.

was treated as a female; her womb was seeded by the ascetics in the form of an offering to Sūrya. The ritual of *Sūryārghya-dāna* is also prescribed for the life-cycle rite of first impregnation (*garbhādhana*), which is performed with the object of getting a son. The life-cycle rites are among the oldest Hindu rituals that are still practiced today. Although the *garbhādhana* is not often done nowadays, the idea that the sun is a source of generative power is perpetuated in this vernacular ritual. (Inden and Nicholas 1977:51)

The explicit representation of the female genitals, although it was called a "sun altar" (Sūrya *vedi*) in the Gājan, was obviously analogous to the Gaurī *paṭṭa* in which the phallic Śiva was seated in the temple. However, in this case the Gājan *sannyāsīs* did the impregnating; and they did so in the form of offerings to Sūrya not to Śiva. The theme of fertilization ran consistently through the Gājan; the idea that the sun is the source of fertility was explicitly enacted in this ritual. On the penultimate day of the Gājan, late at night during the Nīla Pūjā, the role of impregnator was restored to Śiva when he and Durgā were symbolically united in sexual intercourse (Nicholas 2008b:101–11).

Dharma

Śiva and Sūrya are ancient Hindu deities known throughout India, abundantly represented in Sanskrit literature. Dharma, or Dharma Rāj, or Dharma Ṭhākur, is the opposite: an exclusively Bengali god with a curious origin and a cohort of low-caste devotees.

There is an extensive middle-period Bengali literature devoted to this deity, who is described as the creator of the world and as the powerful protector of the hero Lausen. Dharma is anomalous among Bengali gods; he is said to be "formless" (*nirākār*) in a world where gods are embodied beings. There are hundreds of temples for Dharma in the West Bengal countryside. In many of them the deity is represented by a crude stone tortoise. There is no obvious relationship between these rude stone objects and the deity they represent. Although Dharma was not a deity of central importance in the ritual life of Kelomal, his role as protector of the hero Lausen was considered significant by many people. Lausen was said to be a king of Moyna, a place not far from Kelomal where there are remains of an old fort. The ancient capital is surrounded by a double moat inside which the present "royal family" of Moyna, the Bahubalindra clan, maintains a group of temples encompassing the Bengali pantheon: Inside the inner moat there are two large temples, the temple of Rādhā and Kṛṣṇa and the temple of Śiva and Śakti. On the land between the two moats are the shrine (*thān*) of Dharma Ṭhākur, the burial shrine (*samādhi*) of a *mahanta* (chief priest of a temple), and the burial shrine (*dargā*) of a Muslim *pīr*. On the mainland, outside the moats, is a *rās maṇḍap*, the place where the clan deity is brought on the full-moon night in Kārtik (when, according to the *Bhāgavata Purāṇa*, Kṛṣṇa danced with the milk maids). Thus, collected all together in that small locality in Moyna are Śaiva, Śākta, Vaiṣṇava, and *laukika* (popular) gods, and a Muslim shrine.

In Kelomal there was one Dharma temple; the deity in the temple was represented by a black stone shaped somewhat like a

Figure 29. Deities in the temple of Dharma in Banamalikalua. There is a black stone image of Dharma represented as a tortoise (*kūrma*, *kacchap*) in the back row, along with a stone footprint of Nārāyaṇa, some shapeless stones also identified as Dharma, a *bāṇliṅga* Śiva, and a *śālagrām*. The pot with a terra cotta head is Maṅgal Caṇḍī. The large spot on her forehead is the residue of innumerable daily applications of vermilion made during worship. There is a flower on each image, left after daily worship. The stone plate for offerings was emptied after the *pūjā* was completed.

tortoise, as well as a variety of other stone images said to be Dharma. There were several other deities resident in the same temple, including Viṣṇu, in the form of a footprint, a *śālagrām*, and an image of Śiva. The most unusual image in the temple was the goddess Maṅgal Caṇḍī in the form of a clay pot with a terra cotta head.

All of the deities were worshiped together morning and evening. The temple sat in the Gājan ground (*māṛotalā*) facing the temple of Śiva where Gājan was performed. Although the Śiva temple belonged to the village, the Dharma temple belonged to a family of Madhya Sreni Brahmans; men of that family performed the daily worship there. Dharma is rarely a domestic deity, and rarely in the possession of Brahmans. In previous generations, Brahmans regarded Dharma as a deity of the lower castes; he was somehow cleansed and supplied with a sanskritic liturgy.

The temple was located in a very public place. According to the family that owned it, there were two *bighās* of *devottar* property attached to the temple. The ancestors of the present Brahman servants of the deity had purchased the temple, which came with the supporting agricultural land, from a person named Golak Pandit. The current owners said that the deed was in the name of the deity Dharma, and that it was a very old document. They felt obligated to allow the Gājan of Śiva to take place on this ground, the former site of a fair (*melā*) held on the last day of Bhādra (July/August), which is known as Dharma *saṃkrānti*. Although they identified Golak Pandit as a Mahisya, the use of Pandit as a surname or title among Mahisyas is very unusual; however, it is common among the low-caste priests in Dharma temples in West Bengal. The Doms who lived in Murarikalua reported their caste as "Dharma Pandit." They held an annual Dharma Pūjā in their neighborhood for their caste group on Dharma *saṃkrānti*, which was the occasion of Viśvakarmā and Manasā Pūjās for other villagers. High-ranking Brahmans did not often worship Dharma; indeed, the significance of Dharma in the pantheon of Kelomal was very small, probably diminished from earlier times, as the Brahmans placed the other deities in the temple with Dharma. The Gājan ascetics included salutation of Dharma in their daily devotions, although Dharma was a secondary figure in the ceremony.

While Dharma has faded from the pantheon, many of the ritual practices of the Gājan of Śiva are derived from the Gājan of Dharma. A combination of elements led to the absorption by Śiva of the spring ritual originally devoted to Dharma. First, Dharma never attained the status of a respectable deity in the eyes of high-ranking Bengali Brahmans. The standard apparatus of a Hindu deity in Bengal—a *dhyāna mantra* describing the deity and a simple Sanskrit verse for offering worship—is not included in priestly handbooks. Second, the rise in the nineteenth century of the Śiva temple of Tārakeśvara in Hugli District, which became a major regional pilgrimage place, created a new focus for the ascetic ordeals of ordinary rural people. Such ordeals are described in connection with the Gājan in the *Dharma Maṅgal* texts but not in the *Śivāyana*. Third, there was an old Śaiva ritual indigenous to Bengal, involving dancing and adopting strange postures, that took place in the month of Caitra (March/April) to which the ascetic ordeals of Dharma worship could be added. The absorption of Dharma into Śiva is historically quite recent and is still taking place (Nicholas 2008b:20–32).

The late Suniti Kumar Chatterji (1945:78), a learned linguist and most eminent scholar of twentieth-century Bengal, noted the connection between Dharma and Siva, commenting on the "strange conception of Śiva as a farmer, a conception not found elsewhere in India, which appears to be an extension of this aspect of the divinity Dharma to Śiva when the latter came to be identified with the former." Moreover, he noted that the Gājan festival of Dharma "is everywhere always accompanied by ritual dances," which he says "is certainly not Aryan." He thinks the dancing was derived from Austro-Asiatic speaking peoples, the tribal population that is now found largely on the periphery of deltaic Bengal. Dancing is also described in the Bengali *upapurāṇas* as an obligatory part of the Śiva festival held in the month of Caitra (March-April). The *Devī Bhāgavata*, *Bṛhad-dharma*, and *Brahmavaivarta Purāṇas* all mention dancing for Śiva, although they do not refer to the festival as Gājan (Nicholas 2008b:22–23).

Haraprasad Shastri (1853–1931) was one of the leading intellectuals of nineteenth-century Bengal. He was a great scholar of Buddhism and advanced the theory that Dharma was a legacy of late Buddhism that lingered on in Bengal. While most scholars today do not accept this idea, his research has continued to bear fruit. In *Obscure Religious Cults* Shashibhusan Dasgupta recounts the following story, which was recorded by Shastri in 1917:

In a temple of Dharma MM. Śāstrī found a priest dividing into two equal portions the offerings to be presented to Dharma. He asked out of curiosity why such a division was made. The reply of the priest was—"He is Dharma and Śiva at the same time and hence is the division." On further enquiry MM. Śāstrī came to learn that the Mantra with which the offerings were presented to the deity was,—"Salute be to Śiva, who is Dharma-rāja" (*śivāya dharma-rājāya namaḥ*). After several years of his first visit MM. Śāstrī went there once more and found that by this time a *Gaurī-paṭṭa* . . . was placed by the Brahmins beneath the stone-image of Dharma so as to Hinduise him completely. (Dasgupta 1962: fn. p.279)

The appearance of the *Gaurīpaṭṭa* in connection with Dharma also occurred in the Dharma Gājan in Birsingha village, in West Medinipur, in 1940, when Professor K. P. Chattopadhyay (1942) observed the ritual. While the Gājan of Śiva takes place during the last week of the month of Caitra, culminating on the last day of Caitra and the first day of Baiśākh (April/May), calculated on the solar calendar, Dharma Gājan takes place on the lunar calendar in Baiśākh, beginning on the third day of the bright lunar fortnight (*akṣay tṛtīyā*) and culminating on the full moon. In both rituals some villagers give up their roles in everyday life to become temporary *sannyāsīs*. In the Dharma Gājan in Birsingha these temporary ascetics fast during the day, just as do their counterparts in the Śaiva festival.

At sunset they bathe, make an image of a female genital near the tank, call it Hara Gauri (Siva and his wife) and offer worship to Sūrya on it, with a *jaba* flower (*Hibiscus rosasinensis*), milk, honey, ghee and *haritaki*. If other materials are lacking, only water may be offered. Then they come to the *mandap*. To the south of this shed is an image of a female genital in stone, known as Hara Gauri. Here again worship is done. (Chattopadhyay 1942:113)

The conjunction of Śiva, Sūrya, and Dharma, and the symbolism of fecundating the earth, which is treated as a goddess, is the remarkable feature that led me to treat them together. In puranic Hinduism Śiva and Sūrya are not connected, and Dharma does not appear at all, except as a name of Yama, god of death. But in rural Bengal they were connected almost to the point of identification. While the name of Dharma as a god has been uttered with diminishing frequency over the last few centuries, some of his most important characteristics have been grafted on to the Śiva of rural Bengal.

In Dharma mythology Śiva is said to be Dharma's offspring, as are Brahmā and Viṣṇu. Dharma is the creator and his creation is unlike much that is usually found in Hindu mythology. Descriptions of his worship in numerous *Dharma Maṅgal* texts focus on ascetic practices and ordeals, including extreme acts of self-immolation. The protagonist in the Dharma myths is the heroic Lausen. Before his birth, his mother-to-be, Rañjābatī, joined the Gājan participants with the goal of conceiving a son. In her final ordeal she leapt onto a bed of spikes, piercing her body in numerous places. Dharma restored her life and gave her the son she desired. Lausen himself is a warrior who leads a self-controlled life and receives critical support from Dharma. His final offering to Dharma is his own body, which he somehow hacks to pieces. In return for his offering not only does Dharma restore him to life; he causes the sun to rise in the west. The proposition that one can gain control of the sun through ascetic ordeals is a covert message of the ritual of offering to Sūrya in the Gājan. Of course, the body of the ascetic is wasted away through fasting and discipline, not literally hacked to pieces; but bodily sacrifice is the unstated significance of the vows of the Gājan *sannyāsīs*. Following the inclination of people in rural Bengal to identify the locations of mythological events in their immediate neighborhoods, this is all said to take place in nearby Moyna. As noted earlier, the Moyna Raj continues to celebrate its connection with Lausen.

The Gājan rituals in Kelomal contain references to Lausen, as well as very unusual practices that are derived from the *Dharma Maṅgals*. The *Dharma Maṅgals* also contain the stories of Śiva's adopting agriculture, quite similar to the ones in Bengali Śaiva mythology. It is not possible to discover the origin of such tales, and it is quite probable that they were in oral circulation and commonly known before they were written. These stories display a deep understanding of rice agriculture, with details about plowing, broadcasting seed, transplanting rice, and water management. Rice agriculture used to rely on locally adapted varieties that matched expected water levels and seasons; and there were also strains favored for their special flavor or aroma. The hundreds of named varieties differ significantly from one text to another, suggesting that the texts were composed in different localities.

The worship of Dharma has been eclipsed in Kelomal, as it has in much of rural Bengal; this god has undergone a subtle merger to form a composite with the Bengali Śiva. The historical fact of the mingling of these deities was not a social fact for people in Kelomal; for them, Lausen, the hero of Dharma mythology, was a local king. They were unaware that elements of Dharma's Gājan—including the name of the ritual itself—were embedded in their contemporary practice.

Bengali Hindus have often been identified as "goddess worshipers." Much of the reason for this characterization is the very high visibility of Durgā Puja, along with Kālī Pūjā, and Jagaddhātrī Pūjā, which give the autumn season in West Bengal a distinctive character, as well as a lot of extra holidays. At the same time, the mark that Caitanya's Kṛṣṇa *bhakti* has made on Bengal is, in many ways as strong or perhaps even stronger, than that of the goddesses. Certainly in rural areas the evidence of devotional Vaisnavism is seen everywhere, in everything from household *tulasi* shrines and Hari *mandirs* to personal names. Yet in many households Laksmi may be worshiped more often than any other deity. Nevertheless, the place of powerful male deities, among whom Śiva has assumed foremost position, should not be overlooked. The Bengalis are not Śāktas, or Vaiṣṇavas, or Śaivas, but they are all those things; and under the puranic personalities of well known Hindu gods there are some elements borrowed from Islam and some that originated in the soil of Bengal.

7. Brata Rituals: Ṣaṣṭhī, Tāriṇī, and Maṅgal Caṇḍī

Bengali Hindus very frequently use the word *brata* (Skt. *vrata*, pronounced something like *broto*), unaware of is long and continuous history in Indian religion beginning in the *Ṛg Veda*. Volume 5 of P.V. Kane's great *History of Dharmaśāstra* begins with a 462-page section on "Vratas (Religious Vows) and Utsavas (Religious Festivals)," in which he reviews the various meanings that have attached to the term *vrata* over the centuries. It soon becomes evident that "religious vows" is not an adequate translation for the term. Bengalis use it to refer to (1) the mental commitment of the person undertaking the ritual; (2) the expression of that commitment in ritual form; and (3) a story that relates the origin, purpose and results of the ritual.

My goal here is to explain *brata* in Bengali practice.

The first element of a *brata* is self-denial. The person undertaking the *brata*—almost always a woman—usually observes a fast during the period of the *brata*, which is normally one day, sometimes a solar day (*divas*), such as a Tuesday or Saturday for Bipattāriṇī, sometimes a lunar day (*tithi*), such as a *ṣaṣṭhī* for the goddess Ṣaṣṭhī. Fasting in Bengal does not mean going without any food or drink, but rather restricting what is consumed by excluding cooked rice, which is considered a significant deprivation. What is permitted during the fast is *jal khāoyā* ("water eating")—"water" in this case is an extensive category that includes a wide variety of uncooked fruits and vegetables and some items fried in *ghī*, including *lucis* (puffed-up bread made of white flour).

The second element is that the *brata* is directed to a particular deity. These observances are often referred to as *bār-* ("day") *bratas* because they take place on fixed days that are marked for particular deities. The objective of each *brata* is relevant to the domain or special power of that deity. Women may honor that deity by making *ālpanā* drawings of appropriate auspicious objects—in rice flour, chalk, or nowdays in some commercial medium—to decorate the floor where the ritual is carried out.

The third element of the *brata* is a story, the *brata kathā*, that illustrates the reason for the observance in simple, didactic terms, like the Lakṣmī *brata kathās* discussed in chapter 4. These stories, which are read aloud or recited as a part of the ritual, mostly belong to Bengali folklore, although some are taken from Sanskrit *upapurāṇas* composed in Bengal. Since most *brata* observances are domestic rites performed by women, the stories may be read or recited by a woman, although it is considered prestigious to have a Brahman tell the story.

Kunal Chakrabarti (2001:250) treats *bratas* as one of the principal avenues by which Brahmans gained access to the ritual lives of ordinary people in Bengal. By creating a role for themselves in existing domestic rituals they created the trust they used to propagate puranic practices and establish priestly livelihoods for themselves. In some cases this Brahmanical role has blurred the distinction between *bratas* and *pūjās*. For example, worship of the goddess Ṣaṣṭhī performed by women for the welfare of their children, with or without the participation of a Brahman, is a *brata*. However, if a Brahman makes offerings to the goddess, the ritual is a *brata* but also a *pūjā*. The rituals on the occasion of Śivarātri, "Śiva's night," were both Śiva *pūjā* for men and a *brata* for women, who fasted, observed a vigil, and listened to a *brata kathā*. The sixth day of the Gājan ritual was the day of Nīla Pūjā during which women who wished to have children undertook the Nīla Ṣaṣṭhī

Brata, fasting during the day and, in the late afternoon, carrying three, five, seven, or even nine pots of water for the lustration of Śiva in the temple. Although most *bratas* were practiced by women, devout Vaisnava men observed an *ekādaśī brata* on the eleventh day of each lunar fortnight, fasting during the day, although without a *brata kathā*. Many of the *pūjās* in the annual cycle of Lakṣmī worship, described earlier, were *bratas* for women although there were often requirements for males that were not considered *bratas*. Kojāgarī Lakṣmī was a major *pūjā*, with an image of the goddess and elaborate worship performed by a Brahman; at the same time it called for a *brata*, with a restricted diet and vigil, for women. Many domestic Satya Nārāyaṇa *pūjās* were also *bratas* for women. There is no clear way of defining a distinct class of *brata* rituals, but there were occasions in the annual cycle that people in Kelomal unhesitatingly labeled *bratas* and it is these that I take up in this chapter.

The rituals that are unambiguously *bratas* have a distinctly vernacular quality, not only in the language of the accompanying stories but also in the ritual symbols, which are things of everyday life. The deities of these rituals are all goddesses: Maṅgal Caṇḍī, Ṣaṣṭhī, and Bipattāriṇī (or Bipad Tāriṇī). Brahmanical influence has won places for two of them in *upapurāṇas* composed in Bengal; Ṣaṣṭhī and Maṅgal Caṇḍī are accorded the status of manifestations of a greater goddess, along with Gaṅgā, Tulasī, and Manasā (Hazra 1963:313, 323,425). Bipattāriṇī is said to be a form of Durgā who saves her worshipers from danger. All three of these goddesses have benign characters, contributing to their accessibility in simple domestic rites.

In general, more numerous *bratas* were practiced in high-caste households. There were also many prosperous Mahisya households that claimed to have practiced certain *bratas* for generations. As I noted earlier, having the service of a Brahman to make offerings to the deity and to read the *brata kathā* was prestigious; but there were many instances in which the entire ritual, including recitation or reading of the story, was conducted by women. Throughout Bengal, *bratas* are thought of as the rituals of women, primarily *sadhabās* (married women whose husbands are living), though a few are practiced by unmarried young women with the aim of getting good husbands. The social universe for *bratas* is usually the individual household or a cluster of related households. Married women come from their natal families to join their husbands' families; familial love must be created in their marital family. A husband's mother (*śāśuṛī*) is quite different from one's own mother. And the wives of a husband's older brothers come from different families; solidarity among in-marrying women is not automatic. *Brata kathās* are filled with advice about and examples of harmony among the women of a household; Lakṣmī *bratas* in particular contain advice about modesty and good conduct. Underlying the injunctions and the performances of women who undertake *bratas* is the theory that the bodily discipline and privations of a woman benefit those who share her body, principally her husband and her children. The concept of their "shared body" (*ekdeha*) is central to the interpretation of the *brata* rituals. When a woman is married, she is ritually transformed into the half-body (*ardhāṅginī*) of her husband. The bodily relationship with her children is created by their birth out of her body. (Inden and Nicholas 1977:39–57) June McDaniel (2003) has done an extensive study of a wider range of *bratas* practiced in West Bengal that focuses on their social functions.

Ṣaṣṭhī

Ṣaṣṭhī is the ordinal number "sixth"; the worship of this goddess is usually done on the sixth day of bright lunar fortnights. She is often depicted as a married woman with a child on her lap and surrounded by children; her conveyance (*vāhana*), a cat, is often included in illustrations. In some parts of West Bengal she is depicted as a woman with the head of a cat. She is worshiped by women to protect their children and/or in hopes of begetting children, usually sons. There are two special occasions of Ṣaṣṭhī worship: before newlyweds have sexual intercourse, in an effort to get a son, and on the sixth day after a child is born, to bless the child with health and a long life. These are *naimittika karmas*, life-cycle rites rather than *bratas* (Inden and Nicholas 1977:51, 56–57).

There was a *naimittika* worship of Ṣaṣṭhī in Murarikalua by a Brahman woman who had lost her first child in birth. At that time she made a commitment to Ṣaṣṭhī, promising to perform her worship if her next child lived. On the day before she held the first rice ceremony (*annaprāśana*) for her second child, a daughter who was seven months old at the time, she offered a *pūjā* at the Ṣaṣṭhī *thān* in her village. A wood apple (*bel*) tree was dressed in a married woman's red-bordered sari. There were several lumps of laterite (*jhāmā pāthar*) at the base of the tree. The priest marked three of them with vermilion and placed a red hibiscus blossom on each, saying that the tree was Ṣaṣṭhī and the pieces of laterite were her children. The priest made a simple offering to the goddess of flowers, water, raw fruit and vegetables, and a bamboo basket, then asked the mother to seat the infant at his right side. He sprinkled some water from the offering on the child and instructed the mother to mark the tree and the stones with vermilion. Then she did the same with a mixture of yoghurt and turmeric. She bowed low to the tree, and then everyone present did so. The mother marked the foreheads of everyone present with a spot (*phõṭā*) of the yoghurt and turmeric. This *pūjā* fulfilled the mother's commitment to Ṣaṣṭhī; it was not a *brata* except for the mother's fasting before the ritual.

Most Ṣaṣṭhī worship consists of *bratas* done throughout the year on *ṣaṣṭhī* days. These practices were more common in upper caste households, but they are also were also followed in many prosperous Mahisya houses. The Nīla Ṣaṣṭhī *brata* was observed by women of several different castes and their procession to the Śiva temple did not display distinctions of rank among them. I have described the ritual of carrying water to Śiva by the Nīla Ṣaṣṭhī *bratinīs* as a part of the Gājan (Nicholas 2008b:98–103). This *brata* is a part of a public rather than a domestic ritual and it is not done on a *ṣāṣṭhī tithi* but rather the sixth day of the Gājan; however, the objective is fertility and obtaining a son, which secures the place of a woman in her marital family.

Despite her appearance in Sanskrit texts and rituals, and her recognizable iconography, Ṣaṣṭhī in Kelomal was also an autochthonous goddess who had emerged at local shrines and was worshiped with simple rites using common household items. There was a Ṣaṣṭhī shrine in Banamalikalua adjacent to the Śiva temple that was the center of the Gājan rituals, where there was a collection of laterite lumps under a pipul (*aśvattha*, Ficus religiosa) tree. The tree itself was said to be Ṣaṣṭhī Buṛī (Old Woman Ṣaṣṭhī) and the lumps of laterite represented children. In the worship that took place there on the occasion of Araṇya (forest) Ṣaṣṭhī, the sixth day of the bright lunar fortnight in Jyaiṣṭha (May/June), the Brahman who performed the ritual marked the tree and three pieces of laterite with vermilion figures (*puttalikā*), signaling that they contained a living presence. Offerings (*naivedya*) of *ātap* rice, fruits, sugar wafers (*bātāsā*), and sweets were brought by the women from several Brahman houses. There was also a special offering made of milk that had not been boiled, soaked *mug* lentils, and sweets. The goddess was given a fan made of palm leaves, a sprig from a pipul tree containing five leaves, and a butter churning stick (*ghol manthani*, a symbol borrowed from a different Ṣaṣṭhī *pūjā*). For each member of the offering household, one white string containing five knots was placed on a lump of turmeric. These were later tied around the wrists of the beneficiaries of the worship, on the right wrist of a male (or to his sacrificial thread) and on the left wrist of a woman. Women fasted until the *brata kathā* had been told, which was not until nearly 11:30 in the morning.

Worship began with a *saṃkalpa*. The name of the senior woman from each participating household was recited by the Brahman, then he presented the offerings to Ṣaṣṭhī, which he did while ringing a hand bell. When the Brahman rang the bell, women blew conch shells. After he had presented the offerings to the goddess, he told the *brata kathā*. While he was telling the story the women who were participating (*bratinīs*) touched a white thread tied around the pipal (*asvattha*) tree. Araṇya Ṣaṣṭhī is also known as Jāmāi (daughter's husband) Ṣaṣṭhī; often this particular Ṣaṣṭhī *pūjā* honors the daughter's husband with a special meal, if he has come to visit. The story told by a Brahman in Kelomal seemed rather distant from this theme, as does another Araṇya Ṣaṣṭhī *brata kathā*. However, the forest does figure in both stories. Tony

Stewart (1995:352–66) has also translated other versions of these stories (as well as some stories that are connected to Ṣaṣṭhī *bratas* not practiced in Kelomal).

The Kelomal Araṇya Ṣaṣṭhī *brata kathā*

A king had three wives but no children, which made him very unhappy. A sadhu came to his court and offered the king a *jaṛi* (*jaṛibuṭi*, medicinal herb) to be taken by his wives so that they would become pregnant. The first and second wives refused the medicine; the third wife took it, but did not become pregnant.

A maidservant in the king's house told the youngest queen that she, the maidservant, could have a baby that she would present as the queen's. The king agreed to send the third queen and the maidservant to a distant place, where he arranged for a house to be built for them. After some time the maidservant sent word to the king that the third queen was pregnant. The maidservant asked for a blind midwife (*dāi-mā*), a blind barber (Napit), and a blind Launderer (Dhopa) to be sent to assist with the birth and the cleansing of birth impurity. The maidservant paid the attendants very well to tell the king that a son had been born. However, the king was not to visit, nor was there to be any of the standard rites, the Ṣaṣṭhī *pūjā* six days after birth, or first-rice ceremony (*annaprāśana*) at six months.

When the boy reached marriageable age, the maidservant sent word to the king that he should send a music party and a palanquin with bearers for the marriage of his son. She obtained a quantity of *kṣīr* (a sweet of thickened milk) and butter from which she made two dolls that she put in the palanquin behind the curtain. The procession set off without a particular direction and entered a forest. The palanquin bearers said they wanted to stop for a drink of water and the maidservant said that she would go into the forest to relieve herself. The procession stopped near a tree beneath which sat an old woman surrounded by a number of children [evidently a reference to Ṣaṣṭhī, though the priest did not use her name]. The maidservant told the old woman that she must look after the bride and groom in the palanquin. When the palanquin bearers and the maidservant were gone, the old woman looked behind the palanquin curtain and saw the *kṣīr* and butter dolls, which she ate. When the maidservant returned she berated the old woman for her failure to care for the "bride" and "groom." The maidservant said that the old woman would have to provide her with a boy and girl from the group that surrounded her. The old woman agreed, specifying only that the maidservant could not take the oldest nor the youngest child in the group.

With a boy and a girl in the palanquin, the procession set off for the king's house. The king at last saw his "son," who was accepted by the other queens.

A "Standard" Araṇya Ṣaṣṭhī *brata kathā*

(There are several published versions of this story, all quite similar.)

There was a Brahman woman who had three sons; each son had a wife. The wife of the youngest son was exceptionally gluttonous (*nolā*). She used to steal all kinds of things to eat, and she blamed the thefts on the black cat of the house. That cat was the vehicle of Mother Ṣaṣṭhī, and it used to tell her all the things that were going on.

After some time, the youngest wife became pregnant. After ten months and ten days she had a son radiant as the moon. She went to sleep at night with her son at her side, but when she awoke early in the morning her son was gone. Everyone in the house searched everywhere but they could not find the baby.

In this way, the youngest wife had six more sons and one daughter; each of them disappeared and could not be found anywhere. She began to acquire a bad reputation in the village and everyone in the house said she was a *rākṣasī*. Sad and friendless, she went off into the forest.

Seeing her sitting in the forest, alone, crying, mercy arose in Mother Ṣaṣṭhī, who appeared disguised as an elderly Brahman woman. She addressed the youngest wife in the familiar (*tui*) form: "Mā, why are you crying? What has happened to you?"

Crying, she replied, "Mother, I am a great sinner (*pāpiṣṭha*). I had seven sons and a daughter, and I do not have one of them now. Everyone in the family hates (*ghennā*) me. That is why I have come to the forest."

Mā Ṣaṣṭhī said, "Well, unfortunate girl. Why did you steal all that food and blame it on the cat? That is why my cat brought your children to me."

When she heard this, she cried and grasped Mā Ṣaṣṭhī's feet. "Mā, forgive me. Please tell me what I have to do to atone (*prāyaścitta*) for my sin (*pāp*)."

Mā Ṣaṣṭhī said, "Go over there and you will see the decomposing body of a dead cat. Take a pot of yoghurt and massage the body of the cat with it. When it has come back to life, bring the pot back to me. Then you will get your children."

Hoping to see her children, the youngest wife did as she was directed. Mā Ṣaṣṭhī gave her the sons and daughter and said, "Put a spot of this yoghurt on the forehead of each child. And if you ever steal food, don't blame it on the cat. Never strike a cat with a stick. Never strike a child with your left hand or threaten him with death.

"On the sixth day of the bright fortnight in Jyaiṣṭha, make an image of a black cat and a wrist-band (*kaṅkan*) of rice paste (*piṭuli*), arrange an offering plate of uncooked fruits and vegetables (*phal-mūl*) and an offering plate of six prepared betel leaves, six areca nuts, and six bananas; wrap a turmeric-dyed rag in bamboo leaves, and bind it with two yards of thread. That thread is called the "attachment thread" (*sat-sūto*). Put oil and turmeric on that thread and worship Mother Ṣaṣṭhī. After worship, take the *sat-sūto* and touch it to the forehead of each son and tie it to his right arm. Then listen to the Ṣaṣṭhī *brata kathā* and eat some of the uncooked vegetables. Do not eat any cooked rice or strong food. If [mothers and] pregnant women observe all of these rules, their children will not die."

Having said this, Mā Ṣaṣṭhī left. Then the youngest wife took her children and returned home, where everyone was astonished. They were amazed by what she told them; they surrounded her and learned the rules of the Ṣaṣṭhī *pūjo brata*. From that time, desiring the well-being (*maṅgal kāmanāy*) of their children, they began to practice this *brata*.

Excellent marriages were arranged for the children of the youngest wife—beautiful brides for the sons, and a *jāmāi* like the moon for the daughter. On the Ṣaṣṭhī day in Jyaiṣṭha, the *jāmāi* received a spot of yoghurt on his forehead and was offered a platter of mangos and jackfruit. All of the other wives followed the example of the youngest wife, and on this day invited their daughters' husbands to visit. For this reason the day has come to be called Jāmāi Ṣaṣṭhī or Ṣaṣṭhī-bāṭā ("-platter").

The fame of the youngest wife became known far and wide. Soon Araṇya Ṣaṣṭhī was practiced throughout the land. (Vidyāratna n.d.:26–8)

In this story the actors are women and the beneficiaries are children. Ṣaṣṭhī is already a known goddess. In *maṅgal kāvya* stories the goddess is generally unknown to people at the beginning of the story; she makes herself known, usually in an unpleasant way. In the Ṣaṣṭhī *brata kathās* it is the particular occasions of worship and their special demands that were previously unknown. The use of sacralized threads as symbols and reminders of goddesses is a widespread practice. In this story, honoring the daughter's husband is a bit of an afterthought; it appears to be a later addition to a story that is about other things, specifically, the relationship that is posited between the conduct of a woman and the well-being of her children. In many of the Lakṣmī *brata kathās* the connection is made between the conduct of a woman and the prosperity of her marital household.

Ghāṭ Ṣaṣṭhī. The sixth day of the bright fortnight in Bhādra (August/September) is known in Kelomal as Ghāṭ Ṣaṣṭhī, because it is done on the bathing *ghāṭ*, the steps leading to the water of a pond. The almanac calls it Cāpṛā ("clod of earth") Ṣaṣṭhī or Carpaṭā Ṣaṣṭhī; clods have a place in the *brata kathā* though not in the practice of the ritual in Kelomal. It was known in Kelomal as Manthān Ṣaṣṭhī, referring to the butter-churning stick or paddle that was used in this *pūjā*. Women of several related houses who ordinarily used the same *ghāṭ* for bathing, and for washing clothes and dishes, gathered there for worship, though they made separate food offerings to Ṣaṣṭhī in their individual houses. The symbolic offerings presented to the goddess by the priest on the *ghāṭ* are all everyday utilitarian items: a fan made of palmyra leaves, a grinding stone (*noṛā*), and a butter-churning stick (*ghol manthani* or *ghol mauni*). While the fan is meant to give comfort to a guest, the grinding stone (which is rubbed over grain or spices on a flat stone called *śil*) and the churning stick are agents of refining, producing more-desirable out of less-desirable food. Food offerings were also common parts of the diet, including ordinary *dāl*, mustard, *ātap* rice, rice paste, turmeric, and yoghurt. A sprout of *jhiṅge* (ridged gourd) with a blossom planted in a ball of mud was situated on the *ghāṭ* with the other offerings. The priest made the offerings quickly and then read the *brata kathā*, which is quite an unusual one.

Cāpṛā Ṣaṣṭhī *brata kathā*

There was a merchant who lived with his wife, three sons, three sons' wives, and their children. The merchant and his wife were especially fond of the son of the youngest's son's wife.

The merchant's wife complained to her husband that she attracted criticism from the neighbors because she had to use someone else's bathing place (*ghāṭ*) for her Ṣaṣṭhī *pūjā*. He immediately agreed to dig a private pond for her use. When the digging was completed, however, the pond would not fill with water, even after the rainy season. One night Mother Ṣaṣṭhī appeared to the merchant in a dream. She told him that in order to get the pond to fill with water he would have to sacrifice his youngest grandson; when his blood was in the pond, it would fill with water. The merchant cried in distress, but did as the goddess instructed him. The child's mother, the youngest son's wife, knew nothing of what had happened.

When the pond suddenly filled with water everyone in the house was joyous, except the merchant and his wife who knew the reason. The others gathered at the *ghāṭ* and worshiped Ṣaṣṭhī. They made rice-paste images and put clods (*cāpṛā*) of earth in the water for her. As they did so, the boy who had been sacrificed emerged from the water. His mother was quite astonished. When the merchant and his wife got the news they rushed to the *ghāṭ* and embraced the boy. The merchant's wife told everyone the whole story; the youngest wife fainted. Thanks to the grace of Mā Ṣaṣṭhī she awoke.

Each of the three wives took a son in her lap, covered herself modestly, and listened to Mā Ṣaṣṭhī's *kathā*. Everyone in the house received Ṣaṣṭhī's grace and they prospered. The merchant's wife praised her; throughout the country, she told how to worship Ṣaṣṭhī. Soon this *brata kathā* spread from one country to the next and Mā Ṣaṣṭhī was worshiped in every house. (Bhaṭṭācaryya and Kaviratna 1964:89–92)

Bengali *maṅgal kāvyas*, *pāñcālis*, and *brata kathā* are filled with stories of the resuscitation of people—often children—who were killed to impress on ignorant or flawed humans the power of a deity. However, stories telling of human sacrifice, like that of the merchant's grandson, are very rare. Much more common are stories in which a pious young married woman brings happiness and prosperity to her marital household by worshiping a deity or practicing a *pūjā* unknown to others. A story such as this one, in which a young woman gains power in the family into which she is married, although not realistic, has great appeal.

Śītal Ṣaṣṭhī brata. The Śītal ("cold") Ṣaṣṭhī *brata* bears a strong resemblance to the *arandhan* worship of the goddess Manasā described earlier. Women who observe this *brata* do not eat warm food or touch anything warm on the sixth day of the bright fortnight in the cold month of Māgha (January/February). *Bratinīs* are supposed to eat rice left over from the previous day (*pāntā bhāt*) and raw food. This is a considerable hardship, especially for women who, despite fasting themselves, must cook the principal meal for their families; this *brata* was less often observed in Kelomal than Jāmāi Ṣaṣṭhī and Ghāṭ Ṣaṣṭhī.

The Śītal Ṣaṣṭhī *brata kathā* is about the senior woman (*ginni*, *gṛhinī*) of a large family who, on a cold Śītal Ṣaṣṭhī day, directs her hesitant but obedient sons' wives (or grandsons' wives in some versions) to prepare hot water for her bath and a hot meal. The following morning she finds everyone in the house—the dog and cat, the cows, her sons and their wives and children, lying dead.

She knows that she has offended Ṣaṣṭhī by bathing in hot water and eating hot food; she casts herself on the goddess's mercy. Ṣaṣṭhī instructs her about how to restore life to the dead, beginning with the cat, and, of course, reminds her that she must not forget the rules for Śītal Ṣaṣṭhī in the future. (Bhaṭṭācaryya and Kaviratna 1964:171–74)

Durgā Ṣaṣṭhī and Nīla Ṣaṣṭhī. I have elsewhere discussed how the religious year of Bengali Hindus is structured by the opposition between the spring season, marked by the ritual of Gājan, and autumn, which is the season of Durgā Pūjā, often seen as the hallmark of Bengali Hinduism. Durgā Pūjā begins with the awakening of the goddess, which may take place as much as a fortnight before the principal days of the *pūjā*. The major celebration begins on the sixth day of the bright fortnight in Āśvina (September/October). In houses where Durgā Pūjā is held, there is a lot of work the women must do; there is no time for self-denying acts. The *brata kathā* for Durgā Ṣaṣṭhī recognizes the peculiarity of this day. It does not say anything about how or why to worship Ṣaṣṭhī; rather, it provides an account of Durgā's desire for children, how she came to have two sons, Kārtik and Gaṇeśa, on this *ṣāṣṭhī* day, and how Gaṇeśa acquired his elephant head. There is no role for the goddess Ṣaṣṭhī in their creation.

Nīla Ṣaṣṭhī, as noted earlier does not take place on a *ṣāṣṭhī tithi* but rather on the sixth day of the Gājan, which is calculated on the solar calendar. Despite this distinction, it is the occasion for a Ṣaṣṭhī *brata* that is widely observed, particularly by women who desire sons. The Gājan, which is underway at the time of Nīla Ṣaṣṭhī, is a ritual of fertilization; the *brata kathā* for Nīla Ṣaṣṭhī is closely articulated with the Gājan. It tells of a Brahman couple whose five sons and one daughter all died. They made a pilgrimage to Banaras (Kāśī) where they encountered Ṣaṣṭhī in her often-used disguise as an aged woman. Ṣaṣṭhī asked the Brahman couple why they were so sad, heard their story, and advised them to observe the Nīla Ṣaṣṭhī *brata*:

During the entire month of Caitra you should take *sannyāsa* and worship Śiva. Fast for the entire day on the day before the final day of the month.

At sunset, worship Nīlavatī and place a light in the temple of Nīlakantha Śiva. After you have saluted Mother Ṣaṣṭhī then you can eat a light meal (Vidyāratna n.d.:171).

In Kelomal most *sannyāsīs* took vows for a week, not for the entire month of Caitra. The women who observed the Nīla Ṣaṣṭhī *brata* were not *sannyāsīs*. The light in the Śiva temple was maintained by the *sannyāsī* who had the special office of temple attendant. What the *bratinīs* brought to the temple were pots of water for the lustration of Śiva (and Durgā). Why the occasion is called Nīla ("blue") Pūjā and Nīla Ṣaṣṭhī is uncertain. Some people said it was derived from Nīla-kantha ("Blue Throat"), an epithet of Śiva, a reference to his drinking the poison brought up by the churning of the ocean, which caused his throat to turn blue. But this is not an epithet used in the Gājan. Nīlavatī is a common pronunciation of Līlavatī, identifying Durgā as the "playful one." No one whom I spoke to could connect Nīlavatī with this occasion, although many people mentioned her name (Nicholas 2008b:103). Such uncertainty notwithstanding, there were many women in Kelomal who observed this *brata*.

Bipattāriṇī

The goddess Tāriṇī is depicted with a fair complexion and benign, attractive countenance. I have never seen a statue of this goddess used in worship. She was not commonly invoked in a pot, but was sometimes worshiped as a presence in a *śālagrām*, a fossil ammonite that usually represents Viṣṇu. Yet she seemed to be constantly present for people as a protector. The name Tāriṇī means "Protectoress" and the prefix Bipad means "danger": she protects from danger. The Tāriṇī or Bipattāriṇī *brata* is observed on just one day in the year. In about 1959, for the benefit of succeeding generations, the late Bisnu Pada Sarkar wrote down the details of his clan's religious observances. He filled two notebooks in a neat hand, one dealing only with Durgā Puja and the attendant autumnal celebrations, the other containing instructions on all the others. Under the heading "Month of Āṣāṛha—Tāriṇī Brata" he wrote:

The almanac says that the days of Tāriṇī *brata* are the Tuesday and Saturday following the first chariot procession [of Jagannāth] in Āṣāṛha, but it is not our custom (*prathā*) to observe this *brata* on Saturday. [In our family] it is done only on Tuesday. The thread that is given in this ritual must be worn on the left arm for a year, until the time of the next [Tāriṇī] *brata*.

The offerings that are made to Tāriṇī are all common items that were readily available in the village, though the detailed prescriptions are more elaborate than those for most *bratas*. Bisnu Sarkar noted that early on the morning of the preceding day, *mug dāl* should be put in water to sprout. The sprouted *mug* was used in a preparation with molasses, yoghurt or unboiled milk, and tamarind. Some peeled raw vegetables or fruits were to be offered with this mixture. Next, in one dish the following items were to be arranged: a group of 13 betel leaves, a group of 13 areca nuts, one *harītakī* (emblic myrobalan, a medicinal fruit often used to represent the fruit of worship), one areca nut, and five measures of sun-dried rice. On a flat wicker basket (*cāṅgārī*): 3 groups each of 13 betel leaves; 3 groups each of 13 areca nuts; 3 red threads, each containing 13 knots; and 13 additional items drawn from a long list of possibilities. There is no explanation of the number 13, except that it is Tāriṇī's number.

Bisnu Babu wrote that *ālpanā* designs should be drawn on the floor of the family temple where the offering basket and pot were to be placed. One pot to embody the goddess was required together with a five-leafed mango twig to be inserted in the pot. Flowers and flower garlands were to be supplied by the Malakar for a fee of 2 annas. Incense, both stick and resinous types; a ceremonial lamp; and a sitting mat for the Brahman, who was to receive a *dakṣiṇā* of one anna. Bisnu Babu concluded his instruction, without mentioning the obvious fact that a Brahman had to read the *brata kathā* after worshiping the goddess:

> The women who observe this *brata* will fast until the *pūjā* is completed and, at the end of the *pūjā*, they will eat a light meal (*jal khāy*). On this day women who observe this *brata* may not eat boiled rice, puffed rice, or any other items made of rice. They may eat various kinds of bread (*luci, ruṭi, paṛotā*).

Previously we arranged in this *pūjā* to give large cardamoms, small cardamoms, cubeb peppers (*kābābcini*), cloves, fried bread puffs (*luci*), sweetmeat balls, cakes of thickened milk, etc.—4 groups of 13 of each item—but because of the shortage of help and because of various other difficulties, these items have been discontinued.

Such obsessive concern about details, while it is spelled out explicitly by Bisnu Babu, is common in the practice of *pūjās* in Bengal. The concern is that if some detail is not performed correctly, the entire ritual will be spoiled.

The *brata kathā* that was read by the Brahman is an interesting one, both because of the peculiar nature of the danger involved, and as an illustration of the generous character of Tāriṇī. It begins with a visit by the busybody sage Nārada to Śiva and Durgā on Mount Kailāsa. Nārada inquires about what *brata* should be observed by women who wish to avoid calamities. Śiva answered that the *brata* of Bipattāriṇī Durgā protects from calamity, and illustrated with this story:

The king of Vidarbha had one queen. She made the acquaintance of a woman of leather-worker caste (Mucinī). The queen said she had never seen beef, so the Mucinī secretly brought her a basket of beef. The queen concealed the beef in her room, but a servant saw it and reported it to the king. The king was in a rage and questioned the queen. Fearful of what he might do about such a horrible offense, the queen prayed to Bipattāriṇī, who transformed the beef into fruits and flowers. The king was happy and the queen became a devotee of Bipattāriṇī, propagating her *brata* throughout the land (Vidyāratna n.d.:38–9).

Tāriṇī protected the queen from the obvious threat from her husband and from the still greater danger that she might lose her caste by eating beef.

Maṅgal Caṇḍī

Caṇḍī is the goddess par excellence of the Bengal countryside. While the same name is, in Bengal, given to the goddess of the Sanskrit *Devī Māhātmyā*—the text is commonly called simply *Caṇḍī*—the goddess who is present in almost every Hindu village as an autochthonous deity who has emerged from the earth of the locality is also called Caṇḍī. Sometimes a modifier precedes Caṇḍī, such as Grām ("Village") Caṇḍī, Ḍhelai ("Clod") Caṇḍī, or Pāgalā ("Crazy") Caṇḍī.

Most often she is represented as a stone or lump of laterite at the foot of a tree such as that depicted in Figure 3. Goddesses who attain renown for responding to petitions are sometimes recognized by a small brick surround, marking off her space from the footpath. If she is regularly worshiped, then the stone is smeared with vermilion. If a petitioner's prayer is answered, he may provide silver eyes or other facial features for the stone; and a silver repoussé crown may follow. By gradual stages, clothing, limbs, and other adornments transform an inchoate lump into an icon; and the icon might even get a temple if her powers are recognized by a sufficiently prosperous following. The Śītalā of Maisali village, depicted in Chapter 5, is an example of such a process. There are hundreds of temples all over West Bengal housing deities with such modest origins.

Maṅgal Caṇḍī is such a goddess. The name Caṇḍī connects her to the Sanskrit Durgā and to the goddess of the Bengali *Caṇḍī Maṅgal* poem, but for her worshipers she is a local presence. *Maṅgal*, as was discussed in the Introduction, means "well-being"; whatever it is attached to, the word conveys auspiciousness. This is a goddess who is generous, benign, and helpful.

The usual practice of Maṅgal Caṇḍī *brata* was to fast and worship each Tuesday (Maṅgalabār) during the month of Jyaṣṭha (May/June). Bisnu Sarkar's instructions to his family say:

> Mother Maṅgal Caṇḍī's *pūjā* is held on four Tuesdays of Jyaiṣṭha. In case there are five Tuesdays in this month in any year, the *pūjā* will not be held on the third one. Married women will not eat rice on this day. In its place, fruits, bread, or *luci*, as one wishes, may be eaten.

Offerings to Maṅgal Caṇḍī are mostly familiar items, like those for Bipattāriṇī: but where Tāriṇī received offerings in thirteens, Caṇḍī's offerings are in sixteens. Sixteen is a number signifying completeness: sixteen annas made one Rupee. Bisnu Babu said that for each married woman observing this *brata*, there should be a large brass box or a large wooden vermilion box, a sack made of red cloth, 16 leaves from a jackfruit tree, 16 leaves from a wood-apple tree, 16 sweet basil leaves, 16 pieces of *dūrbā* grass, 16 barley grains, 16 grains of sun-dried rice, an offering packet containing 8 grains of rice and 8 pieces of *dūrbā* grass, and a packet to be eaten containing 16 sweet basil leaves and 16 grains of barley. These are all inexpensive and common items. The contents of the red cloth bag included more expensive items: 16 large cardamoms, 16 small cardamoms, 16 areca nuts, 16 cloves, 16 cubeb peppers, 1 nutmeg, 1 *harītakī*, 1 *beheṛā* (another medicinal fruit), a small vermilion box, some vermilion in the large box, an iron bracelet, a small conch shell, and 2 pieces of sandalwood. All those items were for each of the married women; the goddess received a separate set of offerings including: 16 leaves from a jackfruit tree, 16 leaves from a wood-apple tree, 16 sweet basil leaves, 16 pieces of *dūrbā* grass, 16 grains of barley, 16 grains of sun-dried rice, and an offering packet containing 8 gains of rice and 8 pieces of *dūrbā* grass.

Bratinīs were instructed to prepare a pot for the invocation of the goddess, and a mango twig to insert into the pot; some vermilion; *ālpanā* designs on the floor of the temple, where offerings were to be placed; sandalwood for fragrance; a conch shell to be sounded during worship; a sitting mat for the Brahman; a ceremonial lamp; stick and resinous incense; oil for the lamp; 2 areca nuts; and food offerings including two kinds of sweets; about 500 grams of ordinary (parboiled) rice; flowers and flower garlands, for which the Malakar received a fee of 2 annas, and a small basket to contain the cloth bag and box. Bisnu Babu did not mention the *dakṣiṇā* for the Brahman, who most likely received one anna, which was customary at the time.

Some items were to be prepared for distribution after worship: 16 shares of *mug dāl*, 16 slices of banana, 16 small betel leaf packets, and various fruits and vegetables. Bisnu Babu instructed women who took part to present themselves as proper married women with *āltā* (red dye) on the edges of their feet and vermilion in the parting of their hair. They should listen to the *kathā* of Mother Maṅgal Caṇḍī, then eat 16 handfuls of parched rice, followed by the items prepared for distribution. Few houses followed customs as elaborate as those described by Bisnu Babu, but the conception that there is an exactly correct way of performing the worship was widely accepted.

There are many stories about Maṅgal Caṇḍī in circulation. Kunal Chakrabarti (2001:234–74) traces this goddess to very ancient origins among the common people of Bengal. The Brahmans inserted themselves into the rituals of this goddess; she was adopted and adapted by the compilers of the Bengali *Upapurāṇas*, where she accumulated Sanskrit stories, some of which made their way back into the vernacular. However, the Bengali Caṇḍī, known from *Caṇḍī Maṅgal Kāvya*, dominates the narrative traditions. The goddess's appearance to the hunter Kalketu in his humble home and his ascent to kingship under her benign influence one of the best-known stories in Middle Bengali literature (*vide* Curley 2008, Mukundaram Chakravarti 2015).

8. Conclusion

India's tradition of speculation about transcendental problems reaches even into the lives of ordinary villagers. In Kelomal it was due in some part to the influence of Vaiṣṇava gurus, but, no matter how the concept may have reached them, ordinary people talked about living in the *kali* age. The idea was widespread that once, during the *satya yuga*—often equated with the reign of Lord Rāma—the world was orderly and pleasant. The succeeding ages of relative decline, known as the *treta* (three-spot on dice) and *dvapara* (two-spot) *yugas* were rarely mentioned. It seemed that there were just two epochs, one of them wonderful and the other the harsh present. Rather than *kali yuga*, the expression most often used was *kalir bhāva* (*bhāb* in Bengali), referring to the disorderly material world in which, as the Bengali saying has it, "jackals climb trees and daughters of oil-pressers become princesses."

Kṛṣṇa promises to deliver people from this oppressive age: A few men sought Kṛṣṇa's deliverance as mendicant or semi-mendicant beggars, walking from village to village singing *kīrtans* and accepting small offerings of rice and lentils and occasional coins. Widowed women sometimes attached themselves to Rādhā-Kṛṣṇa temples as *sevā dāsīs*, living from the offerings made at the temples. Some Bengali widows from Kolkata and other urban areas were sent to

Vṛndāvana to live out their declining years (often as little better than beggars) in the environment where Kṛṣṇa danced with the milkmaids. Most people, however, lived with their worldly attachments, struggling in the *kalir bhāva* to cope with its problems and perform their worldly work. For these people, the populous pantheon with its numerous rituals and unending details framed an intellectual order. Theirs was a particularistic universe; their community—limited though it was—was minutely divided and differentiated by supposedly inherited characteristics: each caste possessed moral attributes, a physical capacity, and an occupation linked to its inborn features. This elaborate differentiation and specialization established an interdependence and coherence, which, although it was imperfectly realized, presented an intelligible social order, with some scope for explaining the changes created by democracy, universal adult franchise, and land reform.

From a historical perspective, the apparently heterogeneous collection of religious practices described here looks like a layer cake, with bits from the *Gṛhya Sūtras* heavily overlaid with Brahmanical elements from the *purāṇas*, devotional practices espoused by Caitanya, and a dense frosting from indigenous sources. However, for most people in Kelomal such a historical analysis would have been irrelevant. To them, their calendar of observances and their practices constituted a coherent whole that comprehended significant differences among castes and households. They worshiped Śiva without being Śaivas, they worshiped Durgā without being Śāktas, and while many claimed Vaiṣṇavism, they were Vaiṣṇavas who worshiped Śiva and Durgā just as intently as they worshiped Kṛṣṇa. Sectarianism is far from unknown in Bengal; there are some fiercely sectarian Gauṛīya Vaiṣṇavas. But distinctions of sect went usually unrecognized in the village. There were differences that people thought important: most people would have agreed that Brahmans were the experts at worship, but this belief did not prevent them from following their customary rituals. There were Vaiṣṇavas who, because of what their gurus taught, were unwilling to watch animal sacrifices or eat meat, though they ate fish.

There were a very few exemplary Vaiṣṇavas who, according to general consensus, had obtained *jīvan mukti*, liberation in this life;

they appear to have been people of simple piety, not followers of a strict sectarian code. The metaphor used most often to describe *mukti* was crossing a river by boat, a common experience in deltaic Bengal, where the rivers are often wide and turbulent. Kṛṣṇa was said to be a boatman carrying a person to a distant shore, though the songs were more about the peril of the journey than about a beautiful destination.

Śiva was propitiated not for individual salvation or deliverance but for fertility (in the Gājan) or simply because he is a powerful god (the rest of the year). Among the goddesses, Śītalā was dangerous but also a shield; she was a stand-in for Rakṣakālī, Kālī the Protector, and she was mother of the village. Among those high-caste people who lacked the economic and political power to participate in what I call the sacrificial polity, the worship of Kālī as a domestic rite was a substitute for the worship of Durgā. Although she can be a protector, Kālī is mainly known as a destroyer; so she was treated with the utmost circumspection. She is most often depicted dancing wildly on the cremation ground, where she accidentally treads on the inert body of Śiva; she expresses her dismay at discovering her impropriety by sticking out her tongue. Kālī represented in visible form the distant but inevitable toll of time (*kāla*), which brings everything to an end. Infectious disease and snakebite—the domains of Śītalā and Manasā—were not such distant threats. Lakṣmī was not dangerous like Śītalā and Manasā, but she was dangerous nonetheless: she was fickle and could desert a person without apparent reason. There were many people in Kelomal who felt abandoned by her, poor people who were trying to support families, people who saw their children go hungry.

The reasons people gave for performing worship were, usually, straightforward: "We worship her/him because she/he is a god"; "Our ancestors have worshiped thus for fourteen generations"; or "I was moved by devotion (*bhakti*)." People said that worship of any of their many deities *should* be done, with a hint that failure to worship might be penalized, as it is in the stories about them. However, there was an unstated reason that was just as influential as obligation for performing *pūjās*: Far from being burdensome responsibilities, most occasions of worship were subjects of happy anticipation. *Pūjās* offered moments of beauty and joy in the lives of ordinary people: there were decorations, special food, and sometimes the image of a god being brought into the house. People said they felt *ānanda* ("joy" or "delight") in rituals. The esthetic appeal of a *pūjā* was clear: People decorated their houses, created pleasant places for gods to sit, and arranged beautiful, symmetrical platters of offerings. A Bengali author wrote about *pūjās* that people are not satisfied (*tṛpti*) unless " *rūpa, rasa, gandha, sparśa, śabda*" (form, flavor, aroma, touch, and sound) are all enjoyed continuously (Ray 1951:51). Beyond the joy and esthetic delight of rituals there was also an intellectual function, but no one talked about this; it was realized unconsciously.

Myths and Rituals

The problem of the relationship between myths and rituals is an old one in anthropology and religious studies. In 1942 Clyde Kluckhohn did an exhaustive analysis of that relationship, showing all of the many ways in which myths and rituals are connected—or not connected—in diverse settings. While there are instances in which rituals came first and myths were created around them, there are other clear examples (for example, the Christian mass) in which the ritual was created to enact a preexisting myth. Kluckhohn provided ethnographic examples of cultures rich in ritual but possessing little mythology, and of cultures with elaborate mythology and few rituals. Hindu Bengal—like India as a whole—has an abundance of both. Earlier I introduced the Bengali term *śubha karma*, "auspicious action," as a good approximation of ritual. However, there is no comparable term that comprehends all of the narratives that a westerner might classify as "myths." Generally, Bengali Hindus recognize as authoritative the stories in the Sanskrit *purāṇas* ("Old" texts) as well as the Bengali language *maṅgal kāvyas* ("Auspicious Poems"). *Brata kathās* do not seem as weighty as *purāṇas* and *maṅgal kāvyas*, but in fact some of them are Bengali translations of stories in Sanskrit *purāṇas*, and mostly come to the same kind of conclusion as the *maṅgal kāvyas*: a protagonist learns his lesson and takes up worship of a deity previously ignored. I do not see a fruitful way of distinguishing myths from folk-tales in this context. Some educated people treated *brata kathās* as just-so stories, while regarding the *Mārkaṇḍeya Caṇḍī* as an account of historical events in a different epoch. Most people spoke about the *Rāmāyaṇa* and *Mahābhārata* as if they were historical records. At the same time, even in Kelomal, there were educated skeptics who said that religious narratives were imaginary. The important point is that the truth-value assigned to any of these narratives by various members of the community was irrelevant to the ritual.

In previous books, about Gājan and Durgā Pūjā, I dealt with the very different ways in which mythological narratives were engaged in the rituals. Gājan was directed to Śiva; but the word Gājan and key practices are derived from earlier rituals directed to the god Dharma Ṭhākur, a god unknown outside of Bengal whose mythology is entirely in Bengali. The term Gājan and the practice of temporary *sannyāsa*, or renunciation, are briefly discussed in the *Dharma Maṅgal Kāvyas* and not in Śaiva narratives. However, there are also episodes from Bengali Śaiva myths that are enacted in the Gājan. When the "cooked food offering" (*bhoga*) was being given to Śiva, late at night, there was a recitation that mingled references to Śiva with references to Lausen, hero of the *Dharma Maṅgal*. However, overall there is no obvious way in which the Gājan can be said to correspond to any myth.

Durgā Pūjā was quite different from the Gājan with respect to mythology. The magnificent Sanskrit *Candi* was chanted daily throughout the time when the goddess was present. The narrative, a chapter from the *Mārkaṇḍeya Purāṇa*, consists of three episodes; each successive episode is twice as long as the previous one, and each details the destruction of more and more dangerous anti-gods (*asuras*). In a threefold parallel, the central rites of Durgā Pūjā took place on three days—the seventh, eighth, and ninth day was increased in an similarly exponential way. Like Russian dolls, each successive day of the ritual encompassed the preceding days and added something to it; each episode of the myth did the same thing, increasing to include all that preceded it while introducing new elements. Slaughter of the sacrificial animals and the goddess's slaughter of the enemies of the gods were consciously analogized.

Thus, the correspondence between the myth and the ritual was close and explicit.

Worship of Śītalā by the Kelomal villages was regarded as very important; worship included a performance of at least the central episode of the *Śītalā Maṅgal* by accomplished singers, who had to be accommodated, fed, and paid for their performance. However, while the performance of the myth was an integral part of the ritual, there was no connection between the myth and the offering or other ritual actions by which the goddess was worshiped. Offerings given to this goddess varied considerably from one village to the next. Differences of practice among villages marked them as different social entities. Thus, taken as a whole, the annual cycle of worship in Kelomal provided a miniature illustration of the diverse possible relationships between mythological narrative and ritual performance.

Durkheim (1995:79, 122) regarded myths as secondary in the study of religion: Rituals, which brought people together in sacralized social groups, were fundamental; myths were derivative. On the other hand, Lévi-Strauss (1976:158–64) thought it possible to decode the elements of social structure from myths, which, being intellectual products, were not contaminated by the disorder of actual social life. As we have seen, there are important examples in the Bengali case of myths that provide the structure and content of rituals; the rituals, in turn, foster social solidarity just as Durkheim thought.

However, although rituals promote social solidarity, trying to find models of family and social structure in Bengali mythology is challenging. It is certainly true that the assumptions of the caste system, of patriarchal families, and of young wives' subordination to their husbands' mothers are implicit throughout numerous myths and other narratives, and *brata kathās* are didactic about the family code of conduct. However, many other well-known myths present less-than-ideal models. The opposition between wife-givers and wife-takers can be discerned in a few places, but it may take a counter-productive shape, as it does in the famous story of Śiva's destruction of the sacrifice offered by his wife's father, Dakṣa. Śiva and Durgā might constitute a heavenly family, with either two or four children; however, Śiva is anything but a model husband. Rather than an ideal, the Bengali mythology about Śiva depicts what is for many women quotidian reality. Kṛṣṇa and Rādhā are not a proper couple at all; Rādhā is a married woman, so theirs is an illicit love, yet one that humans are supposed to strive for (though only in pure, devotional terms).

Brass workers craft attractive figures of Śītalā, but she is described in the *Śītalā Maṅgal* as an unmarried and unattractive hag riding an ass, accompanied by the horrendous Fever Demon, whom she treats with affection as if he is her son. Manasā, also unmarried, is described as being physically attractive; but she is surrounded by poisonous serpents. The fickle Lakṣmī is married to Nārāyaṇa, but they don't have offspring; and, in most Bengali narratives, Lakṣmī operates quite autonomously, as is clear in the *brata kathās* related in chapter 4. Nevertheless, Lakṣmī is held up as a model for feminine conduct. For an unmarried woman, the *brata* for *Śiva rātri* is said to help secure a husband like Śiva. However, young women would doubtless prefer to avoid a lazy narcotic addict whose idea of supporting his family is begging. While Lakṣmī, Sarasvatī, and Viṣṇu are generally well-behaved and serene, most Bengali mythology does not present models for social structure. Rituals, by contrast with myths, are orderly and elegant; gender and caste roles are enacted properly, even when they are not so tidy in daily life.

The Ritual Calendar

Gājan in the spring and Durgā Pūjā in the autumn constitute the main axis of the ritual year in Kelomal. In addition to the Gājan, the hot, dry weather of the spring was, historically, the season of smallpox epidemics, and thus the time for worshiping Śītalā. The secondary turning points in the calendar are the solstices: The summer solstice corresponds to the beginning of the monsoon rain, marked by the observance of Ambubāci, the menses of the earth, during which digging in the earth and use of the plow are forbidden. The earth as female and the work of men in the earth as analogous to sexual relations is explicit. Ambubāci is followed by plowing and transplanting rice, the most intense period of agricultural work. (The growing crop is treated as a fetus and the earth is given a ritual of increase like the *sādh*, satisfying the cravings of a pregnant woman at *Nal Saṃkrānti* in the autumn.) The beginning of the rain is also the time when the great Jagannāth *Rath Yātrā* takes place in Puri, a key marker in the Vaiṣṇava ritual cycle. When rain floods the fields, snakes are driven to higher ground and to more frequent encounters with people, so it is the season in which worship of Manasā, goddess of snakes, is most widespread. At the opposite point in the cycle, at the winter solstice, the earth yields the rice harvest in Kelomal and all of the surrounding area. It is the time of the new-rice ceremony, and also of the vernacular Banāi Pūjā that ties rice, prosperity, and Lakṣmī to the houses of the cultivators. Like the Rath Yātrā of the summer solstice, the observances of Makar Saṃkrānti, the winter solstice, are important far beyond the bounds of individual villages. Many people from Kelomal go to Tamluk, capital of their erstwhile kingdom, for the great Pauṣa Vāruṇī Melā; many others from throughout the region go to Sagar Island, at the confluence of the Ganga with the sea, for a bath that is supposed to wash away many rebirths. The sun begins its northern course on this day, and there is usually ample rice in the granary to justify a celebratory moment.

Rituals define the social order for families, castes, and communities by enjoining the enactment of proper relations. At the most obvious, practical level, the work of men and women in domestic rituals follows a normal social arrangement: women work and men provide the structure; that is, they perform the *saṃkalpa* that designates them the beneficiaries of the worship. But in community rituals—whether neighborhood, village, or country, the responsibility for preparing the food offerings falls on the men, and it is the community in a collective sense that provides the structure and reaps the benefit of worship. In the major rituals of the former *zamindārs*, the social order of caste is enacted in the arrangement of servants (*karmacāri*, "workers") who carry out the subordinate responsibilities of the ritual: drumming, wielding the sacrificial blade, bathing sacrificial animals, carrying lanterns, providing flowers, making images, and so on. Women still prepare food offerings within the house; thus, although the effects ramify widely in the community, the ritual remains a domestic one. Both domestic and communal rituals usually acknowledge the role of the Brahman as intermediary and as the occupant of the most exalted position in the ritual, unless it is a ritual performed by the householders.

The division of labor in rituals is a transparent affirmation of the social order, and one that occasions little reflection by villagers because it is an obvious continuation of daily experience. However, there is a less explicit message contained in the ritual cycle, one that deals both with the complexity of society and the disorder of the *kali yuga*. Bengali rural society, though it varies in detail from place to place, is an apparently heterogeneous mixture of castes, descent groups and households, rulers and commoners, kingdoms and communities, sophisticated people and simple ones, farmers and people with minutely specialized occupations. The ritual cycle comprehends all of these divisions and, as an ensemble, creates an intelligible picture of a highly differentiated and particularistic universe. Although there have not been any real kings in the vicinity of Kelomal in two centuries, the displays put on by the Rājās of Tamluk, Moyna, Kashijora, and Mahishadal evoked the institution of kingship, while mythology kept the model alive; the origin of the former landlords of Kelomal in these local courts lent some vitality to the image.

A Coherent System

People in Kelomal distinguished the rituals of the "big people" (*baṛo lok*), who were of high caste and wealthy by village standards, from the rituals carried out in the houses of the great majority. The distinction was spelled out in the difference between Durgā Pūjā and Gājan, the latter largely the responsibility of the cultivators and artisans. However, all of the rituals belonged to a single order, a system in which vedic and puranic rites were not distinguished from one another, and which did not recognize that some rites were purely *laukika* (popular). These distinctions are made in the almanac, sometimes implicitly and sometimes explicitly. The worship of Lakṣmī at the time harvests were taking place elsewhere in Bengal, even though there was no harvest locally, was identified as *śiṣṭācār* ("learned custom") or *sadācār* ("good custom"). These "cosmopolitan" observances, common in refined families throughout Bengal, were distinguished from *deśācār* ("custom of the country"), the practices of people who lived within Tamluk *parganā*. Rituals that were carried out by particular clans according to their custom were called *kulācār*. The usually unwritten practices of ordinary villagers were described as *laukika* or *lokācār* by learned observers, but not by the people whose customs they were; for them, these were rituals equal in standing with all of their other observances.

Deśācār, "custom of the country" practices are by definition localized and often unique to particular localities. Worship for the *deś*—whether the larger, vaguely defined country served in the Gājan, or the bounded village served when the village mother is worshiped—may include practices that are distinctive to a specific place. Śītalā mythology, which is performed as an element of village *pūjās*, is standardized but the performances are usually given a local setting and references is made to notable people in the village. More important, while the mythology is the same, the practices of worship—offerings to the goddess, visits to village shrines, sacrifices—differ markedly even between adjacent villages. Even though she is said to be a single goddess, each village Śītalā is deemed to be a different personality and she is represented in a different image. Although Śītalā is regarded as the mother of most villages in East Medinipur, villages in other parts of Bengal have mothers who are regarded as manifestations of other goddesses.

In Gājan the *deś* that receives the fruits is unbounded. There is not a Gājan in every village; people who become *sannyāsīs* for the duration of the ritual often have to go to Śiva temples in villages other than their own. Many participants begin their *sannyāsa* with pilgrimage to the temple of Tārakeśvara in Hugli district, an experience that brings them into a transitory community with *sannyāsīs* from all parts of Bengal. Although the rituals practiced at Tārakeśvara have lent common elements to many Gājans throughout the region, still no two are the same; distinctive local tradition is strictly honored in the Gājan rituals I have observed, yet the fruits of these strenuous rituals are supposed to be the same everywhere.

If the world can be divided between "splitters," who see differences and divide everything into numerous categories, and "lumpers," who are disposed to see commonalities and to create a few large categories, the Bengalis would seem to fall into both camps. In everything from varieties of rice, to castes, to gods, even ordinary villagers make innumerable distinctions. Yet, at the same time, they are ready to unify every duality and to rejoin divided categories. All Śītalās are one, despite their obvious differences of personality and appearance; and in a further step, they are all manifestations of an undifferentiated Devī. In the very influential *Mārkaṇḍeya Caṇḍī*, the master narrative of Durgā Pūjā, various, increasingly fierce forms of the goddess emerge from within her, then, in her final battle, she resumes them all into her single body. While most people in Kelomal could identify Advaita as one of the principal disciples of Caitanya, very few could say anything about the non-dualistic philosophy for which he was named. Nevertheless, alongside their cultural proclivity for fine distinctions, their worldview is constructed on the premise of non-dualism. Some educated Bengalis in the nineteenth century carried this premise to a logical conclusion, declaring that Hindus were in fact monotheists. The religion of Hindus in Kelomal is by no means monotheistic, but when one deity is being worshiped, that deity is treated as foremost among the gods, and all of the many others are relegated to the large residual category of *sarva deva-devī*, "all the gods and goddesses." And, although the opportunity would seem to offer itself, there are no caste distinctions among the gods.

Brahmans are distinguished from one another by origin and ritual practice. Earlier I discussed the many different classes of Brahmans that are found even in rural East Medinipur. However, despite the clear distinctions among them, they are all accorded high social standing. The position of Brahmans in Hindu society and in relation to rituals has been much discussed. I do not want to take on that issue in the abstract but rather to look at it from the perspective of the people in Kelomal. Regardless of wealth, power, or learning, non-Brahmans treat Brahmans as possessors of the highest rank in society. Male Brahmans are addressed as *ṭhākur*, "lord." Brahmans who serve lower castes are nevertheless treated with respect by higher caste people. No one in Kelomal said that Brahmans were distinguished from other people by their "purity" (*pavitratā*). People of all castes prepared for rituals by bathing; they purified themselves in the same way as Brahmans. However, as gods on earth, Brahmans were regarded as capable of making offerings that were acceptable to other gods. As a corollary, food cooked by a Brahman could be eaten by everyone from Brahman to Dom, whereas food cooked by a Dom would be accepted only by other Doms.

Not all Brahmans knew how to conduct rituals, which required specialized education. Most Brahmans consulted the *Pañjikā*, the almanac, which contains a short list of instructions for the conduct of the most ordinary rituals; many of them also consulted the *Purohita Darpaṇa* ("Mirror for Domestic Priests"), a much more detailed handbook. Use of these resources requires a modest knowledge of Sanskrit. But use of the array of ritual objects employed in even simple ceremonies—the *koṣā-kuṣi* for water, the hand bell to accompany certain *mantras*, flowers, oil lamps, a conch shell, *durbā* grass, etc.—require training. The gestures used by priests, both the formal *mudrās* prescribed in *tantras* and the elegant movements employed in displaying objects before a deity in the *āratī* must be learned from a guru. There are *pūjās* that are not in the handbooks—Banāi Pūjā, Nal Saṃkrānti, and most importantly Gājan—that are *deśācār*, "customs of the country," tied to localities and caste groups, that are unfamiliar to Brahmans from other parts of Bengal. At the same time, there are *pūjās*—Durgā Pūjā foremost among them—that are considered so demanding as to be beyond the capacity of local Brahmans. The Ghosh Bari called upon a Brahman from a distant locality—a reputed specialist in the recitation of the Sanskrit *Caṇḍī*—to perform their Durgā Pūjā. But, there was no Hindu caste—regardless of rank or poverty—that did not have some kind of Brahman to perform their rituals. And all the villages relied on Muslims to make offerings to Olābibi. The premise that, in *pūjās*, there is an intermediary between the worshiper and god is generally accepted, but, at the same time, direct access to gods through devotional rituals—processional *kīrtans*, offerings of Hari *luṭ*, and serving the *tulasī*—were equally widely accepted. Thus, there were rituals that enacted social hierarchy and rituals that minimized hierarchy going on in the same setting without a sense that there was a contradiction between them. The contrast between the axial points of the ritual cycle, with the explicit organization of hierarchy in Durgā Pūjā and the radical equality of the *sannyāsīs* in Gājan, spelled out this duality most completely. What might appear to be a contradiction embedded in the ritual life of Kelomal (and many hundreds of other villages throughout West Bengal) was not identified as a problem, either intellectual or social.

The complexity of the pantheon and of the rituals that address it map a complexity in society and the attendant conceptual universe that seem dramatically out of balance with the scale of the community. Most Indian villages are made up of numerous castes that are distinguished from one another in exquisite detail. The capacity of everyone, whether illiterate or well educated, to make such particularistic distinctions is symptomatic of a mode of thought that deals in fine social differentiation. Farmers talk about soil and seed in categories that are unknown to those who do not plow and plant. Potters see five grades of clay where others see just earth; Doms see twenty kinds of bamboo. People who are taught from childhood to be scrupulous about whose food they eat and whose water they drink know the differentiae. They live in a myriad of details all their lives, so the array of gods—each with numerous mythological narratives, each with variant forms of worship—matches their society. The fractionated and intractable problems of daily life in the disorderly *kali yuga* only add to the long list of categories. Described in abstract terms, this ceaseless differentiating is impressive, but when that capacity is wedded to the presupposition that differentiation is unreal and that all dualities are resolvable it gives these villagers the appearance of astounding philosophical sophistication.

I do not mean to imply that there is not a very large difference between the order of society—and of the universe—as people imagine it, and as it exists in quotidian reality. Even allowing that the *kali yuga* is understood to be disorderly and difficult, the lives of most people in Kelomal were hard. For the very poor, work was laborious and scarce. For the small farmers, landholdings were inadequate and agriculture was perpetually uncertain. The many households that did handloom weaving to augment agricultural incomes were usually in debt to the middlemen who supplied yarn. Descendants of the former *zamindārs* no longer enjoyed the standard of living of earlier generations and often turned to salaried occupations, which they called "service" (*cākari*), a less dignified status than that of an independent landholder. The concept of a social order described in the old model was outdated in 1968, and it was being unconsciously revised, often grudgingly, to acknowledge modern reality. However, it was not so dramatically inaccurate or misleading as to produce a social breakdown.

Sacred Symbols and Peasant Religion

I have tried to discuss the practices of people in Kelomal in terms that would make sense to them, but I began from Durkheim's approach to religion through "sacred symbols" and Weber's conception of a "peasant religion" that is closely tied to nature, "inclined toward magic," and "mystagogues," although capable of great transformation by "exemplary prophets," among whom the Buddha was perhaps preeminent. None of these terms corresponds to anything in the Bengali lexicon, but they place the religious practices of rural Bengal in a comparative context. Elsewhere (Nicholas 2008b:17–18) I have discussed the application of the anthropological concept of symbols (or signs) in Bengali culture. Like most Hindus, Bengalis makes abundant use of what I regard as "icons," and, moreover, they treat symbols—which I think have arbitrary meanings—as indexes, indissolubly connected to "roots" (*mūla*) embedded in them. In addition to this "concrete" theory of symbolism, the present work describes the frequent use of commonplace objects as sacred symbols, identifiable by their special treatment, by the way people "pay attention" to them, as Jonathan Z. Smith (1987) has said. Weber points to other significant areas of investigation. It is probably obvious that peasant life is tied to nature insofar as agriculture and household labor are tied to the cycle of seasons. However, despite the great importance of Lakṣmī and the vernacular rites of fertilizing and harvest, there is no sense in which the ritual life of Kelomal can be described as "nature worship," or as closely linked to the natural environment. There are numerous Indian examples of what Weber called "mystagogues," quasi-religious figures who use sleight of hand to persuade people of their miraculous power. Some people in Kelomal had heard of such miracle-workers, but they did not figure in the religious landscape of the village or its vicinity. There was magic in the rituals described here, but it was a kind of magical practice that was also integral to the rituals of the urbane and educated: this was *tantra*. Tantric rites use verbal incantations and gestures that are said to affect natural objects, to induce a deity to inhabit water pot or a clay image, and to endow inert images with vision and breath. The origins of *tantra* are obscure, but it has a place in Bengali Hindu ritual that is far removed from Weber's conception of a simple peasant religion.

Weber was correct about the transformative influence of exemplary prophets in the religious practices of peasants. Caitanya, although he has been gone for almost 500 years, continues to exercise a powerful influence over the thought and conduct of Hindus throughout rural West Bengal, and to play a significant role in devotional Vaiṣṇavism in much of India. Caitanya himself has been elevated to divinity. He was treated as a joint incarnation of Kṛṣṇa and Rādhā during his own lifetime; he is usually spoken of as Caitanya Deva ("God") and Mahāprabhu ("Great Lord"). His ecstatic displays of *bhakti* are models for contemporary Vaiṣṇava practice in Bengal. Some households had gurus, learned Brahmans or Vaiṣṇava preceptors, who visited at intervals and—as exemplary persons, though hardly on the level of Caitanya—were also treated as divinities, worshiped in person and in photographs, fed and offered gifts in a manner analogous to the treatment of other gods. On a further step down, parents also received expressions of *bhakti* from their children. Adult children sometimes asked me to take photographs of their elderly parents, and to be certain to make their feet visible. They wanted photographs they could hang on the wall, to which, after their deaths, they could offer *namaskār* and in which they could touch the feet. There was an abundance of exemplary figures in the lives of people in Kelomal, though the range and depth of influence of Caitanya was unequalled.

Bhakti, devotion, is a major element in the way people in Kelomal talk about religion. Displays of devotion, whether through demonstrative singing of *kīrtan* hymns, the faithful performance of *bratas*, or the personal decision to offer a *pūjā*, are received with approbation by others in the community and regarded as expressions of a pious disposition. The devotional movement among Hindus is often said to be a reaction against elaborate and expensive *pūjās*, which seemed to value pomp over piety, and which were, in any event, out of the reach of common people. In Kelomal—and I think in most contemporary Bengali practice—*bhakti* and elaborate rituals exist comfortably together and interpenetrate one another. Both are conducive to *maṅgal*, "well-being," and both produce *ānanda*, "joy" among those who practice them.

Worship of Kṛṣṇa, Viṣṇu, and Satya Nārāyaṇa was usually undertaken with the expectation of *ānanda*. However, there was very frequently a sense of obligation attended by anxiety connected to the worship of other deities. *Pūjās* that have been practiced by families or clans for long enough to be regarded by them as "traditional"—especially for a *kuladevatā* or Durgā—are given up with great misgiving. Discontinuing an old practice is a betrayal of the ancestors and also likely to incur the wrath of the god—or, more often, goddess—whose worship is foregone. Missing Lakṣmī *pūjā* is risking poverty, or, perhaps, the possibility of getting out of poverty. When a person has made a *mānasik* or *mānat*, a vow or promise of worship in return for a boon—birth of a child or recovery from illness—than there is the additional fear that the sought-for boon may be revoked unless the commitment is fulfilled. And the community itself fails if it does not perform the annual worship of the village mother or the Gājan. Failures of these sorts generally occur in connection with natural disasters or economic calamities, but cause and effect are easily confused: *maṅgal* disappears and deities go unworshiped. *Bratas* impose hardships almost entirely on women, whose fasts and domestic acts of worship are supposed to confer benefit on their husbands and children. Even ordinary people with little education were rational about the causes of hardship, but many of those causes were out of the reach of effective this-worldly action. Even very pious people saw the obvious, that rituals did not always lead to particular results. However, rituals almost always produced joy and satisfaction in those who practiced them, and even in people who came only to watch and listen.

Some of the well-being and joy that were produced by rituals can be attributed to their social functions. There were numerous reasons for brothers to quarrel, and—if local lore is to be believed—even more reasons for their wives to do so. However, even after they had partitioned their property and "ate from separate hearths," families of brothers very often came together to perform domestic rituals. Among lower castes, such as Fishers and Weavers, collective rituals united local caste groups. Villages were riven by factional conflict played out in electoral politics. Weighing against the typical factional posture of total opposition to one's enemies in every sphere of activity was a generally shared conviction that failure to perform the collective worship of the village mother would be equally damaging to all. The gods enforced cooperation and social cohesion, at least for a temporary period. The cohesion of the village as a community with something in common among all its residents—represented in Śītalā Pūjā—was crosscut by the recognition of caste differences and their complementarity acted out in Durgā Pūjā. The village caste system acquired a different shape after the abolition of *zamindāri* land tenure and land reform, but it did not disappear, and the high standing of the Kayasthas and the significance of their Durgā Pūjā for the integration of the village in its hierarchical posture remained.

It was not only objects of everyday life that were sacralized in rituals, but also the locality, the landscape, familiar places. Even faraway Mount Kailāsa, the dwelling of Śiva and Durgā, was treated as a place that could be located on a map of India, like Banaras and more nearby pilgrimage places. Moreover, when Śiva and Durgā were worshiped, they were present in the village. Śītalā resided in the individual Kelomal villages. Vraja, where Kṛṣṇa played with the Gopis, was a real place, brought near on full-moon nights when *kīrtan* parties played and sang throughout the village. The river voyage of the faithful Behulā with the corpse of her husband Lakhindar was said to have taken place on the nearby Rupnarayan River. The landscape of everyday life became the sacred landscape, though this transformation did not erase the imperfections of the present benighted age, the *kalir bhāva.*

Conclusion

This project began with an ethnographic objective. I knew that the annual ritual cycle was complicated, and that there was an elaborate array of deities and rituals. What emerged as the fieldwork progressed was a clear structure of the ceremonial cycle organized by a primary axis running between the vernal equinox, the Bengali new year, and the autumnal equinox, and a secondary axis running between the solstices. On the primary axis there was a sharp contrast between the relatively egalitarian Gājan, fertilizing the earth and water in the spring, and the hierarchical worship of goddesses in the autumn, which enacted a social order organized under the last residue of king-like authority. Kingship figured strongly in mythology and in the cultural conception of the *zamindārs* or large landholders. The idea that the *zamindār* was the local ruler still persisted in the experience of many villagers, although land reform and democratic social changes had permanently undermined that order. The goddess Durgā—visibly represented with her weapons, killing the anti-god Mahiṣa, and receiving blood sacrifices—symbolized the old organization of rural society.

The secondary axis opposed the season of rice planting—near the summer solstice and the beginning of the rains—and the season of harvest and new rice—just before the winter solstice. There were numerous rituals clustered around these secondary poles. The summer solstice was the time of the *laukika* observance of Ambubāci, the menses of the earth, when farmers stopped plowing and digging for three days; of the Rath Yātrā, when the god Jagannāth came out of his temple on his grand carriage pulled by devotees; and of the worship of Manasā, goddess of snakes. The winter solstice, known as Makar Saṃkrānti, was the occasion for the *laukik* Banāi Puja, tying Lakṣmī to the house, of the great annual fair of the kingdom of Tamluk at the Barga Bhīmā temple; and of the pilgrimage to Ganga Sagar, where the Ganges flows into the Bay of Bengal.

Inconsequential as it was, Kelomal was—and is—an heir to Indian civilization. The *Rāmāyaṇa* and *Mahābhārata*, the ancient rituals of the *Gṛhya Sūtras* and the more recent ones directed to Bengali deities like Śītalā and Manasā, are all part of its legacy. And the elaborate division of labor among castes was also a part of that inheritance. The complicated religious history of Bengal—Buddhist, Jain, Brahmanical, and Muslim—contributed further to the complexity. For the analyst, the constituent elements have to be teased apart, but for the villagers they were all of a piece: They had a fairly coherent universe, one populated with numerous deities, a highly differentiated ritual repertoire, and multiple levels of understanding. Each religion creates a picture of the universe as it is in ultimate reality: The universe of the people in Kelomal, as it was in 1970, was extraordinarily rich and complicated, bearing a lot of very specific detail and *dharma* sufficient for the whole of Indian civilization. They were not more or less misguided than the adherents of any other religion, and the categorical complexity given them by this system offered rich potential for the future of analytical thought.

References Cited

Bandyopādhyāy, Amal Kumār (1979). *Paurāṇikā: Paurāṇikā Abhidhāna*. 2 vols. Kolkata: Firma KLM Ltd.

Bell, Catherine (1997). *Ritual: Perspectives and Dimensions*. New York: Oxford University Press.

Bharati, Agehananda (1965). *The Tantric Tradition*. London: Rider & Co.

Bhaṭṭācāryya, Āśutoṣ (1951). *Early Bengali Saiva Poetry*. Calcutta: Calcutta Book House.

______ (1962). *Bāiś kabir Manasā-maṅgal*. Calcutta: University of Calcutta.

______ (1977). *The Sun and the Serpent Lore of Bengal*. Calcutta: Firma KLM Private Ltd.

Bhattacharya, France (2007). *La Victoire de la déese Manasā: Traduction française du Manasā Vijaya, poème Bengali de Vipradāsa (XVe)*. Pondichéry: Institut Français de Pondichéry.

Bhaṭṭācāryya, Gurudās (1960 [1882]). *Bāṅglā Kāvye Śiva*. Calcutta: Indian Associated Publishing Co.

Bhaṭṭācāryya, Nārāyaṇ Candra (1968/9 [1375]). *Prati Bṛhaśpatibārer Śrī Śrī Lakṣmīdevir Brata Kathā*. Calcutta: Rajendra Library.

Bhattacharyya, Narendra Nath (1982). *History of the Tantric Religion*. New Delhi: Manohar.

Bhaṭṭācāryya, Sukumār and Śaśibhusana Kaviratna, eds. (1964 [1371]). *Meyeder Bratakathā*. Calcutta: Orient Library.

Bhaṭṭācāryya, Surendranāth (n.d.). *Bṛhat Lakṣmī-caritra*. Calcutta: Akṣay Library.

Bhaṭṭācāryya, Surendramohana, ed. (1380 [1973/4]), *Purohita Darpaṇa*. 2 vols. 37th ed. Revised by Yogendra-candra Vyākaraṇatīrtha Vidyāratna. Calcutta: Satyanārāyaṇa Library.

Chakrabarti, Kunal (2001). *Religious Process: The* Purāṇas *and the Making of a Regional Tradition*. New Delhi: Oxford University Press.

Cakrabartī, Pañcānan, ed. (1964). *Rāmeśvar Racanāvalī*. Calcutta: Baṅgīya Sāhitya Pariṣat.

Chatterji, Suniti Kumar (1945). "Buddhist Survivals in Bengal." In, *B.C. Law Volume*, Part I, ed. by D. R. Bhandarkar et al. Calcutta: Indian Research Institute, pp. 75–87.

Chattopadhyay, K. P. (1942). "Dharma Worship." *Journal of the Asiatic Society of Bengal. Letters* 8:99–135.

Curley, David (2008). *Poetry and History: Bengali* Maṅgal-kābya *and Social Change in Precolonial Bengal*. New Delhi: Chronicle Books.

Dasgupta, Shashibhusan (1962). *Obscure Religious Cults*. 2nd ed. Calcutta: Firma K. L. Mukhopadhyay.

De, Sushil Kumar (1961). *Early History of the Vaisnava Faith and Movement in Bengal*. 2nd ed. Calcutta: Firma K. L. Mukhopadhyay.

Dimock, Edward C., Jr. (1962). "The Goddess of Snakes in Medieval Bengali Literature, Part I." *History of Religions* 1: 307–321

______ (1963). *The Thief of Love: Bengali Tales from Court and Village*. Chicago: University of Chicago Press.

______ (1966). *The Place of the Hidden Moon: Erotic Mysticism in the Vaiṣṇava-sahajiyā Cult of Bengal*. Chicago: University of Chicago Press.

Dimock, Edward C., Jr., and A. K. Ramanujan (1964). "The Goddess of Snakes in Medieval Bengali Literature, Part II." *History of Religions* 3:300–322.

Durkheim, Émile (1995 [1912]). *The Elementary Forms of Religious Life*. Trans. by Karen E. Fields. New York: The Free Press.

Eaton, Richard M. (1993). *The Rise of Islam and the Bengal Frontier, 1204–1760*. Berkeley: University of California Press.

Geertz, Clifford (1973). *The Interpretation of Cultures*. New York: Basic Books.

Ghosha, Pratapachandra (1871). *Durga Puja. With Notes and Illustrations*. Calcutta: Printed at the Hindoo Patriot Press.

Hazra, R. C. (1963). *Studies in the Upapurāṇas. Vol. II: Śākta and Non-sectarian Upapurāṇas*. Calcutta: Sanskrit College.

Inden, Ronald B. and Ralph W. Nicholas (1977). *Kinship in Bengali Culture*. Chicago: University of Chicago Press.

Kane, P.V. (1958). History of Dharmaśāstra. 5 vols. Poona: Bhandarkar Oriental Research Institute.

Kluckhohn, Clyde (1942). "Myths and Rituals: A General Theory." *Harvard Theological Review* 35:45–79.

Lévi-Strauss, Claude (1976). *Structural Anthropology, Volume II*. Trans. By Monica Layton. New York: Basic Books.

Lopez, Donald S., Jr., ed. (1995). *Religions of India in Practice*. Princeton: Princeton University Press.

Maity, Pradyot Kumar (1966). *Historical Studies in the Cult of the Goddess Manasa*. Calcutta: Punthi Pustak.

Marriott, McKim (1966). "The Feast of Love." In, *Krishna: Myths, Rites, and Attitudes*, Ed. by Milton Singer. Honolulu: East-West Center Press, pp. 200–12.

McCutchion, David J. and Suhrid K. Bhowmick (1999). *Patuas and Patua Art in Bengal*. Calcutta: Firma KLM Private Ltd.

McDaniel, June (2003). *Making Virtuous Daughters and Wives: An Introduction to Women's Brata Rituals in Bengali Folk Religion*. Albany: State University of New York Press.

Mukundaram Chakravarti (2015). *Kavikankan Mukundaram Chakravarti Chandimangal*. Trans. by Edward Yazijian. Gurgaon: Penguin Books.

Nag, Dulali (1998). "Lakshmi and Alakshmi: The Kojagari Lakshmi Vrat Katha of Bengal." *Manushi*, no. 104, pp. 9–11.

Naskar, Debabrata (1999). *Cabbiś Parganār Laukik Devadevī: Pālāgan o Loksaṃskṛti Jijñāsā*. Kolkata: De's Publishing.

Nicholas, Ralph W. (2003). *Fruits of Worship: Practical Religion in Bengal*. New Delhi: Chronicle Books.

______ (2008a). "The Constitution of Kelomal: Frontier Bengal in the Eighteenth Century." In *Societies and Cultures in India*. Vol.II. A. K. Haldar and Pradip K. Bhowmick, eds. Kolkata: R. N. Bhattacharya.

______ (2008b). *Rites of Spring: Gājan in Village Bengal*. New Delhi: Chronicle Books.

______ (2013). *Night of the Gods: Durgā Pūjā and the Legitimation of Power in Rural Bengal*. New Delhi: RCS Publishers and Orient BlackSwan.

Pañjikā (1999–2000). *Gupta Press Directory Pañjika*. Kolkata: Gupta Press.

Rāy, Yogeśacandra (1951). *Pujā-pārvaṇa*. Kolkata: Viśvabhāratī Granthālaya.

Risley, Herbert Hope (1892). *The Tribes and Castes of Bengal: Ethnographic Glossary*. 2 vols. Calcutta: Bengal Secretariat Press.

Sarkar, Bihani (2012). "The Rite of Durgā in Medieval Bengal: An Introductory Study of Raghunandana's *Durgāpūjātattva* with Text and Translation of the Principal Rites." *Journal of the Royal Asiatic Society* 22 (2): 325–390.

Sen, Dinesh Chandra (1914). *Baṅga Sāhitya Paricaya*. Calcutta: University of Calcutta.

——— (1954). *History of Bengali Language and Literature*. 2nd ed. Calcutta: University of Calcutta.

Sen, Rajendra Nath, trans. (1922). *The Brahma-vaivarta Puranam*. 2 vols. Allahabad: Sudhindra Nath Vasu at the Panini Office.

Smith, Jonathan Z. (1987). *To Take Place: Toward Theory in Ritual*. Chicago: University of Chicago Press.

Smith, W. L. (1980). *The One-eyed Goddess: A Study of the Manasā Maṅgal*. Stockholm Oriental Studies 12. Stockholm: Almquist & Wiksell International.

Stewart, Tony K. (1995a). "Satya Pīr: Muslim Holy Man and Hindu God." In, Lopez, ed. (1995), pp. 578–97.

——— (1995b). "The Goddess Ṣaṣṭhī Protects Children." In, Lopez, ed. (1995), pp. 352–66.

Turner, Victor W. (1967). *The Forest of Symbols: Aspects of Ndembu Ritual*. Ithaca: Cornell University Press.

Vidyāratna, Kālīprasanna, compiler (n.d.). *Meyeder Bratakathā*. Ed. by Vinay Caudhuri. Kalikātā: Akṣay Library.

Van Buitenen, J. A. B. (1966). "On the archaism of the *Bhāgavata Purāṇa*." In, *Krishna: Myths, Rites, and Attitudes*, Ed. by Milton Singer. Honolulu: East-West Center Press, pp. 23–40.

Weber, Max (1946). "The Social Psychology of the World Religions," in *From Max Weber: Essays in Sociology*, pp. 267–301. H. H. Gerth and C. Wright Mills, ed. and trans. New York: Oxford University Press.

——— (1968). *Economy and Society*. Ed. by Guenther Roth and Claus Wittich. 3 vols. New York: Bedminster Press.

Index